The Middle Way

The Middle Way

*Theology, Politics and Economics
in the Later Thought of R. H. Preston*

Edited by
R. John Elford
and
Ian S. Markham

SCM PRESS

ISBN 0 334 02793 4

First published 2000
by SCM Press
9–17 St Albans Place, London N1 0NX

SCM Press is a division of
SCM-Canterbury Press Ltd

Typeset at Rowland Phototypesetting,
Bury St Edmunds, Suffolk
Printed in Great Britain by
Biddles Ltd, Guildford and King's Lynn

Contents

Acknowledgments

The Editors would like to express their appreciation to the following who made this book possible. To Professor Ronald Preston who has faithfully engaged with the hard questions in the political and social spheres. To Professor Simon Lee, Rector and Chief Executive at Liverpool Hope, for his support for this publication. To Margaret Lydamore and John Bowden at SCM Press for their encouragement and patience. To The Rt Revd Lord Habgood for writing the Preface. To Professor Charles Birch for the collaboration in ch. 12. To Claire Maxwell and Mr Alfred Westwell for assisting the editors in all the painstaking technical work that was necessary as we finished the manuscript. To John McLaren for assisting the editors in getting the permissions from the publishers.

We are grateful to the following who gave us permission for reprinting articles that have appeared elsewhere: *Crucible* for chapters 1, 8 and 17; *Theological Themes* for chapter 3; Blackwell Publishers for chapter 4; *Expository Times* for chapter 5; *Theology* for chapters 6, 7, 13 and 14; *The Ecumenical Review* for chapters 9, 10 and 11; *The Way* for chapter 20 and HarperCollins for chapter 21.

Sources

The chapters first appeared in the following publications:

1. A Bishop Ahead of his Church
   Crucible, The Quarterly Journal of the Board for Social
   Responsibility, April–June 1984
2. The Collapse of the SCM
   Theology, Vol. 89, No. 732, 1987
3. Remembering Reinhold Niebuhr
   Theological Themes, Vol. 1, No. 2, Northern Baptist College,
   Manchester 1992
4. Christian Ethics
   Peter Singer (ed), *A Companion to Ethics*, Blackwell Publishers
   1991, pp. 91–105
5. Looking Back on the Twentieth Century
   Expository Times, Vol. III, No. 1, October 1999, pp. 4–9
6. Not out of the Wood Yet
   Theology, Vol. 84, No. 698, March 1981, pp. 83–87
7. Christian Socialism Becalmed
   Theology, Vol. 91, No. 739, 1988, pp. 24–32
8. Fifty Years on from the Oxford Conference
   Crucible, The Quarterly Journal of the Board for Social
   Responsibility, January–March 1988, pp. 2–10
9. Critics from Without and from Within
   The Ecumenical Review, Vol. 37, No. 1, January 1985,
   pp. 121–26
10. Convergence and Divergence in Social Theology
    The Ecumenical Review, Vol. 40, No. 2, April 1988,
    pp. 194–203
11. Humanity, Nature and the Integrity of Creation
    The Ecumenical Review, Vol. 41, No. 4, October 1989,
    pp. 552–53

Preface

JOHN HABGOOD

Social ethics is a subject on which most people have opinions, but few – and that includes theologians and church leaders – have the expertise to analyse contentious issues in sufficient depth to point the way towards effective action. Ronald Preston is one of the few. He has fought a life-long battle against the neglect of professional knowledge in the formulation of Christian social policies. As a former economist he has constantly complained of what he has called 'the churches' utopian naivety'. And he has warned against the temptation to contract out of the difficulties and ambiguities inherent in all realistic attempts to secure greater social justice. His thoroughness, persistence, and down-to-earth approach, coupled with a clear grasp of the strengths and limits of theology, have enabled him, for more than half a century, to lead the way among British Christians as a highly respected teacher, writer and spokesman in this much disputed and politically sensitive field.

I had the privilege of working closely with him over a number of years during the early 1990s in a series of critical encounters with the World Council of Churches. A number of old hands, who had served the WCC in happier days, met to share their distress about its growing tendency to disparage expert opinion in the balanced assessment of difficult social and ethical issues, and to favour a more simplistic, prophetic and confrontational style based directly on personal sufferings and discontents. The new approach, labelled 'eschatological realism', set little store by the use of secular academic disciplines in the critical analysis of such practical problems as poverty and environmental degradation, but aimed instead for a kind of gesture politics, expressing attitudes and hopes arising from on-the-ground experience and from the direct application of biblical promises. It was rhetorically powerful, but gave little guidance to those faced with the problem of what should actually be done. Throughout our meetings, of which more is said in the introduction to this volume, Ronald Preston was tireless in his exposure of muddle, ignorance, and high-sounding platitudes. He was equally tireless in his attempts to understand why the WCC was taking this course, regretting its neglect of its own history, and conscious of the strong internal and external pressures then driving it. But he was as always a friendly critic, because he longed for the WCC to recover the intellectual vigour and political relevance it had once possessed, and seemed to be losing. When after a series of frustrations the group decided there was not much more it could do, it was entirely characteristic of Ronald that, instead of walking away, he wrote a book about the issues, setting them in their historical context.

Intellectual integrity and commitment are part of his nature. His academic career was fuelled by a strong desire to bring the Christian gospel to bear on the worldwide social problems of his day in ways which were true to his faith, economically sound, and likely to make a real difference. As some of the articles in this book demonstrate, he is equally at home in casting a critical eye over Papal Encyclicals as in exposing the inadequacies of an early work by John Milburn. His long experience of ecumenical social ethics can still provide depth and perspective at a time when there is a danger of some of the early lessons in such bodies as the SCM and the WCC being forgotten. As a bonus the collection contains a fascinating article on Keynes.

Christians who have had direct experience of the responsibilities of public life are only too well aware that it is no easy task to bring traditional theological insights to bear on complex modern problems. There is a narrow dividing line between compromising one's theology and failing to make proper use of the best secular knowledge. Ronald Preston's way of treading this line has frequently exposed him to criticism from both sides – which is perhaps another way of saying that he has maintained a good Anglican sense of the fruitful tension between opposing truths. The longer I have known him the more convinced I am that he is a trustworthy guide through this difficult territory.

Those who are already familiar with his many books will welcome this collection of articles from his post-retirement period, which show that he has lost none of his incisiveness. I hope it may also encourage new readers to explore his other writings. The two editorial articles offer proof enough of the importance of his work, and of how much there is still to be learnt from his wide experience, sharp insight, and trenchant prose.

Introduction:

Ronald Preston's Theological Ethics

R. JOHN ELFORD

Ronald Preston's theological ethics is, in important senses, both auto-biographical and collaborative. The following discussion will inter-weave these themes just as they have been in the development of his thought and career, which culminated in his appointment as the Samuel Ferguson Professor of Social and Pastoral Theology at the University of Manchester 1970–80. He is now Emeritus. We will see that he brought immediately to the Chair a coherent intellectual position which had been honed during a long period of theological, political and economic formation.

His first degree was taken at the London School of Economics in economics and economic history, chosen in preference to history because he wanted to understand why the world was in such a mess following the Wall Street crash in 1929. Here he came under the influence of modern classical economists and of R.H. Tawney, of whom he was a student. Tawney's book *Equality* was particularly influential.[1] A third influence was that of Reinhold Niebuhr.[2] His career then began as the Industrial Secretary for the Student Christian Movement in 1935. During this time he came to two important realizations. First, that pacifism was no gospel for a civil society and, second, that Marxism was not a scientific theory, as many at the LSE and in the UK had believed, because it contained no basis for prediction, though it did throw some light on the 1930s economic depression and the rise of Nazism. After a degree in theology at Oxford, taken because he wanted to be as equipped in theology as he by then was in economics, and ordination in the Church of England, followed by a curacy at St John Park in Sheffield, he returned to the SCM as Study Secretary until 1948. By this time the fundamentals of his theology and its relationship to politics and economics were in place. It is rooted in the classical tradition of Anglican moral theology, its development in the incarnational theology of F. D.

Maurice in the nineteenth century and of Kenneth Kirk, and the personal influence of William Temple in the twentieth. We will see why it is also indebted to the writings of C. H. Dodd on the Gospels. It also includes reference to all the elements of the Christian drama: creation, fall, 'under Pontius Pilate', and the last days (without which, he claims, the Christian faith would be a mockery for the majority of people). The life of the Christian church and its sacraments are equally important. His vision for a Christian social ethic reciprocates with all these things.

His 'return' to Christianity after a schoolboy lapse was gradual and he often muses on the fact that friends have observed that he has never been 'converted'. Those who have been and then had to work out the implications of it for these wider matters might, of course, think him the better placed for this reason! From this time he was and has remained doctrinally critical, but not to the point of believing that God is an entirely human construct. He has never written on this later point, since he believes it to be an issue in philosophical theology on which it is beyond his competence to write, although he has often spoken on it informally. The modesty of this disclaimer might or might not be justified, but it does demonstrate a deeply personally held belief that theology should only ever operate within defined fields of competence and definition. He describes his ecclesiastical journey as one from Liberal Protestant Modernism to a radical Liberal Catholicism and attributes this to the seriousness with which he came to value the worship and witness of the church.

All this led to the realization that theology had to establish a basis for civil society in spite, and more to the point because, of the fact that one cannot be found in the New Testament. Central to this there had to be a workable understanding of the relationship of love to justice which is applicable to civic life. This, he came to see, could be based on the radical kingdom ethic of Jesus, providing only that it was recognized that this could never be fully realized *in via*. 'The key to the ministry of Jesus,' he writes, '(in word and deed) is its proleptic and future eschatological character.'[3] As a result, justice is the nearest expression of collective love but, like love, it too remains incomplete this side of the parousia. This 'realized eschatology', as it came more widely to be known through the work of Dodd on the Gospels, was the basis for hope in civil society and that, in turn, for Preston put him on the political left. He has been a member of the Labour Party since 1975. None of this, as we shall see, led him to membership of the Christendom Group, which started in 1922, as it did for so many of his contemporaries who were coming to otherwise similar conclusions in the light of the momentous times.

He did not join the Christendom group because it claimed to stand for a 'natural' social and economic order. They did not, therefore, study either discipline as such though they pronounced confidently on social and economic issues. As a consequence, they were vulnerable to what he describes as 'economic quackery' such as C. H. Douglas' Social Credit system.[4] Many leading Anglicans of the time were taken in by this. He does, however, appreciate the way in which the Group pointed out that many social sciences such as sociology were often based on secularist assumptions inimical to Christianity. He remained convinced, however, that many members of the Group were, bluntly, intellectual frauds. They held the simple idea that profit and competition were inherently sinful, because they did not understand the relevance of basic economic theory to the sort of problems every society has to deal with. As a result, they thought that the ethic of Jesus was both realizable in the present social and economic order and that it pointed the way to its future.

Preston also eschewed Christian Socialism, but for different reasons. He has never, as we shall see, accepted their view that competition and profit are inherently sinful. This resulted, again, in woolly utopian thinking which showed no regard for the importance of basic economic concepts or for the problems they are designed to address. His preference has always been for an understanding of market forces which are controlled in the interests of all. The subsequent collapse of soviet-style economies has, of course, entirely vindicated his stance on this central economic issue.

The order of priorities so established was to remain throughout his work: theology, politics, economics. Only by tackling given issues in this order could there be hope of making progress. He insists throughout his writing that politics is prior to economics. This makes the political framework within which the market is allowed to operate crucial.[5]

In 1949, Ronald Preston became a part-time lecturer in Christian Ethics at the University of Manchester. It is difficult for us now to appreciate what a seeming novelty the so-styled subject was at that time. There was only one other such job in England, in Oxford, though there were those in Practical Theology in Scotland. It had previously and more generally been known as 'moral theology' in Roman Catholicism and also had a long history in the Anglican tradition. Largely as a result of his personal labours, this new nomenclature is now widely accepted. An association bearing the phrase exists for its promotion: the Society for the Study of Christian Ethics. One of the things it signified was a new emphasis on the way in which theology engaged not only with ethics in general but with its empirical dimensions in particular. In short, it took empirics seriously by insisting that careful analysis always had to prevail over ideology whenever this or that was claimed as being the case. By this means, the subject never, easily at least, allows opinion to prevail over 'fact'. This might seem a self-evident and therefore unnecessary thing to point out and value, but ethical debate is so redolent with opinion masquerading as fact that it is far from it. One of Preston's latest pieces of collaboration, with Charles Birch, a natural scientist, points out persuasively why the World Council of Churches is now guilty of this very error in the way it uses the phrase 'the integrity of creation'.[6] Instead of studying the natural order of creation to find out dispassionately what it is actually like, the WCC studies use the phrase to *read into* creation the fact that it is self-sustaining. To the contrary, it is now known that it not self-sustaining and, as a result, will end. The upshot of this mistaken view is that the Council encourages an attitude to environmental management which is close to benign neglect, beyond approving popular measures such as climate control, when what is actually wanted in the face of the problem is something far more interventionist which recognizes the divinely-created importance of the role of humans as co-creators. Preston's point here is his oft repeated one; empirics must prevail over ideology if we are even to begin to discover how God's love relates to the actual circumstances of our lives and the created order.

This attention to empirical detail was the reason why Christian ethics, so understood, became, and still is, noted for its interdisciplinary activities. Ethicists have to turn to others when they want to achieve the empirical accuracy which is essential to their work. For this reason, the context of a secular university was vital to this newly-styled academic discipline in the UK with its pronounced empirical curiosity. It did much to separate the subject from ecclesiology where moral theology had previously largely been located, particularly in the Roman Catholic tradition. Above all, this created a secular profile for the subject, principally in the university. As a result, over the years, its interdisciplinary integrity became widely recognized, especially among those who had previously mistakenly thought that theology was about polemics rather than empirics. In this way, it established itself as an integral part of the wider intellectual life of the university campus where it is and has been found teaching and researching in collaboration with a number of secular disciplines. Among these are: social policy and administration, sociology, politics, medicine and, at one time, military studies and psychology. Just one of the benefits of this to students of all the disciplines involved is that they find themselves pursuing common objectives with others who are often seemingly from disparate subjects. Such interdisciplinarity is nowadays so widely and generally accepted that we can easily overlook how long-standing some of its modern origins of this kind actually are. For all this outreach, however, the subject was clearly rooted in a wide range of traditional theological studies on which it constantly drew.

For Ronald Preston there followed years combining the supervision of academic research and teaching with the Wardenship of St Anselm Hall and, from 1971, with that as a Canon Theologian at Manchester Cathedral. By 1980 he was recognized, on wide consultation, to be the ideal first incumbent of the new Samuel Ferguson Chair in Social and Pastoral Theology. As well as bringing this wealth of intellectual experience to the Chair, by that time he had also become established in the affairs of the World Council of Churches and they remain an active scholarly interest. For effectively the first time in an otherwise busy life and ministry, the Chair created the opportunity for complementing teaching with writing which became prolific and, thankfully, still continues. The post also maintained a heavy commitment to teaching the subject at undergraduate and post-graduate levels with, at times, considerable numbers of the latter present at any one time. The Chair, of course, also embraced pastoral theology, a cognate subject but one with parameters of its own. Here he depended on the labours of colleagues whom he supported and encouraged. All this extended the interdisciplinary range of the so-combined subjects. In all this, Preston brought to bear his personal gifts for making each and every individual student feel valued and encouraged. I am just one of many who are personally indebted to him and this volume, on my part at least, is an expression of appreciation for that, as well as it is for the pleasure of many shared personal endeavours and long friendship.

The work at the University of Manchester, thankfully, continues under the now third incumbent of the Chair in visible continuity with Preston's pioneering vision which dated, as we have seen, from 1949. The subject elsewhere is also studied in ways which are similar and which show the like influence of Preston's example. For reasons which Professor Markham examines in the conclusion to this volume, however, Preston's style of theological ethics is not as fashionable as it once was and this has meant, sadly, that he is probably not as widely read as he once was. It is hoped that the appearance of this volume will help, at least in part, to redress that. His profoundly theological ethics, for we shall see that this is what it is, clearly stands in a deeply-rooted theological tradition on the one hand and reaches widely into secular affairs on the other. We will now examine the method of Preston's theological ethics and then discuss some of its main applications.

Preston holds the view that Christian ethics requires three things to be held together; the Bible, Christian doctrinal and ethical tradition, and moral reasoning in a contemporary context.[7] There is no easy way in which it is possible to move from either or both of the first two of these to the third. All the first two can do is to give us what he calls our 'basic orientation' and from there we have to work things out for ourselves. In doing this Christian ethics has to engage the actual world around it, whatever the diversity, complexity, and to use a favourite word of his, 'ambiguities', of that world may be. This, he claims, is because realized and future eschatology is the key to Christian ethics. It is, on this view, markedly Christocentric. 'Jesus got it right' is a favourite phrase. The knowledge of the last things, as seen proleptically in the ministry of Jesus, enables Christians to understand the triumph of good over evil which will come to fulfilment in the eschaton, but which remains incomplete this side of it. 'This hope', he writes, 'is epitomized in the thought of being "with Christ" and of having a new resurrection "body"; and thus it transcends what is within history and continuous with our space and time, and hopefully looks to what is discontinuous with it and with our bodies with their present space and time equipment.'[8] Clearly for Preston, Christian engagement with the actual circumstances of human life is made possible by the knowledge of God in Christ. He writes: '. . . in Jesus the moral goodness of God himself was realized to the fullest possible extent in the life of a human being.'[9] So understood, Jesus' ethical teaching links what God has already done for human salvation with what is yet to be achieved in the eschaton. In the meantime, the life of faith requires a constant striving, by the grace of God, for the realization of love and justice not only to human affairs in general, but also in their minutiae, where the human lot can be most directly affected and improved. Jesus, according to Preston, not only endorses common morality, he systematically radicalizes it. This can be seen, for example, in the fact that: there is to be no limit to the forgiveness of injuries (Matt.18.12ff.); that enemies are to be loved (Matt.6.14ff.); neighbour love is to be unrestricted (Luke 10.29ff.), and so on. This radicalism challenged the self-esteem of the righteous and contrasted that with the righteousness of sinners and the socially outcast. 'He goes beyond,' Preston writes, 'the world of claims and counter claims, of rights and duties and something owed to others, as St Paul clearly sees when in Romans (13.8) he says "Owe no one anything, but love one another." Jesus calls for a certain flair in life, a certain creative recklessness at critical points.'[10] The ethical direction in all this is towards an unself-regarding and spontaneous reaction to the needs of others, according to the moment rather than some rigid code. In fact, Jesus repeatedly refused to legislate in morality when he was so frequently asked to do so, with the seeming exception of his views on divorce (Mark 1.1–12). Rather, he turned questions back to those who asked them and in so doing seemed to cause deliberate confusion and uncertainty. Preston's interpretation of Jesus has since become more fashionable in New Testament scholarship than it generally was when he initially put it forward. Jesus is now widely seen as a radical teacher of subversive wisdom.[11] Accordingly, it might be argued, his moral message can be reduced to: do not always trust convention, think carefully before you do anything, and throw yourself on the mercy of God when you do. What matters above all is that the right thing is done for the right motive and, if possible, for the right reason (if sentimentality is to be avoided), which according to Jesus was based on the radical extent to which we are to love one another because God loves us.

Preston brings to this interpretation of Jesus a belief in the equality of all human beings before God as well as the recognition of the need to create political and economic institutions which promote, realize and maintain that equality amid the actual circumstances of human life. On this view, it is not enough simply to hold that equality only as a future heavenly hope. Over the years, this has put him at odds with writers like Jürgen Moltmann, who have written of hope without accounting satisfactorily for its relationship to the present. Such references to the present as can be found in Moltmann's work, for example, are almost entirely pessimistic. Preston is aware that this belief in human equality often provokes incredulity among those who think that inequalities are so manifest in the natural order of things that they must be taken for granted as being both given and unalterable . His own view is premised on an 'eschatological realism' which envisages the possibility of attaining, even if only in part, a new heaven and a new earth. This is what leads to a new life in Christ, regardless of the perceived differences between people. This belief in equality before God, in turn, leads to a parallel belief in the importance of the pursuit of justice in every area of human concern and activity, in order that liberty and fraternity might become a reality. This belief explains the theological coherence between the otherwise seemingly diverse subjects on which Preston writes.

For all these reasons, equality and justice are not written on only abstractly or philosophically. They are, rather, rooted in the actual stuff of everyday life and, generally, subsumed under a wider concern to articulate the terms and conditions of the moral order of a free, or as he prefers to call it, civil society. Preston rejects attempts to 'engineer' such freedom as is found, notoriously, in Marxist pseudo-'scientific' economic and social theory, respectful though he remains of its more lofty and noble sentiments which focus on the fact that human beings can and, whenever they can, ought to change things for the better. Such freedom, rather, is to be sought amid the actual circumstances of everyday life, however marred they may be by human sinfulness. Here again the influence of Reinhold Niebuhr is writ large. It is, perhaps, strange that Preston, unlike Niebuhr, has paid comparatively little attention to the role of repentance in a free society. This is implicit rather than explicit in his work. Like Niebuhr, however, he agrees that most serious human corruption arises not out of manifest human sinfulness, but as a result of perversions of human virtue. This is so often why evil is difficult to spot until it is too late. In his Gifford Lectures, of course, Niebuhr wrote eloquently of the complicity with which religion so often conspires to disguise the perversion of virtue in this way.

For Preston, this is why it is necessary to remember the importance of the notion of 'ambiguity' in all human moral endeavour. This side of the future kingdom of God, even the best of human endeavour will fall short of glory, as we remain inescapably beset with confusions arising from our inherent sinfulness and arising too, equally importantly, from the incompleteness of our knowledge in areas where we most need its guidance. All this, he writes, requires a 'robust faith' which is able to live with 'ambiguities'.[12] These require the acceptance of 'trade offs' as an inherent part of ethical decision-making. This call for continued realism in the Christian moral life is obviously a main reason why Preston has sustained his interest in such a wide-ranging set of topics.[13]

His use of the term 'social ethics' also needs brief comment, if for no other reason than that the word 'social' is often thought by some to be vacuous and even harmful to whatever it prefixes. First, it stands for the reminder that ethics does not only relate to what is personal and individual and it does so importantly since that is precisely what the word so often enjoins in the popular mind. It relates also to social structures and to questions raised by the exercise of power in society. Whilst these issues had been raised by F. D. Maurice and others, they had lain dormant in the twentieth century until their partial revival by William Temple, who called for a greater attention to competence in social issues. It was this general milieu which was addressed by the Oxford Conference on Church, Community and State in 1937 at which Preston was the Joint Secretary of the Youth section, for under twenty-fives.

In what follows I will briefly appraise some of the main themes of Preston's writing which feature in this collection and elsewhere in his work. They are his views on: free markets, the relationship of technical expertise to Christian moral decision making, and ecumenism and the church and society in general.

Free Markets

Preston is opposed to the resigned acceptance of the ideology of the free market because it treats people as things, denies common justice, and is, therefore, unChristian. It not only victimizes far greater numbers than it rewards, it also invariably rewards the unjust, the unscrupulous and the downright lucky. Criticisms such as these are common enough on the political and economic left and usually lead those who make them to opt for command economies of one sort or another. Preston, however, resists this temptation because he is equally acutely aware of the failings of those alternatives as, for example, has been evidenced by the recent and dramatic collapse of so many of the Soviet-inspired economic experiments.[14] He prefers, rather, to accept the givenness of free market economics because of its obvious successes and argues that it should be treated as an 'institution' which needs a firm political framework, rather than as an untouchable ideology or an uncontrollable natural phenomenon. Here he is clearly breaking with so much of his own Protestant individualist tradition which has long accepted free market ideologies without demur. The prospect of free markets being so controlled raises the central question of the role of the state in economic and social policy and it is at this point that Preston has considerable sympathy with neo-Keynesian economics for the simple reason that it considers the role of the state to be a central one and this, of course, raises again fundamental questions about political organization, social justice and liberty. Whilst it is a constantly evolving and adapting political institution, the democratic state is the most successful means whereby humans have shown they can live together in civil society. Preston sees the three principal types of modern 'party' organization which support democratic states as follows. Conservatives take an organic and hierarchical view in which those on top should be benevolent to those below by allowing their wealth to trickle down. Liberals take an individualist line, stressing freedom and liberty and a level playing field for all. Socialists have an organic view, stressing equality of consideration for all although not equality of outcome.[15] The Conservative view, for Preston, fails on two counts. It embraces an essentially pessimistic view of human nature which does not acknowledge that it is created in the divine image and the *noblesse* does not empirically translate into effective 'trickle down' theories of taxation and wealth re-distribution. It therefore fails the gospel imperative to be mindful of the poor and outcast. The individualism of Liberalism leaves no shelter for the less able and the unlucky. So, the preference is for a neo-Keynesian vision of a state which comes to terms with the way in which free markets operate, recognizes their manifest success and the lack of seemingly any alternatives, but which also assumes responsibility for their control in the interest of all. This is what Preston means by Market Socialism, a phrase which he realizes many will interpret as a contradiction in terms.

This conclusion now, of course, commands something of a consensus as the popularity of left-of-centre politics and economics have significantly changed the political map in the UK, North America and elsewhere. Whilst this popularity might well be largely an instinctive reaction to the excesses of Thatcherite and Reaganite individualism and state minimalism, Preston shows convincingly why it is rooted in a deeper understanding of what it means to be fully human in civil society. The subtlety of this position is an exposé of the shortcomings or the more usual posturings of Christians on the un-reconstructed left and right. An idea, it seems, whose time has come: the so-called 'Third Way', although that term as such is often now used dismissively by journalists. It will be interesting, to say the least, for us all to observe just what effect the exposure of its now widespread adoption will have amid the inevitable vagaries of political and economic experiment and fashion.

Preston is fully aware that there are formidable obstacles which stand in the way of achieving effective state-regulated free markets. One such is the immense and seemingly ever-increasing influence of international and 'offshore' companies and their unaccountability either to national governments or wider international political and economic communities. However, he still believes that difficulties such as these are surmountable. Much of this recently came to the fore in his discussions with Michael Novak, out of which he emerged with considerable credibility. His main criticism of Novak is that '. . . he underplays the defects of the market and is not critical enough of the philosophy of individualism which has been associated with market economies'.[16] The continuing appropriateness of this discussion is self-evident, as political economies generally, and the current one in the UK in particular, try to come to terms with the nature of the often seemingly irreconcilable demands made on the state. On the one hand, it must seek to prevent inflation by the now generally agreed mechanisms of interest rates and money supply and, on the other, it must stimulate private economic initiatives and, in turn, regulate the public interest. In the UK all this now focusses on Europe and, of course, on questions of monetary union and increasing political convergence. Preston is in full support of this and sees no alternative to it, though he remains sceptical about the ability of the European centre to control the diversity of its economic parts by the use of the central management of interest rates alone.

Technical Expertise

Preston has been much engaged with proposals made at the Oxford Conference on Church, Community and State in 1937 about how churches should relate to daily life and technical expertise. In 1939 with Edwin Barker he published *Christians in Society*. In it they wrote: 'It is obvious from the constantly changing and immediate character of Christian decisions, that we are not searching for detailed policies or codes of conduct which could be promulgated as "Christian" ways of behaviour in the contemporary world. That is impossible.'[17] This is followed by a plea, among other things, for the church to recognize technical expertise and Preston's theological ethics, as we have seen, has been preoccupied with this ever since. As a result, he has remained committed to and in turn developed so-called 'middle axioms' (a term which he dislikes, because it gives the impression of drawing logical conclusions from fixed premises). These are statements of policy which occupy the middle ground between specificity on the one hand and generality on the other. They were championed at the, for him and others, seminal Oxford Conference in 1937. They were commended to the churches because they enable them to indicate the general directions which might be taken over any particular issue whilst, at the same time, leaving those who are knowledgeable of the finer and often technically obscure details relating to it to decide exactly what is to be done. They soon found the favour of William Temple, Reinhold Niebuhr and others as a way of enabling the church to recognize the importance for the life of faith of complex political economic and empirical problems and enable something to be said about them in a way which did not claim a knowledge which the church as such does not have. J. H. Oldham and W. Visser 't Hooft describe 'middle axioms' as 'an attempt to define the directions in which, in a particular state of society, Christian faith must express itself'.[18] They are not binding for all time, but are provisional definitions of the type of behaviour of Christians in a given period and given circumstances. In a subsequent defence of this theory Preston writes: '. . . they are arrived at by bringing alongside one another the total Christian understanding of life and an analysis of the empirical situation'.[19] He goes on to point out that, whilst they have a high degree of informal authority, they do not go as far as policy formulation. That, in his view, is properly left not to churches but to individuals and groups of which Christians will be members. The theory was much later criticized, in different ways, by Ralph Potter and Paul Ramsey on the grounds that manifestations of radical evil required denunciations which were more specific than the theory would allow, but Preston, whilst acknowledging this need, has tenaciously defended them in reply.[20]

It must be observed, however, that numerous subsequent church pronouncements have not been of this kind. They have preferred, rather, to venture further than the theory would allow into areas of detailed expertise. As a result, they have often proffered quite detailed solutions to particular problems. A clear example of this is the Report of the General Synod of the Church of England, *The Church and the Bomb*.[21] It did not just call for general nuclear disarmament according to the requirements of middle axiom theory. What it did rather, was to analyse numerous aspects of the then (1982) nuclear arms predicament in some technical detail and propose equally detailed measures for phased unilateral nuclear renunciation. The General Synod of the Church of England subsequently rejected this recommendation as such, although it showed considerable sympathy with it. The situation between East and West was at that time so potentially dangerous, for the whole world, that something more than middle statements were thought called for. There are numerous other examples of recent church reports going beyond middle axiom theory in this way. Whilst they invariably contain the empirical rigour Preston demands, they also go further than he remains willing for them to go in the direction of detailed analysis and often conclusion. He laments that middle axiom theory has not been properly understood, and the debate goes on.

Does 'middle axiom' theory, we must now ask, reflect an older deferential attitude to 'expertise' which existed before the advent of the Thatcherite insistence on public accountability and other influences, such as widespread education and the extent of modern means of communication, brought lively, detailed and widely participatitive debates into the public arena? We now live in information-rich democratic societies and are used, perhaps at times over-used, to calling experts to account, respect their expertise though we may still wish to do. The stuff of our news bulletins and newspapers is full of detailed technical debate of this and that matter and the churches now have had to operate in this milieu. Only time will tell, but the probability is that they will come out of it all rather well as a result of their sustained willingness not to be fazed by technicality or to refrain from expressing their views on particular topics, however tentatively they might at times choose to do so. In all this they are at no more or less advantage than any such other group in society, but they do carry an obligation, for reasons Preston has well made clear, to pay constant attention to complex issues, particularly when they impinge upon human well-being. It is irresistible not to conclude against Preston that not only have the nature of these debates changed since middle axiom theory was formulated, but more importantly the nature of the societies in which they take place has also changed. The churches, no less than any others, have to be involved in the nitty-gritty of making difficult moral and other decisions in a complex, mysterious and frequently frightening world. As they do so, they will not only succeed, they will also fail. And that is a price they have to pay from time to time, just like any others who want to engage in the actual stuff of life, rather than stand apart from it and leave that engagement to others.

Ecumenism and the Church and Society

Preston observes that the notion of ecumenicity arose early in the life of the church as uniformity gave way to diversity, but stresses that it is necessary to distinguish the modern usage of the word from this although the two are related.[22] They share a recognition that the life of the church is but imperfectly realized on earth and, as such, is but a pale shadow of what it could become. He is, however, cautious of aspirations towards a strongly centralized church on the grounds that it would probably be corrupt anyway and would certainly not reflect the diversity of legitimate human responses to the gospel. The only solution is for the church to have a right understanding of the sense in which its diversity is rooted in *oikoumene*, which has had many meanings but has latterly been understood to designate whatever, even approximately, has universal church significance.[23] He welcomes the fact that the modern ecumenical movement has helped to change the attitudes of churches to each other, as well as it has enabled them often to be of a virtual common mind on social and economic issues in general.

Preston has kept up a running commentary on matters of ecumenism and the relationship of the churches to society in general. Ecumenical social ethics, he argues, dates from the World Missionary Conference in Edinburgh in 1910 and was well under way by the end of the 1920s.[24] Ecumenism was rejected by the Roman Catholic encyclical *Moratorium Annus* in 1928, but has since been unstoppable and the Roman Catholic Church has changed. The World Council of Churches, founded in 1948, has been central to it ever since. Preston rejects the view now held by some that the ecumenical movement is dead, though he recognizes that it has lost some of its impetus. Against this he calls for it and the WCC to be taken seriously. By this he means that the work of the WCC must seek to influence the life of the churches through the commanding excellence of its work, something he sadly thinks it has lacked since about 1981. He stresses that the structures of the church must reflect its gospel and that, for this reason, a universal church is an imperative, an impossibility though it seems to remain. There are two main reasons for this. Anglicanism is now a loose federation of thirty-two provinces with effectively nothing at the centre, and the papacy, which is the only real candidate for establishing effective universality, needs such radical reform that it is unlikely to achieve this end. In spite, and perhaps because, of these failures it is imperative that ecumenical Christian witness in social ethics is pursued.

Preston's major contribution to this subject is *Confusions in Christian Social Ethics: Problems for Geneva and Rome*. One result of this is that the attempts of Konrad Raiser and others to construct a social theology based on eschatological realism have been seemingly quietly dropped since he there pointed out that its claims to an intuitive knowledge of what the kingdom will actually be like are as prone to mistaken utopian certainty as are other now discredited ones, such as those of Marxism. He writes: 'It is serious that eschatological realism has dominated so much recent WCC work, and that the present General Secretary is associated with it.'[25] But his criticism of the WCC goes wider than this. He draws attention to the problems of the sheer size and diversity of the WCC, the scale of its agenda as well as to its fissiparousness and downright mediocrity and concludes stridently that: 'Since about 1970 the WCC has not reflected sufficiently on its role, and that of the churches, as change agents or conservers, as catalysts or inhibitors of change.'[26] As a result, he adds, it has sought consensus too readily, implicitly assumed its theology rather than examined it, and not been thorough-going in its empirical analyses. All this has caused it to be utopian in its aspirations and naive about the way power is exercised in the modern world, thereby failing to see that this world is only one of 'two realms' which exist in the sight of God. The other, God's kingdom, impinges upon it in the ministry of Jesus, but it remains in large measure a separate and future possibility. The dubious advocacy of theological powerlessness against all this is, again, rejected.

Whilst recognizing that ecclesiastically, Rome is a very different organization from that of Geneva, it too comes in for criticism. It considers itself to be above the problems it addresses; to have no sense of its own errancy; to fail in seeking consensus (in contrast to the way in which the American Roman Catholic bishops have recently worked by circulating draft documents for comment and discussion); as not recognizing the problems arising from its reliance on one type of natural law thinking; and not showing a willingness to take empirical issues as thoroughly as it ought when discussing human sexuality and other issues.[27]

Against this catalogue of failure and the seemingly little prospect of making any real progress, Preston calls for Geneva and Rome to work together fully (something they have consistently refused to do with the exception of the Sodepax initiative), rather than as they do only in cautious and restricted ways. To achieve this on its side, Rome will have to recognize the richness of diversity within its own ranks.

Geneva, likewise, will have to attend to its problems and re-discover what it means for it to be both a helper-of and a challenger-to the churches.

As yet there is but little sign that either Geneva or Rome will respond at all adequately to this magisterial critical analysis from one of the elder statespersons of the ecumenical movement. It is, therefore, necessary to ask why this is sadly the case, for unless we can answer this question the great twentieth-century ecumenical enterprise in Christian ecumenical social ethics will be seriously at risk.

Preston notes, with approval, that since 1948 the WCC has used 'ecumenical' to refer to the well-being of the whole human race and adds that there is much to be done in re-thinking Christian attitudes to other faiths and philosophies. With further approval, he notes the insistence of Hans Küng on a world ethic for the nations; peace among religions as a re-condition of world peace; and discussion among religions leading to both these things.[28] It is, of course, necessary as well as interesting to ask whether, and if so how, the almost century-long Christian ecumenical aspiration will serve these ends. Its achievements are considerable by any reckoning. At the international level it has maintained running commentaries on issues of the day of naturally varying but undoubted overall quality. By this means, the Christian church has served the wider community well and continues to do so. At local levels the ecumenical movement has engendered mutual understanding, toleration and, most importantly, friendship, and these things have visibly transformed for the better the way Christian communities live together. And all this where only recently suspicion and mistrust fuelled even open hostility. It is a sadness that to some measure this still exists in places like Northern Ireland, but even there is much ecumenical advance and the lingering hostilities have many causes other than religious ones.

Studies of religious pluralism have also done much to further inter-faith understanding, but they have largely left the religions intact as discrete entities. As a result, the churches have probably been guilty of claiming more virtue in their ecumenical aspirations than they have actually achieved. Very few have actually united and others are making, to say the least, but ponderous efforts to do so. Yet others are probably not maintaining their previous ecumenical advances. All this is a long way from the desires of the grass-roots of church membership which is way in advance in its thinking and held back only by institutional restrictions of one sort or another. The questions of now increasingly recognized shared baptism and, to a lesser extent, intercommuion are central to all this. It is to be hoped that all this will put pressure on the churches for reform from below. But will it happen to any significant degree? And what will be the implications for the combined moral witness of the churches to the wider world if it does not? Only time will tell and only then will it be known what the actual legacy of twentieth-century ecumenical Christian social ethics will be like.

Preston's response to all this is that we should go on patiently working and praying for ecumenical advances at all levels and not be surprised or downhearted when it takes much longer than we desire. He does not contemplate any radical re-think of ecumenical first principles, beyond maintaining thorough-going scholarly analysis and following that wherever it leads. This may well be the, and perhaps the only, way forward for the churches in their social ethics and their wider life. But a radical a re-think should at least be contemplated.

This might well begin by heeding the work of Wilfred Cantwell Smith and others who have called for the abolition of the term 'religion' and called for its replacement by 'religiousness' or some such term which focusses on what all religions have in common rather than on what they do not, as is currently and commonly the case.[29] This simple and radical idea could be an extremely powerful agent for change. It points up the folly of so much self-interest which is often but thinly disguised as virtue and does the churches no good in the eyes of those outside them who can see through it for what it is. At the very least, the churches must get their own act together more credibly than they are doing if the *bona fides* of their concern for the wider world and its peace and well-being are to be respected, let alone be effective. In all this, the achievements of a century of Christian ecumenical witness in social ethics will have to be built upon and not ignored in one whit, but it might be necessary to ask more radical questions about the way forward than Preston has shown a willingness to contemplate. As yet, that is.

In this introduction we have briefly seen something of the pedigree, method and specific concerns of Preston's theological ethics. We have noted its emphases: on the ministry of Jesus; on the wider drama of Christian theology and the life of the church; on a right understanding of the relationship of this world to the next; on the need for the Christian church to be ecumenical in both its life and moral witness; and on maintaining a thoroughgoing and professional interdisciplinary at all times whenever it discusses empirical issues. We have also seen something of the rigour with which all these emphases are held together in Preston's work and, in so doing, drawn attention to some of the things which need to be kept in mind when reading it.

In the following selection of Preston's later writings the reader is encouraged to focus on these and other issues, to feel something of the excitement of the ongoing debates and, above all, to want to contribute to them. In that way, the relevance of this particular Anglican tradition and its wider implications for the life of the Christian churches, the world and its concerns will go on being explored and developed. The final chapter by Ian Markham explains why it is important for this to happen.

Part I

Personal Influences and Development

A Bishop Ahead of his Church

Leslie Hunter died in July 1983 at the age of 93. There are good reasons why *Crucible*[1] should contain an appraisal of his life and work, for he was Chairman of the Industrial Committee of the Board of Social Responsibility for many years (indeed of its predecessor prior to the setting up of the Board), but that does not preclude reflections on his wider significance for the Church of England and the ecumenical movement, for he was a many-sided man who influenced the life of the church and nation on a wide front.

Culture

The first was in what in a loose sense is often referred to as the realm of culture. Tissington Tatlow in his *The Story of the Student Christian Movement*[2] refers to his taste as 'fastidious'. The term will do, provided it is freed from any sense of the aesthetic as guyed by Gilbert and Sullivan in *Patience*. He wanted to banish the trashy, not to turn his back on the sordid. He had that hard-to-define but unmistakable when it is encountered quality of robust good taste. His first book, *The Artist and Religion*, was published in 1915 by SCM (long before there was a separate SCM Press), on behalf of a Committee which it had established for work in Colleges of Fine Art and Music. (This was a pioneering venture, characteristic of SCM, which like several other of its pioneering ventures it was not financially able to maintain.) The roots of this aesthetic sense lay in joy in the beauties of the natural world; and it showed itself in Hunter's response to music, art, architecture and liturgy. He had a fine touch himself in playing the piano. He was a good judge of church music, instrumental and choral, and one of his many concerns was to raise musical standards in the diocese of Sheffield where the choirs and organists were more hearty than discriminating. Not that he objected to heartiness. Far from it. He took a particular interest in hymns. He filled the cathedral with choirboys' services devised by himself. He published in his diocesan monthly an acute criticism of the mediocrity of the revised *Hymns Ancient and Modern* of 1951 (as compared with the *BBC Hymn Book* of the same year). The low standards of much church furnishing also distressed him, as did much of the architecture of the church buildings. Sheffield, like most British cities which grew rapidly in the nineteenth century, has much indifferent Victorian gothic architecture and little of its best. The Chapel of Whirlow Grange, the diocesan conference house, and a pioneer among them, is a splendid example of Hunter's taste in its imaginative use of the site in terms of the light and space, restrained but beautiful ornaments, and thought given to the smallest detail, including chairs and kneelers. It speaks of awe and graciousness, strength and calm, beauty and homeliness. To my mind the hymn which best expresses Hunter's spirituality is Robert Bridges' well-known paraphrase, of which the first verse is:

> Happy are they, they that love God,
> Whose hearts have Christ confessed,
> Who by his Cross have found their life,
> And 'neath his yoke their rest.

He was a pioneer in encouraging good quality 'religious' drama in church life, as against the banal which too often characterized what little there was, particularly by his backing of Pamela Keily. He had a fine liturgical sense, and it is unfortunate that he was too old to play a part in the recent revisions of basic services embodied in the *Alternative Service Book*. He had been a moving spirit in liturgical experiments in the 1920s (such as the Grey Book) which were seeking to break away not from the principles of the *Book of Common Prayer*, but from the limitations of its late mediaeval theological and cultural outlook. At this time it was done by supplementary services and alternative intercessions rather than alternative basic texts such as we have now. Hunter was good in his advice on making the best use of the *Book of Common Prayer*. Three years after he retired he published *A Diocesan Service Book* which gave examples of what he had devised as auxiliary to the *Book of Common Prayer*. Those congregations, for whatever reason, who do not wish to remain static, can learn much from him on how to use the Book of Common Prayer intelligently in the twentieth-century.

Parish Life

Hunter gave much thought to the renewal of parish life. He was an early supporter of the Parish Communion movement at its half-way stage, that is to say where the emphasis on fasting beforehand led to the idea of some kind of parish breakfast afterwards. But the renewal of parish life means an articulate, well-informed and active laity, which was noticeably lacking in the Church of England. So lay training, as it was then called, was a priority for Hunter, who lamented that for so many of the laity the confirmation class was their last experience of systematic reflection on their faith. Behind the parish lay the largely unreformed financial structure of the church. So Hunter was a leading figure, perhaps the leading figure, in the group which produced *Men, Money and the Ministry* in 1937, and a sequel, *Putting our House in Order*, in 1941. I suppose the New Synod Group would be the nearest equivalent today, together with the Movement for the Ordination of Women. Hunter took the ministry of women very seriously, and frequently lamented the failure of the church to use the services of well-qualified women, and indeed its fear of them. Many of these themes occur in his primary visitation of the diocese, *Let us Go Forward* (1944), and in a wider and more reflective setting in the one he conducted not long before his retirement, *A Mission of the People of God*.[3] His *A Parson's Job* (1931), largely written out of his experience as vicar of Barking from 1926–30, is an earlier version of these later themes.

Ecumenism

Hunter's concerns, however, extended much beyond the Church of England. He remarks on the isolated position and isolationist spirit of the Anglican Communion, and there is only too much evidence since he retired of how much of this is still retained by, at least, the Church of England. There may be more verbal protestations to the contrary these days, but not the action to match them. Hunter led the way in promoting an Anglican and Free Church Council in Sheffield in the middle of the war, and also an Association of Christian Communities in Sheffield to include the Roman Catholics who in those pre-Vatican II days found any form of co-operation difficult.

Hunter was particularly exercised on the insularity of Anglicans *vis-à-vis* their fellow Christians in Europe (where, of course, the relatively few Anglicans are overwhelmingly expatriate). Next to Bishop

Bell, he was the most tireless of the bishops in keeping and renewing contacts with Christians in Germany, particularly seeing the ecumenical significance of the presence of German prisoners of war in Britain. He was heavily involved in the international side of the work of the British Council of Churches from 1947–61, particularly Inter-Church Aid. He was a leader in the developing Conference of European Churches and, among them, gave special time to the Finnish Lutheran Church. He was one of the first in this country to see the significance of the Taizé Community, and members of it were frequent visitors to Sheffield.

Social Responsibility

However, it is in the area of the social order and Christian social responsibility that Hunter made his main contribution, not least because in it he was so much ahead of his time. This was so from the earlier days of his ministry. In the aftermath of the COPEC Conference of 1924 he was instrumental in the formation of the Tyneside Council of Social Service, which employed Dr Henry Mess (later to become Reader in Sociology at Bedford College, London) as a research officer. He was in thought far in advance of the concentration on 'ambulance work' which was as far as even most of the socially sensitive church folk had got, though he did not neglect practical service to the unemployed, particularly in his time as Archdeacon of Northumberland from 1931–39. A number of vigorous Anglican priests at this time in Tyneside learned a lot from him, notably 'Tubby' Wilson (later to be Bishop of Singapore and then Birmingham), Billy Greer (later Bishop of Manchester) and Ronald Hall (later Bishop of Hong Kong). Indeed the end process of ideas deriving from Hunter's period in Tyneside can still be found working itself out in the Hong Kong diocese, though more on the margin than in the centre of the life of the church there.

Hunter seemed to have a natural sociological bent, to which I shall return. Sociology is inherently a radical study, in that it asks systematic questions about social institutions and social processes that most people take for granted, whether the practical conclusions drawn are radical or not. The Church of England has still not produced one leader trained in the social sciences (as distinct from the natural sciences), but it has produced a tiny number who have made themselves acquainted with them. Of these Hunter was in the best position to pioneer. He asked radical questions about things which the vast majority of church leaders took for granted. He acquired a fine perception of the quite new type of civilization which industrialism has produced in the history of mankind, and of the alienation between it and a church whose organization and assumptions were domestic and rural, and presupposed a virtually stable social order. I remember once when we were talking he expressed great irritation with the way Archbishop Fisher ran bishops' meetings. According to Hunter it was impossible to get any theological or social issue as such discussed because Fisher turned everything into an administrative question.

Sheffield

Hunter came to a highly secularized diocese, where in any case the main church influence in the past, as far as the city of Sheffield was concerned, had been Methodist (by then greatly weakened). He was the second bishop. The first, Burrows, who had had a long period in office since the foundation of the diocese in 1913, had worked hard and faithfully but without any ideas beyond the task of building churches for the new housing estates which proliferated between the wars. These churches were very badly attended. Sheffield was a strong Labour town in politics, with strong Trade Unions, and both were at best apathetic, but also to an extent relatively unusual in England actively hostile to the Church of England, which was thought (rightly or wrongly) to have been against the workers during the great economic slump from 1929. This had hit Sheffield very hard. When I arrived there as a curate there were boys in the choir who had never seen their fathers at work, many of them skilled men like fitters and turners, until they were ten or eleven years old (and whose fathers only got work then through rearmament). Hunter was not disconcerted, even when shortly after his arrival he asked if he could speak to the Trades and Labour Council, and was told he could have nothing to say to them of interest. He set out over a long period to cultivate links with the world of industry, and that was the genesis of Industrial Mission, which has now spread all over the world. Much has happened since Hunter brought Ted Wickham to Sheffield to start it, but nothing to invalidate the insights which led to that start. Hunter realized that the usual church congregation was quite incapable of coping with the alert industrial worker, should he show any signs of wishing to join it, and that there might well have to be a para-church for at least two generations. The few known active Christians among them were almost invariably of the 'pietistic' type and were no help.

of William Temple College in 1947, of which Hunter was a leading protagonist and fund-raiser. (He could never persuade the church officially to give it any money.) It began by providing an extended lay training for women in theological and social studies, in the hopes that they would find jobs paid for by the church, but fairly quickly moved into short course lay training for those in industry, and then into background research. It has now changed its name from College to Foundation, and operates in informal association with Manchester University's Business School, Faculty of Theology, and Extra-Mural Department.

His Significance

Those who knew Hunter like to share personal reminiscences of his pungent remarks, his brief and devastating letters, and the incidents which arose from his notable silences, which many found so disconcerting, and from his almost total absence of small talk. But this is not the place to indulge in them. Four reflections occur to me in thinking on the life and work of a most distinguished leader whose significance might, if we are not careful, be overlooked.

1. *Where should we place him in the spectrum of thought within the Church of England?* The main intellectual and personal influences on him were those of his father, Dr John Hunter, a noted Congregationalist Minister, von Hügel, the liberal Roman Catholic lay theologian and Dick Sheppard (to whom he was curate for a short time at St Martin-in-the-Fields). Later, in the late 1930s, as with a number of others in Britain, he found the social theology of Reinhold Niebuhr a powerful clarification of thought. I remember an informal session at a 'Battle of Britain' ordination retreat when I sat on the floor beside the stool on which he sat and discussed with him the significance of Reiny's thought for the dramatic days through which we were living. It is clear that Hunter cannot be fitted into the 'high' or 'low' category into which it is so often and so lamentably the custom to divide Anglicans. The great majority are not and have never been either; and Hunter is a good example of the non-*necessity* of either if the riches of our own tradition and of the ecumenical movement are to be drawn upon to arrive at an adequate faith and life in our advanced industrial society.

2. *What was the source of his sociological understanding?* There is nothing in his background and training which accounts for it. And at the time sociology was scarcely represented in university studies

except in London and Liverpool. In my judgment it was his experience on the staff of the Student Christian Movement from 1913–21. He was not responsible for anything of the kind in the life of the SCM – his jobs were: Theological College Travelling Secretary 1913–14, Bible Study Secretary 1914–19 and Literary Secretary 1919–21, but anyone with experience of membership of the staff of the SCM at a formative stage of one's life will know what an enormously widening and enriching experience it can be, and the number of contacts it will open up and make possible in the church and social life of the country. Hunter remained in fairly close touch with the SCM. When I offered for ordination and my home diocese, Canterbury, said I should go somewhere industrial, it seemed the natural thing that I should go to Newcastle, where Hunter was then archdeacon. (Subsequently when he moved to Sheffield he moved me there.) I had been involved in developing work for the SCM among students going into industry, which it had pioneered from the early 1930s. They were mainly engineers, who were almost unrepresented in the life of the Movement. To me it seemed the most natural thing that Hunter should start an Industrial Mission in Sheffield; he was developing on a wider front what I had been doing on a narrower one, and with the same preoccupations about the church and industrial life in mind. Indeed the SCM had been hoping to appoint Ted Wickham as Industrial Secretary but Hunter secured him for Sheffield instead. It was also, of course, the SCM which gave Hunter his ecumenical vision. When one considers all that it pioneered and developed its collapse in the student troubles at the end of the 1960s must be seen as a serious blow to the churches. One is constantly looking for people who have had the experiences which life in the SCM provided and failing now to find them. The causes of the collapse and the lessons to be learned from it remain to be investigated. There are now clear signs of recovery, but it is too early to say how far it will go or what precise nature it will take.

Apart from the SCM experience, Hunter was a very good listener, and indefatigable at getting significant groups together on whose experience he could draw. And he was an excellent talent spotter in bringing to the diocese men of very great gifts.

3. *How can the church best ensure continuity in leadership?* Sheffield Diocese was led from 1939–62 by a man whose insight was unsurpassed at the time. But one gift, and that a humble one, was denied him. He had no small talk. That meant that he could not easily and quickly relate to people, nor easily commend his policies

to the diocese and city. He was also liable to be inaudible in a public gathering. It was sad when he was given the Freedom of the City to hear some of the civic leaders still mulling over their grievances from the past about the church, and many of them only half understanding what an ally they had had living and working among them. If Hunter's good work was to be harvested it needed a successor who would follow his policies but have a greater capacity to commend them. He describes in the book he edited, *The English Church*,[4] what he knew of the process of consultation that went on in connection with his successor, but the result was a successor, John Taylor who, whatever his merits, had no such understanding of the mission of the church as Hunter. The troubles that followed in the Industrial Mission were a tragedy. Doubtless there was more than one factor in them, but a main one was the problem of an enterprise which, church-wise, depended very much on episcopal backing and which was faced with a new bishop with a very different understanding. Of course we have been prone to rely too much on episcopal leadership. It can on occasion move matters more rapidly, but it can be precarious if there is a change of bishop. It will always be a necessary element and, that being so, those responsible for appointments need to be aware of the element of continuity as a factor which often needs to be taken seriously. It is probable that this is now taken note of in the new procedures for appointing diocesan bishops. In the case of deans the system remains unreformed.

4. *Has the church caught up with Hunter?* He was a bishop ahead of the church, but it was the church which was behind the times. To some extent it has. It is more alert to the issues to which he was alert, and it has more developed organs for dealing with them. Has it now anyone forging ahead as Hunter did in his time? It is perhaps invidious to speculate. At any rate Archbishop Habgood, to judge from his recent book *Church and Nation in a Secular Age*,[5] although trained as a natural scientist is extremely well read in the sociology of religion and judicious in his social judgments. It is good that there is in York an Archbishop who can cope more precisely with the issues which his predecessor William Temple dealt with in a more general and all-inclusive manner. Hunter had a sharper and more incisive, more mordant, approach then Temple. Both are needed in the life of the church.

The Collapse of the SCM : A Case Study

The collapse of the Student Christian Movement in the 1970s was spectacular. There are signs of revival, but the difference in scale of operations now as compared with twenty-five years ago is striking. Why did the collapse happen? What significance has it for the churches? Have they learned from it? These reflections have been provoked by an article in the prestigious quarterly academic journal *Religious Studies* for September 1984. It is by Dr Steve Bruce of the Department of Sociology in Queen's University, Belfast, and its title 'A Sociological Account of Liberal Protestantism'.[1] In it the SCM is referred to as an illustration of the inherent vagueness and lack of cohesiveness of Liberal Protestantism. I think Bruce's association of the two is fundamentally mistaken. It also has wider implications, for it is clear that in his view the whole ecumenical movement suffers from the same defects.[2] As there are many anti-ecumenical Christians who also assume it involves theological vagueness and a disintegration of belief, and some other sociologists of religion besides Bruce take the same view, it is important to look into this alleged reason for the collapse of the SCM as a case study, lest it too easily becomes quoted as an established fact. Four questions are involved; (1) the error in Bruce's analysis, (2) why did a sociologist of religion make this mistake?, (3) what alternative explanation of the collapse can be offered?, (4) is there a place now for a body like the SCM?

I address myself to these questions in what is meant to be a basis for discussion rather than the product of detailed research. However, I think that research is needed, for matters of great significance in understanding twentieth-century church life are involved. People of middle age or under have had no experience of a large and vital SCM and have some difficulty in grasping the intensity of its vision and the excitement of belonging to it. The book by Davis McCaughey is probably the best source.[3] My references will be entirely to universities, though of course the SCM works in other institutions of tertiary education. I also confine myself to this country, though the SCM is affiliated to the World Student Christian Federation, and the factors involved in its collapse were to a large extent common to continental Europe and the English speaking world (though not to black Africa or India).[4]

Bruce's thesis on Liberal Protestantism is that it is an inherently precarious position because its beliefs are diffuse, it has little or no sense of church, and it accepts as primary the agenda of the secular world and sets out to build bridges to that world. However, bridges carry traffic two ways, and far more used them to walk out of the Christian group than to walk into it. Indeed, if it is believed that all will be saved, what incentive is there to belong? (Bruce shows some theological naiveté here, for it does not take much theological acumen to realize that if you think you have good news, a gospel which enriches life, you want to share it.) In fact Liberal Protestantism is parasitic on an evangelical faith which formed many of its adherents when they were young. Bruce has a point here to which I shall return. As a sociologist he is concerned with how movements grow and spread, with goal changes, with organizational maintenance and with oligarchies and structural differentiation. He maintains that exclusiveness, simplicity and strong commitment are organizationally necessary for survival, whereas Liberal Protestantism essentially breeds divergence; in particular the effort to be relevant undermines it within and between generations, and as far as student generations go this is a potent factor as they change every three years.

We can agree on the need for strong commitment: Christianity cannot survive on Laodiceans who blow neither hot nor cold but are lukewarm. We can agree on the need for simplicity, in the sense that the Christian gospel is not abstruse nor does it require a high IQ to grasp it, provided it is allowed that believers need to show the same quality of thought about their faith as they are capable of using in their life generally and can see how the two must be integrally related, a point of particular importance to students. But what of exclusiveness? If Bruce is right the whole ecumenical enterprise is condemned from the start on sociological grounds. Clearly the concept of exclusiveness needs unpacking. This is not the occasion to deal directly with it, but indirectly all that is discussed here bears on it. Nor is it the occasion to discuss the adequacy of this analysis of Liberal Protestantism. There is certainly some truth in it, for some of its adherents doubted whether, or denied that, the church was an authentic outcome of the ministry of Jesus.

Was the SCM a Liberal Protestant body? It undoubtedly came out of an evangelical milieu which was moving at the end of the nineteenth century towards a more liberal Protestantism.[5] In this thesis Bruce gives a good account of its origin and development. He is particularly good on the personal and family wealth behind many of the early leaders, and their natural network of connections through marriage and other inter-personal relationships. He is good, too, on the split of what came to be known as the Inter-Varsity Fellowship of Evangelical Unions (or IVF) from the SCM. It had begun by 1910. There were further discussions after the 1914–18 war, and the separation became complete from about 1923. The IVF has been known since 1975 as the Universities and Colleges Christian Fellowship. He points out that the IVF subsequently imitated the organization of the SCM in point after point. Why, then, has the IVF held together when the SCM did not? The reason is the fixity of its beliefs. Among other things this has meant little inter-generation conflict in the three-year student cycle. On the other hand, according to Bruce, the SCM has the same definite market as the IVF but no particular product. It was not narrow enough or specific enough to achieve an identity concrete enough to produce any great loyalty. From the late 1950s it reaped the harvest of the 1940s and 1950s. It lacked identity because it lacked a coherent ideology. In particular it is poorly placed for proselytization, which requires the presentation of certainty and assurance. It suffered from poor product identity and brand loyalty. Bruce's conclusion is that the difference between the IVF and the SCM is the difference between Conservative and Liberal Protestantism. He is no sociological reductionist. He fully allows that theology is an independent variable, as this conclusion makes clear. However, it seems to be a travesty of the 1940s and 1950s. But before indicating why I think so, it is useful to attend to one more feature of Bruce's analysis. He holds it to be a weakness of the SCM to be constantly inventing activities which subsequently moved away from it, or wanted to. He gives five examples.

1. The SCM Press, which at one time wanted to drop the name. In fact the reason was that it had expanded far beyond being a publishing house for a student body, and it thought that its name was a puzzle or a hindrance or both to many prospective book buyers. For a short period the name Torch Press was also used, but in the end the original name was retained, and SCM Press remains one of

the largest specialized and unsubsidized religious publishers in the United Kingdom, perhaps the largest.[6]

2. First Conference Estates Plc, which runs conference centres at Swanwick in Derbyshire and Hoddesdon in Hertfordshire. Bruce says this 'followed its commercial interest at the expense of the Movement'. But this is not the point. It has provided centres for ecumenical conferences all the year round, not just sites for summer student conferences and camps. Swanwick was available as long as the SCM wanted it. The company was a pioneer in what is now a commonplace activity, and has succeeded in surviving in a very comparative market. The requirements of the student constituency has moved away from it.

3. The SCM in schools, later known as the Christian Education Movement, which went in for Local Authority finance (and has suffered from its present financial cutbacks). This was because the need was seen to be on a scale far beyond what a voluntary body based only in the sphere of tertiary education could cope with.

4. The Auxiliary Movement (1913–51) among former SCM members, which began to enrol non ex-SCM members and was taken over by the British Council of Churches as an Ecumenical Fellowship. This seems an admirable idea, to further the growth of grass-roots ecumenical experience; the SCM always wanted to feed its ecumenical experience to the life of the church (*pace* Bruce), and not let it remain as a nostalgic memory. There are, however, two practical factors to consider; (1) ex-students move rapidly in the years soon after graduating and it is difficult to keep track of them, (2) it is doubtful whether they ought to be organized in a general society (rather than vocationally) in view of the development of local ecumenical activity in Councils of Churches. The William Temple Association has had this problem. Another attempt at a Graduate SCM is being made; it may well suffer the same fate.

5. The London Medical Group, which has become the pioneer of groups in the Medical Schools of nearly all universities which have one, and is associated with the Society for the Study of Medical Ethics and the quarterly *Journal of Medical Ethics*. This is because the philosophical-theological basis of medicine in Western civilization has been the combination of classical humanism and Judaeo-Christian faith which underlies Western culture. Therefore Christian medical students can study its ontological basis and its ethics with others, and can (and do) make a specific contribution alongside them.

There are other SCM initiatives one can think of. Among them:

6. Pioneering work with oversees students, particularly in London (Student Movement House) and Edinburgh, when there was little other initiative but where now there is a good deal.

7. The Higher Education Group, which has developed from a movement among Christian Dons under the impulse of the SCM. I shall return to this later.

8. Freshers' Pre-sessional Induction Conferences, which were pioneered by the SCM in Newcastle and Durham.

9. Work with students going into industry, mainly engineers, who were usually in jobs which involved much more than technical skill. Out of the method explored in this has come Industrial Mission on a wider basis, whilst Business Schools and Management Courses have proliferated where there were none. A Movement which could generate initiatives such as these with, in most cases, the idea that they must let go of them once they had proved themselves in pioneering stages, would seem to be characterized by boldness and coherence, not wishy-washy indefiniteness.[7]

Bruce's doctoral thesis itself contains evidence that the SCM from its early days was not just a Liberal Protestant body. Tatlow, the General Secretary, worked hard to bring in leaders of the Anglo-Catholic movement in the Church of England, such as Neville Talbot, C. Gore, H. H. Kelly, and W. H. Frere. These, or their successors, were a powerful influence in it when I first met the SCM as an undergraduate. They ensured that it was *inter*-denominational and *non*-denominational (like the IVF); in particular it never infringed any church discipline, nor encouraged its members to do so in the question of, for example, receiving communion, which still causes difficulty. However, in the 1930s the church struggle in Germany made the SCM much more church conscious and in a more fundamental sense. With its WSCF connections with young Germans like Bonhoeffer, the SCM was far ahead of the British churches in appreciating the nature of the German church struggle and of Nazi totalitarianism. It was also ahead in paying heed to the thought of Karl Barth (at least it was in England, I am not so sure about Scotland), and in welcoming the Biblical Theology movement. Indeed I thought it overdid it, though I was not against the tendency. Many of us thought, with Reinhold Niebuhr (who with C. H. Dodd in Biblical Studies was a great influence at the time) that it was necessary to move to the Left politically and to the Right theologically. But how far Right? There I had doubts. But at least the Movement made me take the church seriously, to the point of offering for ordination. Many other former staff members did so and are still doing so. One of its strong features was its emphasis on the Student Volunteer Missionary Union, whose roots lay in the slogan 'the evangelization of the world in this generation' and out of which the SCM originally grew. There was some naive theology with respect to other faiths latent in it, as well as a good deal of cultural imperialism, but my point is that its influence was so strong that (despite disclaimers from SVMU members) the impression tended to be created that the truly committed Christian would offer for missionary service overseas. There was some tension in the SCM between those who tended to think in this way and those more concerned with the Christian commitment in 'secular jobs' e.g. industry, and in the political and social issues of citizenship, but it was a creative tension. The SVMU was disbanded in 1952 because the fundamental witness that lay behind it was seen to require a different instrument in the changed setting between the beginning of the century and half way through it.

I am an illustration of the falsity of Bruce's thesis. I was making a lot of un-thought-out Liberal Protestant assumptions and was forced by the SCM radically to re-think my position both about the Bible and the church. Later, in the next decade, I was to be the encourager from SCM headquarters of a very large number of Bible study groups (as well as many others). This strong Bible-church emphasis continued in the SCM until well into the 1950s, if not longer; but it was always combined in this period with an equally strong commitment to the 'secular' world. From the late 1930s this included a critical concern for the institution of the university itself.

An outstanding Christian who was a Liberal Protestant, saw what was happening and did not like it, was Charles Raven. The SCM did its best to keep in touch with him, for it respected him deeply, but he did not feel at ease with it. He thought that the Movement had reneged on what were to him vital Christian positions.[8] Among the major theologians who were influential in the Movement at this time were Barth, Berdyaev, Brunner, Buber, Maritain, Reinhold Niebuhr and Tillich from outside the United Kingdom; and within it Donald and John Baillie, C. H. Dodd, Alan Richardson, Ronald Gregor Smith, A. R. Vidler and William Temple. It is hard to think of any of them as Liberal Protestants. They could only be called Liberal if the term is used so widely as to mean open to new ideas, and this would have to include many theologians of different confessional traditions, including Roman Catholics; and they could only be called Protestant in the sense of not identifying truth with one group of people or one verbal expression of it, devoid of awareness of cultural content, and this would also have to include the same wide group of theologians.

Why has Bruce got it so wrong? I do not think it is because he is, as he tells us, an atheist. An atheist is perfectly capable of appreciating all the points I am making. It is true that some atheists, including some who are sociologists of religion, seem to have a vested interest in assuming that authentic Christianity is obscurantist, and any attempt to present it in relation to a changing intellectual situation is an indication of its disintegration, but there is no explicit evidence that this is the case with Bruce. Part of the difficulty is the sociological thesis that religious bodies must be exclusive to cohere. This cannot be established by sociology alone; it needs also the disciplines of social psychology and theology. Bruce is too impressed by the first of these, but in principle there is no reason why the concept of exclusiveness cannot be unpacked and differentiated from a pluralism which amounts to incoherence. I think the main reason for Bruce's disastrous error is that he has specialized in investigating extreme evangelical sectarian Protestant groups (Belfast is a good base for this), in which he has been a participant observer, and has come to know many leaders and members well. I think he has taken over their attitude to other Christians without sufficiently probing it. The fact that it fits in with a too simple version of a sociological theory has led him to ignore a mass of evidence from the SCM which goes against it, some of it in his own thesis. How one labels a movement or an individual depends of course on where one starts from oneself. I can see that from a certain evangelical Protestant standpoint all other Protestant and Anglican positions can be called Liberal. In my schooldays Lady Houston was so far on the Right that she called Stanley Baldwin a communist. But it is not a helpful classification to lump together such diverse attitudes under one designation; and it is false to ascribe to all of them certain opinions about the Bible and the church which most of them explicitly repudiated.

If Bruce is wrong, why did the SCM collapse in the 1970s? What do the churches need to learn from it? Is there a place for anything like it in the future? I turn to these questions, and begin by suggesting three reasons for the collapse, as a basis for further reflection.

   1. The growth of denominational chaplaincies. This is not sufficient explanation because Oxbridge has had college chaplains for centuries

and SCM flourished in it. Some other universities have also had them. However there is a spaciousness of life in Oxbridge and an ease of communication which makes a diversity of activities much easier. There is also an established niche in them for the chaplains. It is not so in most universities. In them the establishment of chaplaincies caused problems for the SCM. Its strong point has been that while as a Movement it has been wholly committed to the Christian faith, its membership has always been open to explorers and enquirers. In a century of intense religious enquiry and criticism many who could not conscientiously join a church and whom any church would have difficulty in accepting could be members of SCM. To make this open membership possible the student leaders of branches have had to be of high quality and Christian commitment, for the strength of the Movement has been that it is very much a student led body, with young graduates serving on its staff as peripatetic advisers, and with a more senior but relatively short-term leadership at the centre (Tatlow's length of office has not been repeated). These committed leaders have had to hold their faith in an open way. The vast majority of such leaders have been young men and women who have come to the university as church members, and from the SCM have caught a vision of the unity and renewal of the churches which vastly deepened their understanding of Christian faith and life. It meant that they were ahead of the general life of the churches, and their subsequent contribution to it has been vital for the growth of the ecumenical movement. At the same time they were encouraged by the SCM to be intensely loyal to the church, which was constantly stressing that it was not itself a church.

This was one reason for its undoing. It depended on the churches leaving a space for the SCM. In my young days I naively thought they had done so. I used to say in speaking or preaching about the SCM that they had made an ecumenical move at the university level by letting the SCM act for them. I was quite wrong. Until the end of the last war the churches had hardly awoken to the universities, apart from Oxbridge and a few others. When they did discover them, Anglicans and Methodists in particular established chaplaincies. (The situation is different in Scotland where the Church of Scotland has never had its own student society, perhaps because of its great numerical preponderance over other non-Roman Catholic Christians, and where significantly the SCM did not collapse to such an extent as in the rest of the United Kingdom.) In establishing chaplaincies the churches spoke fair words about the SCM but in effect took away much of its leadership. The SCM, true to its churchly connections, could not object to the establishment of denominational chaplaincies and, indeed, spent much time in trying to get the different Christian societies to work together ecumenically. It was not easy. In particular if Roman Catholics came in at one door the IVF was liable to go out at another. It frequently took time away from more outward-looking tasks, and sometimes it ended in the elision of the SCM itself.[9]

Given the state of inter-church relationships the development of such chaplaincies was probably inevitable. They were very far from following the principle adumbrated by the Lund Faith and Order Conference of 1952 that they should do together all that conscience does not require them to do separately, and they are still far from following it. Further, the growth of student numbers and of the number of universities and colleges made them beyond the power of a private society on the scale of the SCM to cope. It would have required massively greater church financial support, and it was beyond the powers of the imagination of the churches to think of universities in a creative way and give, jointly or severally, financial support on the scale required when they would not have control over its expenditure. In effect this was a betrayal of the ecumenical enterprise. (Nearly all the leaders of the ecumenical movement came from the SCM and the WSCF.) It was a foretaste of the stalling which has taken place since in England when a point of crucial ecumenical decision has been reached. In England the Church of England bears a heavy responsibility for this. On the whole chaplaincies are run in a 'liberal' way (not in Bruce's sense), and they have undoubtedly taken over a lot from the traditions of the SCM. But they are inevitably more official and less student-run than the SCM. And they do overwhelmingly cater for the already committed. Moreover with the demands made upon by them, and the opportunities open to them in the universities today, few students can have, or should have, the time for two religious bodies. So, with the traditional source of student leadership undermined, the SCM was much weakened and brought near to total collapse.

On the whole the churches are primarily concerned with keeping their students loyal to themselves during the intense years of university life. The chaplains collect sympathetic students round them in a kind of gathered congregation, but it tends to leave out a sense of openness and adventure and it institutionalizes paternalism. The advent of Roman Catholic students and staff as members of the SCM in the new atmosphere produced by the Second Vatican Council has not altered the basic situation. Participation has been fruitful, though of course the great majority of active Roman Catholic students are linked with their chaplaincies, which have been co-operative in a way previously unknown, but those chaplaincies are also primarily concerned with keeping students loyal to the church. A Christian concern for the well-being of the university as an institution is hardly in evidence.

These developments had weakened the SCM by 1960. It soon took a step which hastened its decline. In 1963, when Bishop Ambrose Reeves was General Secretary, it decided that ecumenism had become official and was no longer a matter of pioneering. The churches were proving extremely slow to move. Greater theological flexibility was not matched with institutional flexibility; church structures, which are to a large extent power structures, had proved extraordinarily tough. (Perhaps only a severe inflation will shake them.) Students began to be disillusioned with institutions, in church and society alike. The SCM decided to leave ecumenism to the churches and to be where they thought the students were, by working for a new and socialist order of society. A gentle decline set in, and in the atmosphere of uncertainty it proved impossible to attract a General Secretary of sufficient calibre. No great change occurred until after the Manchester SCM congress of 1969, which was a lively affair, more radical and spontaneous and less structured than the previous large congresses. After that the democratic structure of the SCM proved its undoing.

· 2. Radical criticism of current institutions by students was much more widespread than previously. Having grown up with more resources spent on them than any previous generation in British history, they began to be uneasy about the further pursuit of affluence (though inclined to take for granted and rely on the affluence that already existed). Sensitive to this the SCM was caught up in the student criticism of structured activities. There was a genuine sense of openness and freedom in this reaction. Grass-roots participation and instant communal decisions produced a vigorous atmosphere. One could experience it at conferences. But a heavy price was paid. Three years of unstructured activities in a student body can bring it near to collapse. Moreover, a section of radically politicized students was in fact structured. They came into their own when the SCM was caught up in the student troubles of 1969–70. Its organization, we can now see, had always been open to capture should any group of people with an uncompromising ideological slant, whether political or theological, set out to capture it. This had never happened and indeed had never been thought of. 'Liberal' people (how hard to avoid that term!) who do not take power seriously, particularly in religious organizations, and assume everyone is frank in what they say, are easy to dupe. I experienced that when 'fellow travellers' in the leadership of the National Union of Students bamboozled most of the membership in the years immediately after 1945. To say this is not necessarily to impugn their integrity; most did what they thought their ideals required. The SCM came under the control of a group of people who followed a Marxist or neo-Marxist political analysis and represented only a small minority of students. Decline was rapid, and the SCM ceased to exist in most universities. Once in control of the assets it was possible to carry on with little relation to actual student life. Students themselves contributed almost nothing financially to the Movement, and a General Assembly of less than fifty people, a number of them members of staff and their wives, could control the operation subject only to the very broad requirements of the Trust Deeds.

There was a deliberate attempt to wipe out the historical traditions of the SCM. Radical discontinuity was thought to be necessary. There was more awareness of affinity with student frustrations than with the traditions of the SCM. Quasi-apocalyptic political language was used. Issues were foreshortened; there was no long-term vision. The General Secretaryship was abolished in 1972 and with it any longer term senior leadership. A further element entered, a return to nature from the cities, with the move of the headquarters from London to Wick Court, near Bristol, in 1974. Communal houses were set up which quickly showed all the problems which a theological and socio-logical study of Christian communes in history would lead one to expect. Inherited resources were spent as a windfall to finance radical experiments, with no sense of obligation to the future. There were special projects, but in effect no national movement. Constitutions were manipulated. A period of extremely rapid and chaotic staff turnover began. There were not enough staying long enough to provide some ballast against the changing three-year student moods. It was in the middle of all this that the SCM Trust Association, after a natural reluctance to interfere held it back for some time, appealed in 1975 to the Charity Commissioners to investigate the use of SCM resources, a quarrel which was eventually settled in 1979. It is argu-able that the situation was already on the mend and that an inter-vention earlier might have been better. For one thing the leadership never lost touch with Robert Mackie, Tatlow's successor as General

Secretary until 1968, after which he became an ecumenical world figure and, after retirement, a revered counsellor. He managed to keep contact with the changing and chaotic student leadership.

The lesson of the 1970s would seem to be that Christians should show more wisdom in dealing with political goals and tactics, and realize that this realm is inescapable; and that Christian bodies should see that their constitutions correspond with their insights into the sins and follies of mankind, and so preserve themselves as far as possible from the more dubious forms of power politics.

From about 1976 the SCM began to discover how far it was from the student constituency, and has been recovering its heritage as a mainstream Christian movement, though with more explicitly radical theology and political tendencies than was explicit before. The journal, *Movement*, bears lively witness to this. Bruce should note, however, that these tendencies are not Liberal Protestant ones.

3. There has been a change in the composition of the student body, which is much more heterogeneous. It used to be drawn almost entirely from middle-class families upwards, just the classes in which the churches were, and are, relatively strongest. It is not that large numbers of students from working-class backgrounds now enter universities. The proportion is regrettably low and, if anything, is falling. It is that large numbers of first-generation students from lower-middle-class families have entered, who have had less contact with the churches, and who have not the expectations of leadership in the future to the same extent as university students have had in the past. They are, however, socially mobile upwards, and are mostly destined for suburban life and professional jobs. Nevertheless their role in society is important; without them an advanced inter-locked industrial society could not carry on for a fortnight. They need a personal and social vision beyond that of upward mobility, for the health of their own soul and that of society.

I do not claim that this is an entirely adequate analysis of the collapse of the SCM, which needs more investigation, but these factors point the way to one. They suggest that it had a strong church consciousness and was deeply committed to the ecumenical movement well beyond that of the churches then or now. Hence the initiatives of the churches at a time of rapid expansion of higher education weakened the SCM, which needed far more financial resources to cope. The weakening meant that it attracted less outstanding top-level leadership, and there was less of it, so that it was not able to provide sufficient check against the dramatically changing moods in the student world from the late 1960s, until the General Secretaryship was abolished. Furthermore, the SCM could be charged with having a liberal theology in the sense of having an insufficiently realistic understanding of power politics in both secular and ecclesiastical affairs. This is a study in itself and not, of course, the liberalism of which Bruce wrote.

I come, therefore, to the question: has a body like the SCM a future? It cannot have the predominant role of the past, when it had hundreds of study groups, two large summer conferences, and a winter congress of 2,000 students every four years. This is so on financial grounds if no other. All corporate bodies find that inherited income does not keep pace with rising costs. Some of the SCM's resources were wastefully used in the 1970s. What remains is now being used by a drastically slimmed, but excellent, staff who are helping members to explore Christian faith and practice, as of old, in a self-critical spirit, with no sacred cows, no holds barred, and nothing human considered foreign to the gospel. Inherited resources will not last indefinitely. The SCM has not had wealthy backers for many years. Large legacies are increasingly unlikely. Students are not in a position to contribute much towards overheads in addition to the cost of joining in present activities. Trusts may produce something; but a lot depends on how much financial backing comes from the churches.

Here there are difficulties. It must be rooted in churches but it will also be critical of them. It must move among the many students who have no use for the churches and some who regard them as an actual obstacle to the spread of the gospel (as the theologian Charles Davis did when he left the Roman Catholic Church). Will the churches put more money into a body from which so much criticism of them will come? This is indeed the challenge which the ecumenical movement itself has always presented to the churches. It is a challenge to them that ecumenical causes are relative newcomers on church budgets, which are increasingly under strain in financing long established structures and ways of working. New causes tend to be prime targets for cuts, rather than for increased expenditure. The principle of 'last in, first out' can apply beyond industry. The adequacy of the Christian presence in universities is of enormous importance. I have a suspicion the churches think they have handled this quite well. In fact there is a large gap as compared with the past, and the churches are correspondingly weaker.

Should the SCM continue? Societies can be born to satisfy a need and fade away when their task is done. Indeed if their task is done it is better that they should fade away rather than drag on an otiose existence. I am not persuaded, however, that the task of the SCM is done, and that for six reasons:

1. Chaplaincies inevitably tend to channel students into familiar paths rather than into exploring new ones. They are more local and lack in practice the national and international network the SCM has to offer. The SCM is needed to help them to explore as far as it is possible for them to do so in the brief period of their student days. For most of them such an opportunity will never recur.

2. This experience needs to be fed into the life of the churches. At the moment there is nothing like the feeding into them that there was a generation ago of those who have had a more far reaching ecumenical experience than the churches provide. In searching for people under forty for important jobs who have had the experience that being a leading student in, or staff member of the SCM would provide, one finds that they hardly exist. There is a gap.

3. It is not cynical to say that many evangelical students need the SCM. They have fundamental strengths but they are too narrow. It has often been noted that some of the best Christian students, dedicated to the unity and renewal of the churches, have been evangelicals; they have been given a personal faith for which they will always be grateful, but they find the institutional expressions of evangelical faith narrow and restricting and not liberating. In short they are 'browned off'. The SCM is for them. There is an impression that many ex-IVF members leave the church and form part of what Dr Jack Dominian calls the 'Third Church'; men and women in their forties and fifties who want to be Christians but can't bear the churches. (They may well find some ex-SCM members in the same position.)

4. From what has already been said it is clear that other students need the SCM, for instance the religiously under-developed fresher, and the growing number of students who arrive at the university with no previous religious contacts or commitments, and who begin to take seriously the phenomenon of religion.

5. The religious picture in universities is not encouraging. Chaplaincies do good work. Evangelical societies continue much as before, though with a rather wider spread of concerns. (This is partly because some members would have been in the SCM if there had been an effective branch to join.) But at a time when there is a wide but uncommitted interest in religion, and more studying of it than ever before, there lacks a relatively informal, definitely Christian, but open

student religious society where the enquiring student can be at home. On some campuses, to judge by the notice boards, Buddhist societies appear to be the most active. There are many signs in our society of a feeling after what we may vaguely term 'religion' or 'spiritual values' (neither term appeals to me), but little sign that the churches are able to communicate with such seekers or that it ever enters their head that they might. Of the four traditional themes of student discussion – sex, sport, politics and religion – a fifth has to be added in these hard times, jobs, but religion is still there. Universities are of key importance in this respect, and it is hard to be content with the present state of Christian witness in them.

6. Universities themselves need an SCM. They are not in good shape. They have been very badly treated by the government in recent years, and in such a series of short-term steps that it has been impossible to plan ahead rationally. The individualism of many dons and departments has not helped, but the short-sighted criteria with which the government operates, whilst having some point against a remote academic indifference to the needs of society, is grossly inadequate to understanding the crucial role universities should play in the community. They should be centres of excellence, communities of mutual dialogue in a search for the common good, critics of society in terms of the best professions of the society, and sources of a sense of wonder and mystery in life. A generation ago the SCM called in question the whole 'liberal' basis of the university (Bruce should note this), as a shallowness which collapsed when it was challenged by Nazism.[10] The pretence of even that basis is hardly mentioned now. Universities are driven to sell themselves in the crudest terms of increasing the Gross National Product. Christians, on the basis of their faith, have to call the universities to a deeper understanding of their role and the commitments it calls for, which have to be continually explored and striven for. Students accept too readily what is offered by universities and are not sufficiently alert to the implicit, and sometimes explicit, ideology it conveys to them. The SCM is well placed to raise the questions and to work with chaplaincies on them.

One thing seems clear. In the end, whatever senior leadership is provided by chaplaincies or in other ways, students must find ways of ministering to students, and need an appropriate structure within which to do so. The generations change so rapidly that, as a general rule, only those who are students or who have not long gone down are sufficiently in touch to organize this. Seniors need to be ready with financial and moral support, and readiness to lend a hand when needed. For the sake of the unity and renewal of the churches, as well as the health of the universities, it is urgent that this task be better accomplished than it is at present.

3

Remembering Reinhold Niebuhr

Theological giants of the immediate past, though they have a permanent place in the history of the church, can often lose their prominence in the decades following their death. How far has this happened to two men who were leading figures both in church and state earlier in this century, William Temple and Reinhold Niebuhr? Both were also leading figures in the formative stage of the Ecumenical Movement. One can no longer take it for granted that William Temple can be referred to in the United Kingdom without further explanation. In the case of Niebuhr attention in the USA has never ceased. Three major studies of him are due in the autumn of 1992. Theses on him continue to be written. Also the fact that his younger brother, Richard (who for many years was a Professor at Yale) remains a significant figure, adds to the continued interest in Reinhold. In the United Kingdom an undercurrent of interest in both continues.

Reinhold came suddenly to the fore in the United Kingdom in 1936 with the publication by the SCM Press of his *An Interpretation of Christian Ethics*. In an astonishing rise to fame he was appointed Gifford Lecturer at Edinburgh for 1938–39, and he remained a dominant figure throughout the 1940s. A severe stroke in 1952 restricted his activities and, among other things, prohibited foreign travel. In Manchester we were sad that it prevented him receiving in person the honorary DD that the university had awarded him. However, he continued writing, and by his death had produced more than twenty major books and an enormous number of articles and reviews.

I was one of the first in the United Kingdom to read a book by Reiny (as everyone who knew him called him). It was in 1933. I was an undergraduate at the London School of Economics. An American research student arrived with Reiny's recently published *Moral Man and Immoral Society*. He lent it to Arnold Nash, the member of staff of the Student Christian Movement whose field included LSE. He lent it to me. We were both so excited by it that we suggested to the editor of SCM Press that it be published in the United Kingdom. He was the well-known Baptist, Hugh Martin, whose major life's work was to build up the SCM Press. We found that he had rejected it as an unChristian book! Although it was on the reading list of politics courses in university for many years it was not published in the United Kingdom until the SCM Press made amends by issuing it in 1963. In 1935, *An Interpretation of Christian Ethics* arrived from the USA, and this time Arnold Nash and I laid siege to Hugh Martin and persuaded him to publish it here.

However, before the United Kingdom had heard of Reiny he had had a notable career in the USA. His father had been a German immigrant as a young man, and the family grew up in a German-speaking Christian milieu with both Lutheran and Reformed links. Reinhold and Richard moved to the wider setting of Yale, and after leaving there Reinhold became minister of Bethel Evangelical Church, Detroit, from 1915 to 1928. During this period Henry Ford was developing the model T car (hence the jingle 'Henry's made a lady out of Lizzie'). Reiny's reflections on his pastorate, *Leaves from the Notebook of a Tamed Cynic* (1929), make fascinating reading. I have twice read extracts from it during silent meals at an ordination retreat as an antidote to any lurking spurious piety that might be around. In 1928 Neibuhr was called to a Chair at Union Theological Seminary, New York, and there he stayed until his retirement in 1960. The Seminary was his spiritual home and its chapel his church base. Spiritually he became more alive to Catholic elements in the Christian tradition, chiefly through his marriage to Ursula, an English Anglican; but he never spared the complacencies of institutional Catholicism or Protestantism.

What made his writings such a breath of fresh air in the 1930s? It was a traumatic time. The Wall Street crash of 1929 had led to a serious economic depression with mass unemployment. Capitalism seemed to be collapsing, as Marx had said it would. The Nazis came to power in Germany; the international situation was steadily deteriorating. The League of Nations, in which a lot of hopes had been invested, seemed powerless to prevent a drift towards war.

Christian opinion was confused. After the appalling slaughter of the 1914–18 war, which Christians could only justify by regarding it in crusade terms as 'a war to end war', enormous emotional capital was put into the League of Nations. It was backed up by an unrealistic theology, which spoke of nations as if they could act in the same simple moral terms as individuals, and did not analyse power structures in human affairs (particularly in relation to sovereign states). It did not examine how Christian faith should understand power in human life. At the heart of that faith is a disclosure of divine *agape,* focussed in the Cross of Christ. How does it bear on the collective affairs of humankind? Basically it was a problem of the relation of justice to love. Instead of tackling this, much Christian thought at the time seemed socially irrelevant and to be suffering from moral paralysis.

Niebuhr's writing threw a flood of light on this situation. His more political analyses clearly had theological roots. This came through particularly in his sermonic essays. *Beyond Tragedy* (1937) is a splendid collection of these. It is impossible to convey to anyone who did not hear him the power of the torrent of words which came from him. This was not due to oratorical tricks, but to a mind wrestling as he spoke with basic biblical and doctrinal themes to illuminate grave current events. He ranges over narrative, prophecy, parable and Pauline theological statements. One of my friends, with whom I shared a flat in London, was killed in the Dunkirk retreat of 1940. A fortnight before I heard of his death I had a letter from him in which he said he had taken *Beyond Tragedy* with him into the army and that it had kept him going.

Niebuhr's call for a movement to the Right theologically, from what he would call a simple moralism, and the Left politically, to cope with a dislocated economic system which was extricating itself from depression only through re-armament, seemed indeed a message for the time. Also in the darkest days of the 1939–45 war, Reiny's support for our resistance to Nazism was a great comfort. He had long abandoned his earlier pacifism, and his *Why the Christian Church is not Pacifist* (1940) was written partly to counteract any incipient isolationism among Christians in the USA in the spurious guise of maintaining innocence by keeping out of the conflict. His *Europe's Catastrophe and the Christian Faith*, in the same year, reinforced this.

Then came the Gifford Lectures, *The Nature and Destiny of Man* (1941–43), one volume on human nature and one on human destiny. This is Niebuhr's major work. It is important because Reiny had been thought by many to be merely an acute analyst of sin and a prophet of doom, as his attacks had mainly been on personal and collective sin, and especially on any claims to political or religious perfection. He did that, but he did much more. The Gifford Lectures were intended to be a synthesis of Reformation and Renaissance insights. Here he brought out the 'indeterminate possibilities' of human history, if humans are emancipated from false assumptions of inevitable progress and utopian hopes.

By now Reiny was a world ecumenical figure, and a key person in the launching of the World Council of Churches in 1948. He had also become an adviser to politicians in the USA, including the White House.

So what of the later Niebuhr? How far did he change? His pacifism had gone. Next to go were semi-Marxist socialist arguments. Strictly economic issues, as distinct from political ones, had not been his main concern, but in the early 1930s capitalism seemed to be collapsing. Niebuhr was a founder of the Fellowship of Socialist Christians in 1931. In 1935 he founded its quarterly journal *Radical Religion*, which later changed its name to *Christianity and Society*, as the FSC changed its name to Frontier Fellowship. The journal lasted until 1956. I was at one time the British agent for it, and I possessed what I am almost certain is the only complete set in the United Kingdom. I have presented this to the John Rylands University Library, where it will be very useful to research students.

Roosevelt's New Deal had shown that capitalism could be rescued and Reiny came to support it. After 1945 he became a supporter of 'Americans for Democratic Action', an element within the Democratic party. With the advent of the Cold War in the later years of Stalinism he supported anti-communist government policies, but not in any way the hysteria of McCarthyism. He had opposed a liberal 'soft' utopianism; he was equally opposed to Marxist 'hard' utopianism, Marxist illusions, a temptation to 'fellow travellers' in the 'west', needed exposure. But that did not mean that much of the talk of 'freedom' by the New Right in the USA should be accepted. Its ideological nature needed exposure. Moreover, the kind of political realism as evinced by the Watergate scandal was not what Reiny meant by political realism. It was merely cynicism.

Niebuhr's writings became more concerned with overall historical themes, where he moved from the emphasis on tragedy (as in *Beyond Tragedy*) to irony (as in *The Irony of American History*, 1951). But he never ceased to address the problem of relating ethical insights and goals to the self-interest of groups, especially states, and to explore how to move in the vast and morally ambiguous area of international relations with as much integrity as possible. His theological stance also enabled him to show how, whilst it is necessary to take the social sciences seriously, caution needs to be exercised because of the over-simple rationalist assumptions about human nature which are often operative (and often unavowed) in allegedly ideologically neutral sciences. So whilst Reiny changed his opinions on many particular issues he never changed his basic theological stance in illuminating the paradoxes of human existence.

Criticisms of Niebuhr have been principally two-fold. His analysis of *agape* as heedless self-sacrifice is held to be overstated. This is well discussed in Gene Outka's important book, *Agape* (1972). Feminist theologians have thought his analysis of pride and insecurity as the root of sin to be too masculine, and have stressed that women tend to be too dependent and submissive. Daphne Hampson discusses this in her chapter in *Reinhold Niebuhr and the Issues of our Time* (ed. Richard Harries, 1986), a useful symposium of papers given at a colloquium at King's College, London. Any criticisms by Liberation Theologians have to be qualified by their tendency to take over elements of a discredited Marxist critique of capitalism as if it were an established science. Meanwhile European theologies of hope, influenced by Moltmann (who was in turn influenced by the Marxist, Ernst Bloch), have advocated a recovery of utopian hopes on the basis of the new things God will bring about, as the starting point for ethical decisions. This is sometimes and confusedly called 'eschatological realism'. Its results in terms both of analysis and what is advocated are not impressive.

Reiny remains an inspiration to all who stand for a radical social commitment in hope, whilst remaining alert to the ambiguities of human life, as illuminated by a Jewish-Christian understanding of divine *agape* in Jesus. (He did not deal with the Muslim faith.) Reiny was a pessimistic optimist. He knew that the world of faith and the world of politics cannot be separated. There is a push of duty and a pull of grace. A faith adequate to cope with it needs to relate its partial understandings to the mystery of God's transcendence. In its light there is a constant need for self-criticism (including national self-criticism, more difficult as this is). We must be alert to the hidden falsehoods in our truth as we expose in its light the false elements in the truths of others.

I conclude with one of his most pregnant passages.

Nothing that is worth doing can be achieved in our lifetime; therefore we must be saved by hope. Nothing which is true or beautiful or good makes complete sense in any immediate context of history; therefore we must be saved by faith. Nothing we do, however virtuous, can be accomplished alone; therefore we must be saved by love. No virtuous action is quite as virtuous from the standpoint of our friend as it is from our standpoint; therefore we must be saved by the final form of love which is forgiveness (*The Irony of American History*).

Reading Niebuhr

For someone coming to him for the first time I suggest two books: the sermonic essays which make up *Beyond Tragedy*, and *The Children of Light and the Children of Darkness* (1943). The sub-title of the latter is 'A Vindication of Democracy and a Critique of its Traditional Defenders'; it is a short and good introduction to his social ethics. Some of his later sermons and prayers are included in *Justice and Mercy* (ed. Ursula Niebuhr, 1974). Then one can go back to *Moral Man and Immoral Society*, and then be ready to tackle the Gifford Lectures, *The Nature and Destiny of Man*. Of his later works *The Self and the Dramas of History* (1955) is his most philosophical work. *The Structure of Nations and Empires* (1959) is his chief discussion of international relations. A biography by Richard W. Fox, *Reinhold Niebuhr* (1985), shows a remarkable insight from a younger man who never met him. It is a little weak on Reiny as an ecumenical figure, but good on his early years and his rather sad last years.

4

Christian Ethics

Christian ethics can most simply be differentiated as the way of life appropriate to those who accept the Christian faith. However, in the course of nearly two thousand years Christianity has become a worldwide protean phenomenon. Therefore there are many points of view from which Christian ethics could be analysed, and many ways in which its history could be charted. This account is written by one who can reasonably be said to be in the mainstream of Christianity, as it has been historically expressed. So the plan of this article is to begin with an overall view of the phenomenon of Christian ethics, then to deal with its foundation in New Testament times in the ministry of Jesus and the interpreter of Jesus of whom we have most evidence, St Paul, and conclude with a brief mention of criticisms of Christian ethics made in recent years.

A Survey of Christian Faith and Ethics

The Christian faith, as its name implies, is specifically related to Jesus Christ. It can be said to rest on two presuppositions. The first is the reality of God. But then the question is raised, what sort of God? (since there have been many and diverse gods in human history). The second presupposition is that God is as disclosed in the ministry of Jesus Christ. This has become a single name in common usage, though the term Christ is rooted in the Jewish faith within which he lived. It refers to an expected Deliverer who would be sent by God to put the world to rights. The earliest Christians were those Jews who believed that this had indeed happened in the ministry of Jesus.

The Jewish faith is a strongly ethical one, quite unlike the various mystery religions which were current in the Roman Empire at the time of Jesus. So it is no surprise that the Christian faith is also strongly ethical. Its sources are found first of all in the Bible. The Old Testament is seen as preparing for and being fulfilled (though also in many respects negated) by the ministry of Jesus; the New Testament is seen as a witness to the life, death, and triumph over death of Jesus, and to the new community, or People of God, which came into existence as a result of his ministry. Experiences after his death led the closest disciples to worship God through him. An extraordinary thing for strictly monotheistic Jews to do; and that is why the Christian church commonly ends prayers with the phrase 'through Jesus Christ our Lord'. However, even the term 'resurrection' which the Christians used to interpret Jesus' triumph over death is drawn from the vocabulary of Judaism in the last few centuries BCE.

Initially the traditions about Jesus were transmitted within the new Christian congregations by word of mouth, and in ways relevant to their situation. Later they were incorporated into the four Gospels, each author having his own theological stance. Mark is the earliest, about forty years after Jesus' death. Prior to that we have letters from St Paul to various churches, several of which he founded. These cover both his basic understanding of Christian faith and ethics, and his answers to specific ethical problems which had arisen in the life of these young churches.

It took three or four centuries before it became quite clear which books would be regarded by the church as included in the canon (or rule) of scripture, and thus in the Bible as we know it. So the sources of Christian ethics also include the tradition of ethical reflection in the community of the church down the centuries as it was brought to bear on the changing situations it faced. And the data themselves of these problems became another source of Christian ethics. Underlying all is the conscience (or power of reasoning on ethical questions) which Christians share with all human beings.

The questions which had to be raised ranged from the intimately personal to the complexities of economic and political life, including those of war and peace. A classic typology of five characteristic attitudes to the whole realm of human culture which continually appear in Christian history is that of Richard Niebuhr's *Christ and Culture*.[1] These are (1) Christ against culture, a kind of other-worldly pietism; (2) the Christ of culture, a Christianity which casts a gospel glow over the existing order and hardly challenges it; (3) Christ and culture in paradox, which makes a sharp separation between God's kindly rule in the church and his stern rule (for the sake of order) in public life; (4) Christ above culture, meaning a triumphalist church which seeks control over public life; (5) Christ transforming culture, a leaven in the lump of personal and public life which allows for a legitimate autonomy of secular disciplines and seeks to influence but not necessarily to control institutions. All five positions refer back to the same biblical material, showing how important is the way it is decided to move from the Bible to the modern world. These five types have usually not been exemplified in totally pure ways; they are what the sociologist Max Weber called 'ideal types', in which an attempt is made to distil the distinctive elements and different tendencies in each. But it is suggested that since they have reappeared so constantly in Christian history each is likely to have some basic cogency. For instance, the Christ against culture type speaks powerfully when Christians find themselves against hostile and oppressive governments; or perhaps a small minority in a particularly alien environment. However, this is not to say that all five are equally plausible. All of them originally developed against the background of a social order relatively stable compared to that which the world has known since the scientific and technological changes which we call the Industrial Revolution. This has produced a new kind of civilization, and one involving rapid social change over almost the whole world. Today the fifth type, Christ transforming culture, seems to be much the most cogent, and more so than in the days of St Augustine and Calvin whom Richard Niebuhr finds to be two of the most notable examples of it.

This typology illustrates the protean nature of Christianity. Beginning as a reform movement, associated with a charismatic figure in the Jewish countryside, it rapidly became a predominantly urban movement as it spread along the great road routes of the Roman Empire. The direct Jewish influence soon ceased (particularly after the fall of Jerusalem to Rome in 70 CE), and that of the pervasive Hellenistic culture increased, with its legacy of Greek philosophy and ethics. After the fall of Rome itself four centuries later, Christianity became heir to the rickety Roman Empire, and in due course embodied itself closely in the institutions of one civilization, that of Europe and its later offshoots in the 'new world'. Christianity has now spread globally and this presents it with new doctrinal and ethical issues.

Living through these changes, Christianity has split into five broad confessional traditions, each of which has achieved a certain stability and each with a doctrinal and ethical style of its own. (1) The Orthodox, primarily in eastern Europe and Russia: (2) the Roman Catholic, by far the most numerous: (3) the Lutheran: (4) the Calvinist or

Reformed, met with in the English-speaking world in the form of Presbyterian, Congregationalist and Baptist: (5) the Anglican, to which must be added Methodism as an offshoot bigger than the parent. In addition there are hundreds of other churches: a few are historic, like the Society of Friends or Quakers and other Peace Churches, whilst many are the products of this century, notably indigenous African churches. The ecumenical movement is bringing greater coherence and mutual understanding into both doctrinal and ethical reflection among this variety, though there remains a sizeable minority which is either anti-ecumenical or is so far unaffected by it.

To come closely to grips with Christian ethics, against this general background, it is worth noting that the term is commonly used in Protestant circles, whereas in Catholic ones the more common term is moral theology. There is no agreed differentiation between the use of the terms nor any essential difference in subject matter. Both are concerned with the two basic issues in ethics, how to act from the right motive and how to find what is the right action in particular circumstances. In essence the methods and procedures of Christian ethics are no different from those of moral philosophy; the difference in Christian ethics is its starting point in the Christian faith. (Other systems of ethics will have other starting points, either religious or some form of humanism, for all must have some presuppositions before they can get going.) It will be found that at many points there will be an overlap between different systems of ethics, and this is important in a growingly interconnected but plural world whose inhabitants must learn to live together.

That the two basic issues in ethics are right motive and right action seems obvious, but it is not always realized that they are. For instance Samuel Butler in his nineteenth-century novel *The Way of All Flesh* has this passage: 'The more I see the more sure I am that it does not matter why people do the right thing so long as they do it, nor why they may have done wrong if they have done it. The result depends upon the thing done and the motive goes for nothing.'[2] St Paul, in a benevolent mood in the first chapter of Philippians, seems to take the same view. He says some people are preaching Christ out of envy but nevertheless he rejoices that Christ is preached. However, he would not have agreed with Butler that 'motive goes for nothing'. In furthering action from the right motive Christian ethics is concerned with what is often called 'spiritual formation'. By that is meant a growth in character through private prayers and public worship (both of which involve reflection on the Bible), and discussion with fellow

Christians (and others where appropriate) so that one's insight or powers of discernment deepen. Bringing motivation to bear on particular decisions is traditionally known as casuistry. This got a bad name at the time of the Counter-Reformation because its aim seemed to be a series of rules for the evasion of obvious moral duties rather than to find out and fulfil what was the right action in particular circumstances. For instance mental restriction, equivocation and perjury were said to be legitimate if the welfare of the person, including honour or possessions, was at stake: whilst the doctrine of 'philosophic sin' held that no action was morally sinful unless the agent was actually thinking of God at the moment of committing it. Such absurdities were excoriated in Pascal's *Lettres Provinciales*[3] and they were soon condemned by the papacy. It was a passing phase. The abuse of procedure does not mean that the procedure is wrong in itself. 'Casuistry', whether known by that name or not, is essential. But it can no longer be tied to the precise demarcation of sins, associated with the confessional, as recent Roman Catholic moral theology recognizes. Nor is it to be supposed that there are clear, specific, 'Christian' answers to all the ethical problems that the world throws up. More likely there is a range of possibilities, with some ruled out. Recognizing the ambiguities of choice is part of the task of Christian ethics.

Jesus

We turn to the roots of Christian ethics in the ministry of Jesus, especially the teaching in the so-called Synoptic Gospels, Mark, Matthew and Luke. The fourth, John, can best be regarded as a selective and mature series of meditations on the main themes of the first three, whether the author knew them or only the oral traditions behind them. The crux of Jesus' teaching concerns the kingdom of God, or the way God exercises his rule as king over the world. Jesus saw it as exemplified in his own life and teaching. He reflected on the traditions of his people which were available to him through the synagogues as he grew up, and interpreted them in a new and original way in terms of his own mission. He saw the weight of God's purpose for the world through Israel resting upon himself. The intimacy of his understanding of God comes clearly through the Gospels. His understanding of God's kingly rule was highly paradoxical by conventional standards, so he expressed it less by doctrinal affirmations than by indirect means, parables and pithy sayings (as well as by choice of actions), related to everyday experiences but designed to startle the assumptions of the hearers and viewers and shift them to a new dimension. In particular God's rule is seen not in the punishment of wrongdoers but in bearing the consequences of their wrongdoing. Equally paradoxical ethical teaching followed.

It may be asked how far we can be sure that these teachings go back to Jesus. The broad answer is that the Gospels have been put through a more meticulous and widespread critical examination than any other writings of the ancient world and that, allowing for elements of uncertainty in places, there is no doubt that from them we can know a great deal about Jesus' teaching, even though it has come to us filtered through the concerns of the earliest Christian congregations. One of the indirect evidences for this is that two great themes of post-resurrection (Pauline) Christianity, the dynamism of the Holy Spirit and the universality of the gospel, were not read back into the life of Jesus but only appear as anticipatory hints in the written Gospels.

What is conduct appropriate to a citizen of the kingdom of God? Some of it is at the level of 'natural' morality, for instance the Golden Rule, 'Always treat others as you would like them to treat you' (Matt. 7.12), which is found in some similar form in other ethics, and which can be taken at different levels provided one is consistent between oneself and others. Some of Jesus' words appear to follow 'natural' human judgments in offering rewards for good conduct and threatening penalties for bad. We shall return to this. But the distinctive feature of Jesus' ethical teaching is the way it radicalizes common morality. For instance there is no limit to the forgiveness for injuries (Matt.18.21ff.), not on the grounds that it will win over the offender but because it corresponds to God's forgiveness of us. Similarly love of enemies is enjoined (Matt.6.4ff.) not because it will win over the enemy (although of course it might) but because God loves his enemies. There is no restriction on neighbour love (Luke 10.29ff.). Anxiety is the surest sign of lack of trust in God (Matt.6.19–34), especially anxiety over possessions. So far from motive not being important provided the right action is done, Jesus was penetratingly critical of the self-love of 'good' people (Luke 18.9–14), and it is clear from many passages in the Gospels that he thought bad people to be not nearly so bad as the 'good' thought them. Underlying all this teaching lies the fact that Jesus was a man of faith (trust). Faced with the ambiguities of existence he looked at the weather, sun shining and rain falling alike on good and bad, and saw it as a sign of the unconditional goodness of the creative power of God. A sceptic would have drawn from the same evidence the conclusion that the universe is quite indifferent to moral worth. In this respect Jesus is an archetype for his followers.

His ethics is very different from an everyday ethic of doing good turns to those who do good turns to you: that is to say an ethic of reciprocity. This is invaluable as far as it goes. Social life requires a level of mutuality on which we can normally rely. One of the perils of international relations is that governments have not sufficient confidence in their relations with one another for mutuality to be relied upon. However, in our lives as citizens we do usually count on it. Some people behave better than the rule of reciprocity requires. Some keep it exactly on a fifty-fifty basis. Some get by with the minimum of co-operation. Some who do not even do that are likely to end in prison. Jesus goes much deeper, explicitly warning against loving only those who love you, and saying that there is nothing extra-ordinary in that, the Gentiles do it; rather, what do you do more? (Matt.5.45ff.). He goes beyond the world of claims and counter-claims, of rights and duties or something owed to others, as St Paul clearly sees when in Romans (13.8) he says, 'Owe no one anything but to love one another.' Jesus calls for a certain flair in life, a certain creative recklessness at critical points.

It might be thought that another emphasis in the Gospels, that on rewards, is incompatible with this non-reciprocal ethic. Indeed it has continually been misunderstood. It is true that there is one passage in the Gospels, about taking the lower seat in order to be promoted to the higher (Luke 14.7ff.) which is presented as pure prudential morality, presumably teaching that egoism is self-defeating, as a traditional proverb might. But it is most uncharacteristic. The usual teaching on rewards is found in such passages as Matthew 19.29, where it is eternal life, or Luke 18.22 where it is treasure in heaven, and especially the Beatitude in the Sermon on the Mount, 'Blessed are the pure in heart for they shall see God' (Matt.5.8). This teaching, as that on punishments, must be taken as a statement of fact. In the kingdom of God there is only one reward whether, as in the parable of the labourers in the vineyard, you have worked all day or began only at the eleventh hour (Matt. 20.1ff.). The thrust of the teaching is towards a self-forgetfulness which results in an unselfconscious goodness. Writers on spirituality often call it disinterestedness. Jesus spoke severely against self-conscious goodness, as we noted when referring to Luke 18.9ff. In the allegory of the sheep and the goats the sheep are unconscious of either their goodness or of rewards. The rewards Jesus spoke of cannot follow from the direct pursuit of them. Indeed consciously to pursue disinterestedness is self-defeating. One cannot *pursue* self-forgetfulness. If God is as Jesus said he is, it must be the case that following his way of life brings us to God; and to turn our backs on it must bring us to destruction, vividly symbolized by the perpetual burning rubbish dump outside the walls of Jerusalem (Gehenna). The fact that one can be tempted to do the right thing for the wrong reason, which was the fourth and most insidious temptation of Becket in T. S. Eliot's play *Murder in the Cathedral*,[4] cannot alter that reality. The reward of God's presence must be for those who follow 'the way of the Lord Jesus' for love's sake, not the reward's sake. Indeed only they will be able to appreciate the reward. Whether anyone with full knowledge will turn their back on the vision of goodness lived and taught by Jesus is a question to which we have no answer. If there is a hell of destruction, is it empty?

This teaching on rewards has often not been followed or understood. Almsgiving is a litmus test. Donations and bequests have often been made with the motive of securing God's favour now and after death, and not as a joyful response to a graciousness of God already known.

It is significant that Jesus did not give a precise ruling on detailed ethical issues. When asked whether tribute should be given to Caesar (Matt. 22.25ff.) he said that what was due to God should be rendered to God and what due to Caesar should be rendered to him, without saying which was which. This has had continually to be worked out in varying circumstances. Education is a key area. When asked by two brothers to divide an estate, he refused (Luke 12.14). There is truth in Richard Robinson's contention that 'Jesus says nothing on any social questions except divorce, and all ascriptions of political doctrine to him are false. He does not pronounce about war, capital punishment, gambling, justice, the administration of law, the distribution of goods, socialism, equality of income, equality of sex, equality of colour, equality of opportunity, tyranny, freedom, slavery, self-determination or contraception. There is nothing Christian about being for any of these things nor about being against them if we mean by "Christian" what Jesus taught according to the synoptic gospels.'[5]

Some have thought that the passage in the Sermon on the Mount concerning 'turning the other cheek' is an injunction to pacifism as a political technique (Matt. 5.39ff.), but this is to ignore its literary character as well as the nature of Jesus' ethical teaching. It occurs along with the command to pluck out an eye or cut off a hand rather than fall into evil, and also to give your cloak as well to anyone who asks for your coat (and thus be naked, for only two garments were worn). Like paradox, hyperbole is a way of giving concreteness to abstract ideas. The passage is neither for nor against pacifism as a political technique; Robinson is right.

Divorce is the one apparent exception to the fact that Jesus did not give detailed ethical rulings, but it is very doubtful if it is so. The key passage is Mark 10. 1–12 which deals with God's basic intention for marriage, without any direct reference to ecclesiastical, still less state, law. In Matthew 5.32 and 19.9 this is modified to include a clause forbidding divorce except on the grounds of *porneia*, usually translated as adultery. There has been an immense discussion of these texts. Apart from the inherent improbability that Jesus would give a detailed rule on only one issue, it seems clear that Matthew has made him arbitrate between the two rival contemporary rabbinic schools of Hillel and Shammai on what justified divorce in terms of Mosaic ruling in Deuteronomy 24. 1.

The Fourth Gospel reflects in its own way the distinctive features of Jesus' ethical teaching. There is no ruling on any specific issue. The concentration is on the radical challenge Jesus brings to accepted ways. All is darkness except the white light focussed on him, and through him on his intimate disciples. Indeed mutual love in the first instance is restricted to them, but it is only a provisional restriction, for the world is to be saved and not abandoned (17.20ff.). Love in word, will and action is stressed, even as a condition of knowledge (7.17). There is a parallel here with classical Marxism, which has been picked up by recent liberation theology, that only those who are actively committed to the cause of the poor will understand the Christian faith. It is certainly the case that Jesus challenged society's standards by the standards of the kingdom of God in his attitude not only to the poor, but to heretics and schismatics (Samaritans), the immoral (prostitutes and adulterers), the politically compromised (tax collectors), society's rejects (lepers), those whom society neglected; and to women as a sex.

What is the meaning of love to which Jesus referred when he said that the Old Testament law (Torah) could be summarized in two commandments, love to God and to one's neighbour as oneself? (Matt. 22.34ff.). Without going into a detailed word study, it is well known that the one English word love covers several different Greek words, notably *eros* (a yearning for satisfaction at any level up to the heights of beauty, truth and goodness), *philia* (friendship), and *agape*. This last was a relatively colourless Greek word which Christians took over to express the heart of Jesus' teaching. The two loves are not univocal, for adoration and worship are involved in our attitude to God, but not to our neighbour. Briefly, love of neighbour means being responsible for our fellow human beings, not because of their idiosyncratic qualities but because of their humanity as made in the image of God (Gen.1.22). It does not depend on natural affection in the one who loves nor natural attractiveness in the one loved. It does not imply identical treatment, but putting oneself in the neighbour's shoes. It is not a question of what *you* would want if you were in the neighbour's shoes. It does not mean submission to being exploited; for one thing it would not be for the good of the neighbour to be allowed to exploit you. Nor is it in the first instance concerned with self-sacrifice; it is service to the neighbour, not a loss to the self which is important. Indeed an affirmation of the self is needed. Those who hate or despise themselves cannot love their neighbour. It is pride, sloth and anxiety which are the enemies of the self, and thus the enemies of *agape*.

When more than two people are involved the expression of *agape* involves being fair to each of them. Questions of corrective and distributive justice are in the background of the New Testament, but the relation of them to *agape* is not systematically worked out because it is not a systematic work on ethics. The focus is on the new community of love, a fellowship of repentance, forgiveness and reconciliation. The New Testament is very rich in its picture of the church in this respect, and very sharp in its criticism of the church when it fails to be such a community. But questions of justice remain. Suppose, for instance, parents have two children. They love both equally; but children of the same parents can differ greatly and it is still necessary to be *fair* between them. If this is so in the intimacy of family relations it is just as necessary and far more difficult to arrive at what is fair in the wider collective relationships in which humans are involved. These extend even to issues of war. St Thomas Aquinas' brief discussion of the rudiments of a 'just war' doctrine occurs in the framework of his treatment of love.[6]

The relation of justice and love is complex. It quickly brings in questions which are discussed in moral philosophy, like the place of special obligations. At least it must be said that love presupposes justice; it cannot require less than justice even if it transcends it; otherwise it degenerates into sentimentality.

Love as a motivation does not give detailed content to ethical decisions. That requires knowledge and discernment, a combination of skills and perceptiveness. A love which is unwilling to be formed in this way and is content to 'mean well' is irresponsible and potentially dangerous. Some of the worst sins against love have been perpetrated by those who 'meant well'.

One theological tradition, the Lutheran, has particularly emphasized the gratuitous and unceasing love of God, his 'amazing grace', which is not dependent in any way on the merits of the loved one. It does this because it wants to remove any possibility of human boasting, any trace of a religion of works which thinks it can earn acceptance of God, that a credit balance of meritorious deeds is a prior condition of being 'right with God', rather than the Christian life being a response to God's prior graciousness. In a major modern work, *Agape and Eros*,[7] Anders Nygren ends by comparing human beings to tubes or channels through which God's grace flows to the neighbour. Something has gone wrong when humans are compared to tubes. Rather they are called to share in God's non-reciprocal love which yearns for a response for the neighbour but does not give up when it fails to elicit it. In this it differs from friendship, which is more mutual and changeable, and needs *agape* to save it from self-centredness. *Eros* also, which can move from the instinctive level of sexual libido to the highest levels of aspiration, needs to be set in the context of *agape* to save it from self-centredness.

The church has had trouble with this radical understanding of love. It is focussed in the question of how to interpret the very radical sayings found in the Sermon on the Mount (Matt. 5.7), the most considerable collection of Jesus' teaching. Several ways have been adopted, all having the effect of neutralizing these radical elements and bringing them nearer to common-sense morality. One has been to say that Jesus expected the imminent end of the world and that the ethic was meant only for the short time left. This is probably correct about Jesus' expectation, but it does not follow that the ethic is irrelevant now that the world has not ended. Another way has been to siphon off the more radical elements as 'counsels of perfection' to which a few are called. They are usually to be found in monasteries and nunneries, having taken vows of poverty, chastity and obedience, and are called Religious with a capital R. The rest are called to follow the basic ethical 'precepts' which are binding on all. One way of expressing this is to say that one *must* be just and one *may* be loving. It is a kind of Honours and Pass course in Christian living. A serious feature of it has been to make the married state a second best. Whilst Religious communities still flourish, they are rarely advocated today, even by their members, on such grounds. Still another way is to make a sharp separation between the realm of love in the church and the stern realm of justice and order in the world, or to say that the purpose of Jesus' radical ethic is to convict us of sin and prevent the development of spiritual pride. None of these attempts will do. The radical elements in Jesus' ethic are an authentic corollary of the radical stance of the kingdom of God, calling us past the necessary struggles with justice to a fuller realization of love. It is the more challenging because the more serious sins feed on moral achievements, not on the more coarse and flamboyant ones. Both with individuals and collectives corruption can feed on moral achievement, so that if there is a moral collapse it can be greater than if the achievement had been less. Nazi Germany is the great example of this in the twentieth century. Hence the question has been raised: Is there any point in such a radical ethic which is always being ignored? Would not a less drastic and more practical one be better? It is a question which is frequently asked in this century by adherents of other faiths, such as Jews and Muslims.

One of the first Jewish writers to make a sustained effort to get behind the polemics and persecutions of the centuries and take a new look at Jesus was Joseph Klausner in his book *Jesus of Nazareth*.[8] He has had a number of successors. This is a remarkable change. Christian scholarship at the same time has become alert to the deep Jewishness of Jesus. Klausner's verdict is that all Jesus' ethical teaching is to be found somewhere in Jewish sources but nowhere else gathered together without any commonplace matter. However, it is an ethic for the days of the Messiah and impossible short of them. It breaks up the family, ignores justice, and would disrupt social stability. More than that it has been ignored by all except priests and recluses: and in its shadow every kind of wickedness and vice has flourished. How much better the practical, corporate ethic of Judaism! For instance the rabbis would have been likely to agree with Jesus that 'the Sabbath was made for man and not man for the Sabbath' (Mark 2.27), but they wanted a rule for breaking the normal Sabbath rules and this he did not give. This is not because life can be lived without rules or codes, like an extempore speaker, but because Jesus' ethic is in a different dimension. It always seeks an adequate expression of *agape* whilst transcending particular instances of it. To these charges Christians tend to make two replies. One is to say that it is indeed fortunate that Jesus did not give us detailed and ethical instructions or we would be forever trying to relate them to very different and changing cultures and involved in tortuous exegesis in doing so. Second, and more important, they stress the relevance of an impossible ethic. Its point is to bring us to see that the reward of loving is to learn more of the depth and range of love, so that even those who we consider most 'saintly' are those who are most conscious of gulf in their lives between what *is* and what *ought* to be the case; and this not because they are morbid but because they have grasped more of the inexhaustible nature of love.

Such a perspective is meant to be a spur to action, with both a personal and social reference, and not an excuse for a spurious otherworldliness (as distinct from hope beyond this life which is involved in following Jesus' understanding of human destiny). To paraphrase the rather prosaic words of a modern New Testament scholar: the Christian ethic does not provide a law for either the individual or society, but creates a tension which has transforming results.[9]

St Paul

St Paul is a controversial figure because of the controversies in which he was involved, and those which have focussed on him since, not least at the time of the Reformation. Because of his Pharisaic background and his split from it he cannot be considered apart from the question of the self-definition of the Christian community as against Judaism, particularly after the fall of Jerusalem to the Romans in 70 CE. By then the number of Jews in the Christian community was small. The kind of character that Jews and Christians admired was very similar, and hence Christianity attracted admirers of Judaism in the Gentile world because it commended the virtues of Judaism but without circumcision and the food laws. The dominant Gospel picture of Jesus' controversies with the Pharisees must not be taken as a complete picture: indeed there are indications in them of a positive relationship between him and some Pharisees. The Pharisees were not a uniform party. In an effort to find and follow God's way in every detail of life they were argumentative. Moreover arguments were not finally resolved; minority opinions continued as part of the tradition. Some Pharisees were like the dominant Gospel picture, but it has been a Christian travesty to say of all of them that they were content with a religion of outward observance of moral rules as a means of establishing their moral worth in God's eyes, whereas Jesus probed to inward motives. This travesty was intensified by Luther's struggle against the spirit of late mediaeval Catholicism, as he encountered it, which often became attributed to Pharisaism. Wherein, then, lay the difference between Jesus and the various parties of Judaism, particularly the Pharisees? In the first place it was their exclusiveness, and in the second their understanding of the range and depth of love was not radical enough. But with respect to St Paul, he was a complex thinker and these issues are still much discussed and by no means resolved.

It is clear, however, that St Paul grasped that the basis of Jesus' ethic is a joyful response in life to the overflowing graciousness of God. 'Freely you have received, freely give' (Matt.10.8). The kingdom of God in the First Three Gospels is witnessed to in St Paul's letters as the new life in Christ, which he understood as essentially a community experience. A typical expression is 'We who are many are one body in Christ' (Rom.12.5). The 'law of Christ' is Christ himself (Rom.10.4). The kingdom of God is both a present reality and a leaven in the lump of history (Rom.14.7), and yet it is still to come in its fullness (I Cor.15.24 and 50). Love is the cornerstone of it. The characteristics of love are spelled out in I Corinthians 13, which is somewhat like a Stoic diatribe but quite different in spirit. Jesus was the model for this passage. St Paul does not directly quote incidents from his life but assumes they are known to his hearers and readers by referring in passing to his birth, teaching, crucifixion, burial and resurrection. He assumes that the young Christian congregations know in their own experience that the work of Christ has led to an outpouring of God's spirit which has broken down barriers between people which humans have created; between Jews and Gentiles, men and women, slaves and free. He uses this shared assumption to chide them when they fail to express this reality. In Romans 13 he sums up the Christian ethic as one of love, as has been mentioned.

Moreover what makes St Paul so important for us is that he is the first Christian of whom we are aware who was called upon to bring his understanding of the Christian ethic to bear on particular problems thrown up by the churches, as when a deputation from Corinth puts to him various questions about marriage which he answers in I Corinthians 7. In dealing with them he shows on occasion, as we would expect, that not every corner of his mind was instantly converted to understand all the implications of his new faith. Some of his teaching with respect to women is incompatible with his best insights. Too often the church has taken his instructions as a permanent rule so that, to take a trivial example, it is only in this century that women have been able to enter churches without hats because of what St Paul wrote in I Corinthians 12.5ff. Again, as we would expect, his advice has to be put in the context of the situation of the early Christians in the first century CE. His expression of the imminent end of the world influenced his advice on marriage. However, he took a typically robust attitude in urging the Christians to get on with their daily lives and work just because time is short, and not sit about waiting for it to end. By the close of the first century the church had had a major change of view in this matter (though the attitude has continued among some to this day). The Fourth Gospel reinterprets the return of Christ and the end of time as the gift of the Spirit within the community. Cosmically, St Paul accepted the current view that superhuman powers affect human affairs (though the exalted Christ had now drawn their sting). These ideas have to be translated by us into a realistic sociology. As to earthly powers, Christians were in no position to alter human institutions or affect public policy. In this situation, St Paul takes a favourable view of the pagan Roman state, of which he was proud to be a citizen and to which he had reason to be grateful. The abolition of slavery does not enter his view, though he does show how Christians can transcend its structures (note the letter to Philemon). In short, he gave to people oppressed with a fear of change and of a fate decreed by the stars a present security and a future hope because of his belief in the lordship of Christ.

The problem of Christians in the later years of the first century, as of all Christians since, was to sustain the radical rigour of the gospel ethic without an expectation of the imminent end of time. The ongoing life of the local churches produced a number of standard problems, particularly in the realm of marriage and the family. In the later books of the New Testament we find codes of conduct inserted, often taken from Greek ethics and Christianized with biblical illustrations. Examples can be found in Colossians (3.18–4.1), Ephesians (5.12–6.9), I Peter (2.11–3.12 and 5.1–5), Titus (2.1–3.2) and I Timothy (2.1–6.19). There is here a difference in emotional tone as well as in content from that of earlier letters; piety and perseverance are stressed, and love becomes one virtue in a list of others. There is no reason to object to codes of conduct to cover standard situations, provided the radical ambience of the gospel is kept. However, some of it was lost. The church is settling down too easily in the current

An imaginative venture was the establishment of the Hollowford Church Youth Hostel type of conference and outdoor centre in the Derbyshire hills, with the industrial young workers of Sheffield particularly in mind. There were more church contacts at the managerial level, but little or no linking of faith and work, the two being kept in separate compartments, so much needed to be done here also.

Establishment

Hunter was alert to using the influence of the established church, where possible, for an end for which it was not used to being used, as a base for engagement with 'the powers that be' rather than of subservience to them. He valued his place in the House of Lords when he attained to it, and one of his greatest regrets on retirement was the necessity of leaving it. He would have made a good Life Peer. No city, except perhaps Glasgow, was more in need of a Clean Air Bill than Sheffield, and Hunter made himself expert on the matter in the Lords. His establishment position was made easier by the fact that he was obviously in general sympathy with the aims of the Attlee government of 1945–50, that is to say with the idea of a 'welfare state' and with the task of 'planning for freedom' which was common then. One thinks of the social philosophy of Karl Mannheim, and of the social thought expressed by the World Council of Churches from its start in 1948, or by Joe Oldham's *Christian Newsletter* in the United Kingdom at the same time.

Hunter's social concerns were by no means confined to industry. The development of social service agencies and of professional social work was of great significance to him. In his 1944 Visitation Charge he urges clergy to take every opportunity of co-operating with social workers, warns them not to be suspicious of them, nor of jealously trying to cling to doing things themselves in an amateurish way which now required professional competence. But this did not mean that all social concerns needed to be professionalized – far from it. He saw the necessity in a live democracy for voluntary and statutory provisions in great variety. There has been much reflection and experimentation since his day on this issue. He was an active supporter of the Family Service Units, and of the Marriage Guidance Council and, indeed, provided a half-time salary for Alfred Jowett (later Dean of Manchester) to work with the Marriage Guidance Council, and the other half for him to work for the Anglican and Free Church Council. His industrial and social concerns both coincided in the foundation social and political order. An unfortunate feature of some of the codes is a stress on the duties of the 'inferior' to the 'superior' party, wives to husbands, children to parents, and slaves to masters, without any corresponding stress on the duties of the 'superior' party. Such an ethic of patience and submission is hardly adequate for our world, which is more and more conscious of personal responsibility and the need for social structures which encourage it, or even in some situations of oppression begin to make it possible for the first time.

However, periodic persecutions prevented the church settling down too easily, and we can find elements of a challenge to those who tried to do so in these later New Testament writings. It takes the form of a rigorist reaction against mere conforming, in the shape of references to sins which cannot be forgiven. We do not know what was the 'sin unto death' of John 5.16 (perhaps apostasy), but we are forbidden to pray for anyone who commits it. In three places Hebrews refers to sins which cannot be forgiven (6.4–6; 10.26–31; 12.16ff.), whilst Revelation never considers that any of those who suffer the fearful penalties of John's visions will repent, nor hopes that they will; rather it exults in their punishment. These two tendencies continued. Conformism in the church, especially after the 'conversion' of Constantine, as it is usually referred to – it is not clear how far he was using Christianity as a weapon in his political struggle – led to the rigorist reaction of the Desert Fathers, and then to the beginnings of communal monasticism and to the double standard of counsels of perfection and precepts. Thus by the end of the New Testament period the creative tension established by Jesus had largely been dissolved into disparate elements, though it has always remained as a source of renewal in the church, challenging distortions.

Criticism of Christian Ethics

Problems of moving from the Bible to the modern world continued to be explored, as do the different traditions in thinking about ethical issues which have developed in Christian history. Notable among these has been the incorporation of Natural Law thinking into Christian ethics.

It is necessary, however, that mention should be made of some common contemporary criticisms of Christian ethics.

(1) Christian ethics is intolerant and breeds intolerance. There is much evidence to support this charge. All the major confessional traditions have at times persecuted each other. Indeed it was only at

the Second Vatican Council (1962–65) that the Roman Catholic Church finally abandoned the position that 'error has no rights'. Antisemitism was also a major disease of Christendom (though also found outside it). Toleration came into the 'Christian' world largely through the influence of those who were appalled by Christian intolerance, and Christians learned through the sceptical tolerance of a man like Voltaire to distinguish tolerance from an indifference to truth. There have always been Christians who understood this. Bitter lessons this century have brought it home.

(2) Christian ethics is immoral because it works on a system of rewards (heaven) for good behaviour and threats (hell) for bad; and not on doing what is right simply because it is right and for no other reason. The question of rewards has already been mentioned and seen to be overdone.

(3) Instead of leading to self-fulfilment, Christian ethics is repressive. Most modern psychological analyses of human growth and development advocate as an ethical norm an altruistic, autonomous character. They do not look to Christianity to produce it; rather they think it leads to defensive and restrictive behaviour, and to a static social conformism. This is connected to a further criticism.

(4) Christian ethics keeps people at an immature level, because it leads to stock moral reactions regardless of circumstances. It prevents people from learning from experience. Many immature people are 'religious'. At its worst Christian ethics has certainly had this effect, but at its best its effect has been quite the reverse, as in its traditional teaching on conscience. The traditional teaching has been that it is reasons which justify moral judgments, and conscience has been the name given to the power of reason and discernment brought to bear on moral issues. This is so central to the integrity of the person that the teaching is that 'conscience must always be obeyed'. In saying this no claim is made for the infallibility of conscience, or for more certainty than the very nature of the uncertainties of ethical decisions can provide. The teaching is accompanied by a call for the formation of an informed and sensitive conscience by living in the Christian community, and making use of the resources for the education of conscience which have already been mentioned. Differences between Christians on ethical issues often arise from different weights attached to these different sources. Sometimes this whole teaching has been suspect as leading one to put one's own unregenerate judgments in the place of the guidance of God. Hence, sometimes conscience has been seen as the 'voice of God' within the self, but the problems and

dangers of this, as of all forms of intuitionism, are obvious. Once the complexities of the moral life are faced, the traditional teaching on conscience is seen to lead to vigorous, creative and hopeful Christian living.

Within the spectrum of attitudes among Christians to Christian ethics there is a strong, though not universal, stress on the dignity of the human person, the reality and universality of the community of the church, and a concern for its contribution to the holding together of humanity in a pluralistic world. Christianity must not add to its divisions, but exert a healing influence. These convictions are in conflict in many respects with the 'possessive individualism' which has had a wide influence in Western circles in the late twentieth century. It has produced in some circles a version of Christian ethics in its own image, but one which is not accepted by the majority of contemporary Christian ethicists, certainly not those influenced by the Ecumenical Movement. Rather there has been a growing emphasis on giving preference to the needs of the poor. These two emphases, concern for the unity of mankind and for 'a preferential option for the poor', mark the end of the embodiment of the Christian ethic in church and state which for centuries characterized its heartland, Christendom.

5

Christian Ethics in the Twentieth Century

There are many ways of treating such a vast theme, and the problem of selection is inevitably idiosyncratic. We have all become much more conscious of conditioning factors in our thinking during this century, a Marxist influence which has now been liberated from its origins. The sociology of knowledge has developed during the century as a discipline which studies it. So I make clear some of the factors which have conditioned me in respect of this theme. Britain had a Protestant culture and Roman Catholics were on the margin of it. Now they are part of it, and Christian ethics, which was predominantly Protestant and denominational at that, is now ecumenical, and since Vatican II Roman Catholicism has become a major part of it. Hasting's *Encyclopaedia of Religion and Ethics*, characteristic of the early years of the century, will no longer do. Furthermore, the horizon has to be much less 'Western' and more global. Allied with this is that other faiths are no longer more or less distant from the UK; we must now live with them. I am part of mainstream Christianity, and an Anglican. I cannot deal with the ethics of those outside the mainstream (nor within it with the Orthodox, because for historical reasons they are only recently coming into mainstream ethical dialogue). I am also part of the wealthy one-third of the world, and have experienced the dramatic rise in the standard of living in the 'West' since the end of the 1939–45 war, which even the poorest have experienced compared with the past.

The background to this survey is the assumption that we have lived through a century of dramatic technical, social, economic and political change, which is likely to continue, whereas all traditional confessional theologies took for granted more or less static assumptions, that the structures of society they experienced were God given and maintained by his providential care. Many thought it was only this that prevented them getting worse. In the nineteenth century there was a striking breakaway from this; theology and ethics were widely affected by the belief that there was an underlying trend towards a better future. This century, with its two World Wars and Holocaust, has destroyed that. But the fact remains that a theological ethic which cannot deal with dynamic change is no use to us.

The problem in writing this survey is to find a framework within which to fit the diverse material. The framework I have chosen is the two problems the Christian (or any other ethic) has to deal with. (1) How to act from the right motive, and (2) how to arrive at the right action in particular situations. It is clearly possible to arrive at the right action in particular situations. It is clearly possible to arrive at the right action for the wrong motive (Phil. 1.17ff.) which was Becket's most subtle temptation in T. S. Eliot's *Murder in the Cathedral*. I will deal in turn with what has happened to each in this century. The first involves the formation of a sensitive conscience, and the second how to use it in deciding what to do (whether the decision is a purely personal one or involves collective actions). By conscience is meant the capacity characteristic of human beings of being able to distinguish right from wrong and to know that we ought to follow that which we judge to be right and shun that which we judge to be wrong. It is the use of our reasoning powers in moral issues. That conscience must be followed (*conscientia semper sequenda*) is basic to Christian ethics. But of course we can make mistakes, sometimes through no fault of our own, but sometimes through prejudice, so it is important that we live in a milieu where we are helped to develop a sensitive conscience.

This section can be brief because it is not here that great difficulties arise. How to act from the right motive? What is the right Christian motive? A joyous response to the graciousness of God made known to us through the ministry of Jesus Christ. 'Freely you have received, freely give.' God's graciousness is not something we earn, it is something we receive and respond to. It sets us free from anxiety, and inspires the love of our neighbour and proper love of ourselves. What then of the problem of rewards for good behaviour, prominent in the Gospels? The basic answer to this (which cannot be expanded here) is that the rewards (which must be a fact if God is indeed the God we understand through Jesus), will only be for those who follow for love's sake, not the reward's sake, and they alone will appreciate them.

This right motivation and sensitivity is fostered not in isolation but in the life of a Christian community, through its worship (and private prayer), corporate reflection on the Bible and Christian tradition, and the mutual pastoral care and discussion on the moral issues of one's own day. The Abbé Bremond, in a memorable phrase in the early years of the century, said, 'Worship disinfects conduct from egoism.' Of course it does not always do it, and we are all aware of self-centred complacent worship, but of all the activities humans engage in, worship is most likely to purify our motives as we respond to the Gospel and say the Gloria or, colloquially, 'How splendid'.

All Christians agree that ethics is fundamental. Ever since the teaching of the writing prophets of the eighth and seventh centuries BCE the Judaeo-Christian tradition has known that no worship, however beautiful, is acceptable if divorced from ethics. Even the most pietistic forms of Christianity which have dwelt on the joys of heaven as against the miseries of the world, have never doubted that wrongdoing is a bar to heaven. However, right-doing needs worship to free it from egoism.

This century has seen a steady growth in emphasis on the church and its worship. In the early years much Protestant theology tended to think that the Christian task was to build the kingdom of God in human society, and that this, not the church, was the heart of the Christian life. Then came the totalitarian challenge of Nazism, Fascism and Stalinism. With all their weaknesses, the churches provided a surer standing ground against totalitarianism than any other. 'Let the church be the church' was an early slogan of the incipient Ecumenical Movement. Also the collapse of the Christendom situation in Europe, and the decline in church attendance, has made those who attend more churchly self-conscious.

The church is nourished by the interpretation of the gospel which the great theologians provide in each generation. Some are of enduring significance as new insights and relevances are discovered. This applies for instance to Augustine, Anselm, Aquinas, Luther and Calvin. Some of the great names of this century are Harnack, Barth, Bonhoeffer, Brunner, Bultmann, Rahner, Pannenberg, Balthasar and Moltmann. We have our own from the Anglo-Saxon world, which I forbear to mention. Of course they present different approaches to the gospel, and there are some sharp disagreements among them. But on the basic question of the church as the prime source of ethical formation, and of the fundamental importance of that formation, they would all agree. The Ecumenical Movement has made it clear that what these theologians agree on far exceeds what they differ on, and as far as ecclesiology and ethics go they are at one in stressing the fundamental importance of ethics in the Christian life.

The more the stress on congregational formation is pressed, the sharper the question arises as to how far congregational life corresponds in any strong way with the stress on its importance. Everyone is aware of quarrels and splits within congregations; of concentration on trivialities; of timidity; of inward-looking congregational life; of complacency and of ecclesiastical power politics. 'Judgment begins at the house of God.' We know that the church itself is always in need of reform *(semper reformanda)*. Nevertheless we know that in spite of its failures it does constitute a universal community, transcending particular expressions of its life and capable of transforming individuals and cultures. God's graciousness is not blocked by the church's follies and it remains the best place for growth in sensitivity of conscience, often in spite of itself. The exceptional believer who remains outside it, like Simone Weil, is in fact dependent on it.

How to find the right action in particular issues? How to bring the gospel of the kingdom of God, the heart of Jesus' ministry, to bear on the ongoing details of life? Here there is great confusion. In the early years of the century it was widely held that the Christian ethic was non-controversial (many Victorian agnostics had thought that); it was the doctrine that was controversial. 'Doctrine divides but service unites' was the slogan of the incipient Ecumenical Movement in the 1920s. But this proved too simple. The ethic was far from obvious common sense, and Christians have been as much divided on ethical issues as they have on confessional theologies. That is why many congregations are so timid in encouraging discussions of current ethical issues. They fear there will be quarrels and splits in the congregation, and they have not learned a way of tackling such issues which will encourage Christians in both personal and civic responsibility while at the same time understanding why equally genuine Christians may differ on the details of decisions.

The roots of the difficulty are two, the paradoxical nature of the ethic of the kingdom of God and the difficulties of getting accurate information on current problems. As to the paradox, New Testament studies in this century have shown that there are different elements in Jesus' ethical teaching in the Synoptic Gospels, much of it in accord with Judaism, but the radical and distinctive ethic is one that is not reciprocal. The everyday ethic by which the world rubs along, and very important it is, is one of doing good turns to those who do good turns to you. Broadly speaking we can rely on this. Jesus radically differentiates his teaching from this, demanding an unlimited commitment, for instance to forgiveness, on the grounds that that is how God behaves to us. It is an ethic which is always a challenge but never totally realizable, what Reinhold Niebuhr called an 'impossible possibility'. More especially, there is no civic theology here; no explanation of how love of this boundless character is related to justice. Even in family relations parents may love their children equally, but must still be fair between them. The nearest Jesus gets in the civic area is to tell us that there are things to be rendered to Caesar, but there is no guide as to which. The church has always found this teaching difficult to cope with; witness the many different ways of interpreting the Sermon on the Mount in Christian history. The New Testament has examples of how the earliest Christians tried to live with it, from ardent expectation of an imminent *parousia*, through various efforts by St Paul, to its domestication in the Pastoral Epistles. A civic theology is vital. In the Old Testament it was less complicated because Israel was a theocracy where church and state were one kingdom. From New Testament times Christians have lived in two kingdoms, and have had to relate the ethic of the kingdom of God to the kingdom of this world. Their various efforts to do so are related to their time and circumstances. That is why there is no *direct* link between biblical texts or traditional ethical positions and *detailed* ethical decisions. It has become clearer during the century that the Bible *presupposes* a civic society, with basic structures of sex and family life, economic and political order, and culture. Not being a text book it does not argue about them any more than it does about the reality of God, it assumes them. These are sometimes called Orders of Creation, though theologians in this century have used other terms. A temptation has been because of the static assumptions behind traditional theologies to assume that the empirical feature of these Orders are fixed, just as there has been a tendency to assume that nature is fixed; but that is a gratuitous assumption.

What I have just written is far from being generally accepted in the church. Many Christians shy away from realizing that most ethical decisions involve attention to evidence and assessment of its weight, so that there are inevitable uncertainties, especially about the possible effects of particular decisions, and therefore Christians may disagree. They want certainties. They want to move directly from a biblical text or a traditional position to a detailed conclusion. And the

churches have been little help. All, even those which put more emphasis on tradition, use the Bible in an arbitrary way in their documents.
This could be illustrated from issues in the past now dead, such as
slavery, and usury (not quite dead), or live contemporary ones like
homosexuality, abortion, the recent use of the Jubilee of Leviticus 25
and the position of women.

The Bible gives us a general perspective on human life and destiny;
a broad drama from creation, incarnation, redemption and the church
to the last things. Within this there are theologies with a special
emphasis; feminist, black, green, political and liberation, to quote
five. But from all of them we have to move to a grappling with the
data of particular issues. In this connection we may pause to mention
liberation theology. It reflects the growing influence of Marxism
through the century until about the 1980s. Its strong point is its
stress on 'the option for the poor', based on Jesus' ministry. (Strictly
speaking, it was *all* the marginalized with which he was concerned,
not least woman.) Its basic point has been that unless we are *actively*
concerned with the cause of the poor, we turn the gospel into an
ideology of the powerful. When, however, we ask *how* this active
concern is to be expressed, the liberation theologians tend to take
over uncritically a rather selective version of Marxist theories. These
can be shown to be seriously flawed; and the internal collapse of the
Soviet state in 1989 left many Christians bereft. They had assumed
that, take away the distortions of Stalinism, there was a more just
economic order in Marxism than the 'Western' capitalistic order. In
fact the cupboard was bare.

Behind these theologies, with their special stresses, there are different general theological approaches to the whole of human culture.
Richard Niebuhr in a seminal book, *Christ and Culture* (1951),
showed that there are five which have persisted in Christian history,
all on the same biblical and basic credal bases. They are not all equally
cogent, but the fact that they persist suggests that they are all cogent
in some circumstances. All have found expression in this century.
(There is no suggestion that all have been expressed in one way only
of the five; hybrids are common.) That still leaves the problem of
moving from any of these general attitudes to specific issues.

Perhaps one should list some of the particular ones, and the new
situation in this century in which they have presented themselves. Let
us begin with sexuality, which is clearly (and rightly), a major, even
if too exclusive a concern of the churches. At the beginning of the
century they were clearer on it than they are now. Their attitude was

cautious and negative. No sexual intercourse outside marriage, and none in it that was not open to conception; no contraception; no divorce; no masturbation (and therefore today no AIH, still less AID), no sterilization; no abortion; no homosexual physical contacts. As the century has gone on the importance of relationship in human sexuality has come to the fore and there has been much re-thinking. It was mid-century before any churches thoroughly accepted contraception. Now, cohabitation having become so common, the situation is having to be re-thought and the upshot is not clear. Also feminist issues have become prominent, and the deeply patriarchal culture out of which the Bible came has had to be faced.

New human powers have raised new questions about the stewardship of humans over creation in the shape of environmental issues, and the relation of humans to animals. 'Factory farming', for instance, was unheard of before the 1939–45 war. Again the cracking of the DNA Code by Crick and Watson has led to new medical problems, particularly at the boundaries of life and death, euthanasia for instance. Then there are issues of genetic 'engineering'. The use of that term itself shows deep human uneasiness about our ability to control the new powers we possess.

The rapid development of Information Technology is having dramatic effect on management and on employment generally. The unskilled jobs in which many earned their living are disappearing. Education for many has become vital, and society has to learn to use the personal qualities of the less able if broadly full employment is to be achieved.

The very concept of the term *race* has had to be questioned as a result of the Holocaust and so has the status of the nation state which was unquestioned by Christians at the beginning of the century. Since European nationalism involved the world in two wars, it cannot continue to be unquestioned, and the slow development of international institutions is now part of our continuous agenda. Moreover the development of some weapons of war which are inherently designed for mass destruction has caused a new approach to the traditional Christian doctrine of the Just War. The criteria of prudence and proportion are as relevant as they ever were in handling conflicts, but the new question is how to deal with the possession by certain sovereign states of some weapons which it would never be justifiable to use. So much for some instances of changes in the ethics agenda this century.

This raises the question: 'Are there any moral absolutes?' Here opinions differed greatly. This century has seen the complete collapse in the UK of the evangelical ethic which said 'no' to many things, and most noticeably to gambling and alcoholic drinks. I have already mentioned the traditional 'no's' of the sex ethic. There certainly are some absolutes but there are not nearly as many as many Christians have supposed, and they mostly appear at 'boundary situations'. Fortunately life is not usually lived at these extreme situations. Could it ever have been right, knowingly, to co-operate in the transport and slaughter of Jews in gas chambers? Would it ever be right to torture a child in front of its parents in order to extract information from them, even if it might save lives? The use of inherently indiscriminate weapons of war has already been mentioned. Are there any limits to the ethics of spying? Many blacks in the USA wanted separate institutions as the only method of building up a power base against the whites (and it greatly troubled those of a 'liberal' conscience), but that is different from having *apartheid* imposed by force on a subject population, as in South Africa. What if a white Christian congregation is forbidden to allow a black person to worship with it purely on the grounds of colour? What if Nazi authorities imposed tests on university professors which had nothing to do with or would corrupt scholarship? In some cases there are options to dissemble, or bend principles in order to fight another day, but clearly there are *some* things which Christians ought to have the courage to oppose, suffer and even die for. Fortunately life does not often put us to such a test. But the last war certainly put many Christians in acute boundary situations, and it is not difficult to find peace time ones which can do so.

For the most part, however, we have to decide ethical questions which do not present such unambiguous clarity, but in varying and ambiguous circumstances, and as traditional moral theology says, 'Circumstances alter cases'.

This brings us to the Situation Ethic debate which dominated the third quarter of the century. It was concerned with the bringing to bear of our general understanding of the Christian gospel to the data of particular cases. If one thinks a moral absolute applies, the problem is only that of deciding whether the data comes under the absolute category. Where it does not it is necessary to weigh the pros and cons of possible courses of action and decide which is likely to lead to the best outcome in the circumstances. In either case, but particularly the second, there are problems of getting at the facts and deciding what significance to give them. The process of bringing to bear a general judgment of conscience on a specific question is known as casuistry. It got a bad name in the seventeenth century, for reasons which do not concern us now, but it is essential. If we do not like the term we can call it practical moral reasoning. Normally we take our judgments from parents, school, church or other sources, but at any point we may find that what we had generally decided no longer fits. We are brought up short. Then we have to think in what way the new situation does or does not differ from cases about which we had hitherto been clear, and whether our course of action should or should not change. That is how casuistry works; from the more certain to the less certain. That is why the formation of conscience is so important.

Those who believe that a moral absolute is involved work deductively from that to a particular case; otherwise the tendency is to reason inductively from the data towards the general understanding of the gospel. The situation ethic debate petered out because although it had won its point against those who wanted to settle ethical questions by moral rules, independent of a particular context, its proponents often gave the impression that moral problems could be settled by a kind of intuition as to how love (*agape*) could best be maximized without the discipline of careful moral reasoning characteristic of casuistry. Furthermore, a number of leading Protestant theologians were nervous of wrestling with particular issues because human effort of this kind would lead to a religion of justification by works, not faith. The demand of God must be obeyed in every situation and will be disclosed in that situation. Indeed, conscience itself was thought of negatively by some as being a conviction of wrongdoing (the wrath of God), on the grounds that a sensitive and a good conscience were contradictory and must savour of works of righteousness. One thinks of Brunner and Bultmann, and to a large extent Barth, in this connection. Barth gives a magnificent exposition of the Christian gospel. But his particular ethical judgments are arbitrary. Nygren in *Agape and Eros*, an influential book in mid-century, was so afraid of human effort that he referred to persons as 'tubes' through which God's grace flows to the neighbour.

Be that as it may, the situation ethic debate died down, and attention turned to the nature and formation of the Christian virtues, leaving the method of decision making as confused as ever, and the uses of the Bible in particular as arbitrary.

.This is the place to refer, all too briefly, to Roman Catholic moral theology. It pursued its own way before Vatican II; since then it has become inescapably part of the scene for all mainstream churches.

One of the notable achievements of that Council was to produce a reform of moral theology. The old manuals were cast out, with their stress on precise precepts and prohibitions based on an understanding of Natural Law, which included detailed requirements (as interpreted by official Vatican teaching), binding the theory on all human beings, but enforced on Roman Catholics by the authority of the *magisterium*. The understanding was a-cultural and a-historical, and timeless; many acts were regarded as intrinsically evil, irrespective of context. Since then there has been an intense debate within the Roman Catholic Church between revisionists who interpret the call of Vatican II for a renewal of moral theology in a more radical way, and traditionalists who want a more cogent restatement of it. In 1993 in an encyclical *Veritatis Splendor* the Pope came down heavily in favour of the latter, and the discussion has become more subdued, but it has not gone away.

The question of moral absolutes is the focus of much of the discussion. For example, the encyclical *Humanae Vitae* of 1968 modified previous church teaching by giving more place to the role of sexual intercourse in fostering the marriage relationship, but then went on to require every such act to be open to procreation, and ended with a consequentialist argument on the evils which follow if this is ignored. The basis of this absolute is apparently nature, but the trouble is that to many Christians, including many Roman Catholics, nature seems to deal lightly with many embryos. Many moral theologians think that the position taken by the encyclical cannot be sustained on the arguments it advances, and so papal authority has to be called in though, as is well known, on this matter it is widely disregarded by the laity. On abortion there is no scriptural text to rely on for an absolute, and tradition has not been uniform, so the Roman Catholic Church has taken an absolutist position on the fully human status of the foetus on the grounds that the issue is so vital that we must be absolutely sure on the matter. Most Roman Catholics agree; many others think that the doubt has been greatly exaggerated, and that such an extreme safety-first stance on other ethical issues would lead to a paralysis in human living. The revolutionists maintain the judgments of proportion between human goods and risks must be made. The traditionalists argue that there are a number of human goods which are self evident to human reason and that none of these must in any action be frustrated. One list of such human goods given by John Finnis in, for instance, *Natural Law and Natural Right* (1980) is (1) life itself, including, health, freedom and procreation;

(2) knowledge, of facts and theoretical reasoning as a basis for judgment; (3) play (4) aesthetic experience, including experiencing and creating beauty; (5) sociability, including friendship and living in tolerable peace; (6) practical reasonableness in making conscientious judgements; (7) religion, understood in a broad sense that these previous six reflect a transcendent order in the universe. There is a big step from listing these human goods to the argument that we must never destroy or impede or damage any of them in any action, or the result will be self-alienation, not self-integration. They cannot be weighed in order of importance because they are incommensurable. Hence these values are embodied in exceptionless prohibitory moral rules. The revisionists would say we are constantly having to make proportionate judgments between values and disvalues in particular situations. There is a stalemate at the moment with the power structures in the hands of traditionalists. In practice, it is mostly on sexual issues that the absolutist position is stressed. On many issues of human rights and the dignity of the person, concern for the marginalized, queries on the working of the free market economy, the importance of and conditions in employment, and many others, the teaching of the organs of the Roman Catholic and other mainstream churches is very similar. This is at a general level, either on a general doctrinal basis or on empirical agreed evidenced at a general level. Beyond this last 'middle level', when it comes to detailed proposals there are likely to be different opinions within and between churches, and therefore limits on the likelihood of official church teaching.

A moral absolute which has grown among a significant minority of Christians in the century is that of a pacifist position on principle (not the same as non-resistance). The debate between this and the majority of Christians who do not think that Jesus' ethic is to be expressed in this way in a civic theology has got no further in the century.

The exercise of the practical reason on ethical issues means that Christian ethics cannot be divorced from discussions in moral philosophy, and cannot fall short in standards of analytical rigour and clarity in the use of language. This is a theme beyond the scope of this article. Some understanding of the nature of the human person underlies all philosophical discussions, and Christians would hope that there would be much agreement on the bases of a common morality. They would also expect that elements of faith, hope and love are found in the common experience of living as a human being, inextricably bound in the bundle of life with other human beings, so that some elements of a non-reciprocal morality can be acknowledged without the strong but highly paradoxical basis for this in Jesus' ethic of the kingdom of God. An unfortunate tendency has grown towards the end of the century to stress that Christians and others live in separate communities which cannot converse with one another. This connects with the relation of Christian ethics to that of other world religions, which again is too big a subject for this survey. Suffice it to say that Christians in the course of the century have had to modify some of the sharp doctrinal and ethical separations they made in previous centuries between their faith and others. If humans are to live together in tolerable harmony the adherents of world religions must come to understand and appreciate one another at a certain level. That means that the fostering of a basic reciprocal morality, laced if possible by elements of a non-reciprocal one, is a priority.

It is worth noting the chief criticisms of Christian ethics made this century by outsiders in 'the West', some of them sympathetic, some hostile. There are four. (1) It is immoral because it uses the hope of heaven or the fear of hell, instead of teaching its followers to do the right just because it is right. (2) It is intolerant. (3) It is defensive, restrictive and repressive, instead of producing mature, autonomous persons who can stand on their own feet; (4) related to this, it keeps Christians immature by its fixed code of conduct which prevents them learning from experience. It is important to ask ourselves how much truth there is in these charges.

It seems clear that in a dynamically changing world, and with the new powers humans have acquired in this century, we have greater possibilities but added responsibilities and risks. Assessing risks requires much more attention than Christian ethics has hitherto given it. Risk assessment is governed by the hazards of forecasting. Sometimes, as in economic matters, short-term forecasting, even two years ahead, is difficult. In technology important inventions have been made which even a few years before were un-thought of. Some climate and environmental issues are long-term and the evidence uncertain. Extrapolating on the basis of the present is inherently conservative. We need to be intellectually and emotionally ready to cope with the unexpected.

A radical faith should not cling to an instinctive conservatism. Valuing the past is one thing; having to be dragged into the modern world is another. Knowing we are sure of God's love should give us a sober but not utopian hope that faithful Christian (and human) actions can make the world a better place for human flourishing which God intends for those made in the divine image.

Part II

Christian Socialism

6

Not Out of the Wood Yet

Since the end of the nineteenth century there have been small, explicitly Christian, politically radical groups in Britain, most of them socialist and deriving much of their inspiration from the 'Christian Socialism' of F. D. Maurice and his associates. None of these groups has been very influential, though they have had associated with them some very influential people, like R. H. Tawney or Lord Soper. They have shown the fissiparousness characteristic of left-wing groups, but on occasion have made efforts to unite. One such occasion in 1960 was marked by the publication of a manifesto of their position, *Papers from The Lamb* (the title referring to the name of a pub where meetings had been held). I discussed it in an article in *Theology*, April 1960, 'The Christian Left Still Lost'. Now, twenty years later, another effort at co-ordination has been made, and in September several groups marked this occasion by amalgamating their separate journals for one joint issue. Earlier in the year the latest Christian Socialist statement of position appeared in *Agenda for Prophets*, edited by Rex Ambler and David Haslam,[1] and although it has no direct relation to the latest effort at co-ordination, its appearance is timely, if only as a foil for reflection on political theology in general and the state of the Christian Socialist case in particular.

The sub-title of the book is in fact 'Towards a Political Theology for Britain', the editors correctly commenting on the strange lack of thought in Britain on political theology and its implications for this country. The only specific attempt known to me is by Alistair Kee, in the course of editing a book[2] which reported on a national student Christian Congress run by the Student Christian Movement at Huddersfield in 1973 under the title *Seeds of Liberation*. In it he addresses radicals, disillusioned after the collapse of the upsurge of the late 1960s, and speaks of the need for Christians temporarily to withdraw from the political struggle, and to build up alternative lifestyles based on eucharistic communities which will have better staying power than disillusioned political groups. They will not be so utopian as political groups, will exemplify what they preach to a greater extent than the latter do, and to some extent will have a different emphasis. Communities are important, because individuals can easily be picked off one by one. He ends by asking whether the monastic tradition can contribute anything to sustaining such groups. This is a meagre conclusion. It is true that there will always be a place for Christian groups practising an alternative lifestyle, but one would hope for a more direct political influence than that in a country like Britain, with relatively free political institutions as compared with many parts of the world. So one approaches *Agenda for Prophets* (which does not mention Kee's discussion) with interest roused by its sub-title.

The book is something of a hotch-potch. Many publishers would have dismissed it at once, and perhaps potential readers will. However that would be a mistake. There are indeed 16 sections in only 165 pages, together with an Introduction and Postscript, and 16 contributors, and the contributions are of a very diverse kind, descriptive, historical and analytical. In a sense the book has been thrown together. An address of Tony Benn in 1976 on the Levellers is included. (He modernizes them into an image of himself, not appreciating the significance of their exclusion of 'servants' and 'those receiving alms' from 'the free People of England.') Ken Leech writes on the Christian Left in Britain, 1850–1950, as if it consisted only of Anglicans; and John Kent takes up a tale from 1945 to 1970 in a quite different but quirky vein. Nevertheless the very variety has its own interest, and certain tendencies can be observed, with some exceptions, which it is profitable to discuss.

To begin with, what is political theology? David Haslam's introduction does not throw much light either on this or on the criticisms made of it by the yet more radical liberation theologians. He tells us that the type he favours wishes to begin from an entirely different theological presupposition from those of reformists who want to introduce a political dimension into Western liberal theology, but he does not tell us what those presuppositions are. My own view is that the basic point of political theology is the realization that theological thought is inescapably political, in that it does not take place in an intellectual vacuum of pure, disinterested, reasoning but in a political context in which social, economic and cultural factors are powerful in conditioning that thought. It is the development of the sociology of knowledge which has brought this home to us. To recognize these conditioning factors is partially to transcend them, but we can never do so totally and be entirely 'independent' thinkers. Most academic and popular theology ignores this, and to the extent that it does so is flawed. J. M. Bonino has a short article in this book in which he puts his finger on this point. He asks, Who does theology? and, Who consumes theology? He answers 'a limited section of social class . . . does theology basically for the same community', and adds 'unless theology finds a way to overcome class captivity, it cannot expect to render true service to the "whole people of God", either within the churches or in the wider social body'. He points out that the last ten to fifteen years have seen a theological renaissance in Latin America arising from 100,000 'basic communities', which has resulted in 'a new-gained freedom which helps to uncover the hidden, ideological, class-bound presuppositions and judgments of much that passes for purely objective scholarship'. He concludes that the resulting situation is full of risks, uncertainties and potential conflicts, but also the possibility of creativity in the spirit of Christ.

The root question is, therefore, how to 'do theology'. Political theologians begin with the presupposition that the Christian gospel which derives from the kingdom of God as witnessed in the life and teaching of Jesus involves commitment to the poor; without that it is impossible to theologize properly. Perhaps it would be more accurate to refer not only to the materially poor but to *all* society's rejects as being a particular concern of Jesus. If this point is fundamental, the next question is how this commitment is to be worked out in the life of the church itself, and in the relation of the church as an institution and of each Christian, to the world.

Here we come at once to the dilemma that the church is part of the problem. For this reason many political and liberation theologians are inclined to give up the church in the large sense and concentrate on Bonino's 'basic communities' or Kee's 'alternative communities'. Thomas Cullinan in this book shares in advocating 'Abrahamic communities' as inevitable and necessary because the church as a whole, which takes on all comers, and at all levels of commitment, is bound to be messy and ambiguous. However, he does not leave the church aside. Is it a hopeless task and a waste of time to be concerned with Parochial Church Councils, Synods, Presbyteries, Circuits, Assemblies and the like? I think not, and this book does not specifically say that it is, but it gives no help in the task.

Nor does it say much about the church and its function in society, nor that of individual Christians. To deal with this it would be necessary to analyse group relationships and conflicts as a perennial feature of the human condition. A theology of power is needed, the necessity of its use, and checks on its abuse. Instead the implication is given that the task is to overthrow capitalism and then these problems will be solved. Behind power is violence, but this is discussed only in connection with class war. An over-simple type of Marxist analysis, to which I shall return, has left these questions untouched.

J. J. Vincent is the contributor most explicitly sceptical of Marxist theory. However he is as much preoccupied as the others with new kinds of Christian community, on the margins of the church and of the existing social order, but he sees that the people of God as such do not have directly applicable political policies or solutions. Instead he writes powerfully of the value of acted parables, and of prophecy of Christian groups. As a Protestant Christian he is also preoccupied with using the Bible (particularly the Gospels) as guidance in these tasks of political witness; and this leads him to an ingenious but too simple procedure. Briefly, one finds a Gospel, as redacted in the New Testament, with a broadly similar political situation to one's own and then holds a dialogue with it. Thus Mark comes from a time of eschatological foreshortening to which a policy of 'non commitment' is appropriate; Matthew represents the creation of a new third nation in reaction to Jewish exclusiveness after the Council of Jamnia, so Christians are a new political community; Luke represents long term co-operation with a favourable political regime; John a time when societies are concerned with ideas, philosophies and world views. Apart from debatable points concerning each of the Gospels and the artificiality of being shut up in these four options, Vincent's suggestions overlook the fact that all of them arose from a quite different situation from our post-Christian one. It is impossible to move in this way from the Bible to the modern world; first-century conditioning factors prevent it. The kingdom of God in the teaching of Jesus escapes these factors precisely because of its lack of detail. Consequently it is always seeking a political and social expression but never at ease in any one of them. That is why Christians need an 'eschatological reserve' as they cope with social change and look for a new social order. They certainly need to live for the future in the light of the past, as Rex Ambler stresses, whereas they have had a distressingly static attitude to society and a fondness for the status quo, but on the other hand they do not imagine that they are building a terrestrial kingdom of God of which they have the ground plan. Political theologians are afraid that any talk of eschatological reserve will make Christians pessimistic and passive about social change, and they have much evidence to support them in this. But there is no necessity for it. *All* Christian doctrines have been corrupted into a static quiescence, but that is no argument against their proper use.

So far we have been concerned with how theology is to be done. The other main question is, how to find out 'what is going on' in order to act relevantly. Here the Bible cannot help us. Nor can experience in 'basic communities'; that can tell us where the shoe pinches, but not exactly why, or what to do about it. There is no escape from an empirical investigation. At this point the book operates, for the most part, with a broad and stereotyped Marxist brush, without any defence of it, or even reference to the various subtler forms of the pluralist Marxism which are now available. Capitalism is said to suffer from basic contradictions between capital and labour. There is no discussion of the allocation of scarce resources which any society has to solve, not the handling of conflicts of interest between givers and receivers of orders, or between producers and consumers. McCabe refers to 'the archaic irrelevancy of the market'. Only Cullinan mentions management, and only he the Third World. Yeo talks of Marxism as providing a vision not based on money, price or profit, when Marxism's characteristic claim is to be a *science*, and one would think that for the Christian the vision would be based on Jesus and the kingdom of God. Various writers assume that workers' control solves everything. There is no analysis of the various Marxist societies of which we have now had evidence and of the problems they reveal. Haslam talks of a 'truly socialist community' but gives no indication of its features except that there would be workers' control. There is no coming to grips with the problems of an advanced industrial society, nor of its relations with the Third World, nor of how we move from where we are nor, apart from the vaguest indication, where we move to. In my judgment the essence of the socialist case is its equalitarian emphasis, which it stresses in the cause of greater communal fellowship and as a matter of distributive justice. This has its problems, too, both in the nature of equality in relation to other social values and in the practical questions of how we deal with our inequalities of income and wealth, the latter being an especially stubborn phenomenon. There is no guidance on these matters in *Agenda for Prophets*.

Prophecy is a more complex phenomenon than just transferring the concept from the Old Testament to the present day. The Old

Testament prophets were deepening a doctrine of God in a 'one kingdom' context. Since New Testament times we have been engaged in working out a doctrine of God's kingdom in Christ and how it relates to the kingdoms of this world; a two kingdoms context. That requires an understanding of one's present-day world. The trouble with *Agenda for Prophets* is partly with its basic theological stance but even more with its jejune 'secular' analysis. It raises two key questions for Christians. The first is whether the main point of political theology is right; I think it is. The second is whether its view of contemporary society is well founded; I think it is not. But the debate about this second point is not about Christianity but about the modern world.

7

Christian Socialism Becalmed

The Christian Socialist Movement of today was founded in 1960 as the result of the amalgamation of several organizations, all numerically small, but some with notable members.[1] The amalgamation was marked by a pamphlet *Papers from the Lamb*.[2] Twenty-one years later a more substantial symposium was published, *Agenda for Prophets*.[3] Its twenty-fifth anniversary was marked by a third symposium, in scale midway between the two previous ones, *Facing the Future as Christians and Socialists*.[4] It is in the style of a glossy magazine and includes fourteen articles, together with a brief analysis of many of the Christian Socialist groups which had functioned from 1877 to 1960.[5] This latest symposium is wider in its range of writers (four came from outside Britain) and its contents, since humanistic Marxism is considered as an intellectual source, whereas previously there was a generally sympathetic and sometimes uncritical attitude towards the Soviet Union as distinct from any serious effort to grapple with Marxism. With the exception of the Christian Left of the 1930s, the roots of the various Christian Socialist groups were found chiefly in the theology of F. D. Maurice. In other respects, however, the third symposium shows little change from the previous two. This is worrying in view of the tasks facing the political Left at the present time.

In the traditional Christian Socialist critique of capitalism there have been four strands, only the first of which achieves cogency, though it is of fundamental importance. First, a critique of the philosophy underlying the development of capitalist institutions. This philosophy is often called 'possessive individualism'; it erected the conception of minimum government and a free market into an overall understanding of how men and women should be related in society. Reacting against the *laissez-faire* view of the free market accepted by most Christians of his time as being a law of God, Maurice had maintained that the contention that competition is the key to human relations is a lie. It presupposes a false view of persons in society and is irreconcilable with a Christian understanding of human life.[6] Second, Christian Socialists were prone to go further and say that the concept of competition is itself unChristian. I can see no grounds for this. Rather it seems a necessary element in life, especially in so far as grading is inescapably involved in many human corporate activities.[7] Third, profit has also been a suspect concept. The slogan was 'production for use and not for profit', and the economic motivation was to be 'service not self'. This was too simple. It did not examine closely enough the role of the self and self-regard, including concern for the family as an extension of the self, to distinguish it from selfishness. And it did not come to grips with the perennial economic problem of allocating relatively scarce resources with alternative uses. So it did not consider the possibility that profit might be in many cases a useful directive, whether or not it was an incentive, and whether or not it was private or public profit. It hid this basic economic problem under the demand for 'common ownership', without asking how that in itself could solve it, or whether there were political problems of excessive concentrations of power lurking in the concept. Fourth, it thought of socialism as a model society, often equating it, or a co-operative commonwealth (another popular term) with the kingdom of God in the teaching of Jesus. New Testament scholarship this century has destroyed this notion.

The Aims and Objectives of the present Christian Socialist Movement[8] indicate how strong such positions still are. Its members pledge themselves to work and pray for the coming of God's kingdom on earth and hold that the Christian gospel offers us power to bring this about. It holds that socialist policies are implicit in the *quest (sic)* for the kingdom of God. Its six points to pray, give and work for are:

1. The unity of all Christian people, especially in social purpose. This is a welcome and relatively new note; in the past there were marked sectarian Anglican tendencies in several groups.

2. Reconciliation between nations.

3. World peace with nuclear and general disarmament.

4. Redistribution to close gaps between rich and poor, and between rich and poor nations.

5. The common ownership and democratic control of the productive resources of the earth.

6. A classless society, combining social, sexual and racial equality with personal responsibility and freedom of speech and association.

The utopianism of some of this is evident. Not to be in favour of reconciliation and world peace would be to favour sin. What is missing is the radical eschatological challenge of the kingdom of God as Jesus taught and lived it. If it can be said that Christian theology is always searching for a philosophy in which to express itself, it could also be said that the kingdom of God is always seeking expression in a social order, never at ease in one, always challenging the status quo from the perspective of the underdog in terms of distributive justice; in short applying *semper reformanda* to the social order as well as to the church.

Socialism has historically stressed equality, not out of envy but for the sake of fraternity; and democratic socialism has seen the necessity of bringing in liberty as a criterion as well. The search at any given time is for structures which will best embody these criteria, including the order and law necessary to sustain them. Practical policies will raise fresh problems as existing ones are dealt with; and there will always be the danger of a relapse against which to guard. Within this perspective the free market has its place as a human device to fulfil certain human purposes, a servant and not a master.

In *Facing the Future* there is one contributor who for the first time in these symposia strikes this note. He is Peter Broadbent, who centres Christian commitment to the poor in the gospel of the kingdom of God in the ministry of Jesus, because of whom 'the life of the world has become incarnate in the world and the world can never be the same again'; so we 'live in the already/not yet tension of the life of the kingdom of God' which stands as a prophetic sign over against the established order and proclaims the transformation of relationships and structures.

Apart from Broadbent's article, *Facing the Future* carries on traditional Christian Socialist emphases. Lord Soper continues to identify 'socialism with the kingdom of God as Jesus proclaimed it'. Eric Heffer agrees; so does Edward Charles. (Irene Brennan, however does not agree with this identification.) Charles adds that a world without war is an intermediate stage *(sic)* on the way to the kingdom of God. René-Marie Croose Parry (the founder of the Teilhard Centre) holds to the belief in the human capacity for indefinite improvement, which is tenable if she had mentioned also the subtle temptations that go with moral achievements and corrupt them, but she does not. Indeed she says that 'the next threshold, which humanity must cross in union, *will be as great a transformation as was the change from animal instinct to human thought'*. Evolutionary utopianism can hardly go further. Grace Crookall-Greening, extrapolating from Quaker experience, says that the Christian churches should 'learn to assume and exercise responsibility under divine guidance without needing to appoint leaders' as an example to British politics. So much for the problems of management in industry, commerce, education and social services, and those of representative democracy in politics! The Marxist Rudolf Bahro wants to see the amalgamation of socialism and Christianity in practice and in ideas. But when 'scientific' Marxism is repudiated in favour of an alleged humanitarian early Marxism, and when Irene Brennan wants to exorcise from this the overtones of a distorted religion, it is difficult to see what it can contribute which is not in the Christian tradition already. Moreover, the Marxist critique of religion is a key feature; remove it and much else tumbles besides. Another article praises the 1982 Moscow World Peace Conference for being aware of 'the evolving future of the created world'. Human society is clearly meant. In what sense is it evolving? Paul Derrick argues in favour of workers' co-operatives as a way to express common ownership, in which control is vested in the workers but the productive resources 'are used for the benefit of society as a whole'. This is certainly one model of industry which deserves more attention than it has had, but like other models it has its ambiguities. Workers have their own vested interests as against consumers. Like most of us they like to be left to work in accustomed ways and are loath to face the need for innovation. And if things are going well they are prone to keep a good thing to themselves rather than expand the work force. Experience in Yugoslavia, which has experimented with this form of organization as a reaction from Soviet centralizing, has been illuminating in these respects. Derrick makes no mention of these considerations.

Facing the Future suffers from the defect of not relating its Utopianism to the basic problems of any economy. Socialism is written of as if it is a clear and unambiguous concept, as it is by the Jubilee Group, whose basic leaflet says it stands for socialism, undefined, because 'the capitalist system is incompatible with the Christian gospel'. In my view, as I have already said, its philosophy is, but the free market is not. If it is thought that there is an alternative 'Christian' economic system, Christian Socialists have not provided a model of one, and I do not think it is possible to do so. Nor have secular socialists provided a viable alternative model. Years ago Oscar Lange offered a theoretical mathematical optimization model, parallel to a perfect market, which he claimed would do the job better. Hayek replied that it would not work because the amount of information required would be so great that the chances of getting it right would be minimal. It would also put too much power in the hands of the planners. And in any case it could not cope with change and innovation. The passage of time has not lent enchantment to Lange's ideas; indeed Soviet-style economies are slowly moving away from it.[9] The centralized Soviet model is discredited because of its inefficiencies, particularly in servicing capital goods and with respect to innovation, and also because of its excessive concentration and abuse of economic with political power. Talk of common ownership does not suffice; that can be run by governments of the Right, Left or Centre. Socialism is basically not a model alternative economic system to the capitalists, but a stance which stresses equality, for basically religious or secular humanist reasons. Democratic socialism also brings in liberty as a criterion. There is still a lot of mileage in R. H. Tawney's *Equality*, and it is noteworthy how often thinkers on the Left return to Tawney's approach to socialism.[10]

The problems of the handling of social conflicts, the distribution of wealth, and the creation of wealth are all related. Producers and consumers, and givers of orders and receivers of orders, have conflicts of interest which need legitimate expression, but they need to be handled creatively and neither denied nor suppressed. An important question is put to socialists by Tories like Roger Scruton when they say that Socialists often seem to think of a society in which power is abolished, when in fact the rights of 'man' need a delicate apparatus of law and authority to make them a reality, so that power is controlled by rule of law. A workable economic model has also to relate to the constraints imposed by the international position of Britain, for it is not possible for a heavily populated country like the United Kingdom, so dependent on international trade, to turn itself into an economic national fortress while it pursues domestic ideals undisturbed by foreigners and their pressures.

Welfare capitalism, even in our present diluted form of it, is proving more stable than we expected, though at the cost of grave injustices to a minority. Twenty-five years ago I never thought that between three and four million unemployed would be tolerated. If these injustices are to be corrected as far as distribution is concerned it cannot be done by merely diminishing the wealth of the top five per cent, offensive as are the extremes of income and wealth, which have been getting worse since 1979. 'Middle Britain' will have to pay more, including the better paid weekly wage earner, who has been doing well if in work. In addition economic growth is needed, something like four to four and a half per cent per annum instead of the two and a half to three per cent on which we tend to set our sights. There are feasible plans to achieve this. But any model must show how to combine the higher public spending which this will require as pump priming with the avoidance of an unacceptable degree of inflation. This means some form of incomes policy. Full employment, stable prices and free collective bargaining cannot be achieved together, for they are incompatible. The model needs to point to the best mix in our present situation. It also has to show how the needed flexibility in the economy can be accomplished without undue hardship on those who have to change their skills, and how the extra wealth created can use the personal qualities of the unskilled whose routine jobs are increasingly being mechanized. Capitalism is cruel to those who have little or nothing to trade with; no wealth or particular skills, only physical labour and their human qualities to offer. Various proposals for a basic citizens' wage and for guaranteed jobs for the long-term unemployed fit in here.[11] The Christian Socialist Movement does not engage with these issues but remains irrelevantly on the sidelines. It could have helped to prod the Labour Movement into taking more notice of them, but it has not. That Movement itself has been slow to attend to them, though there are now signs of a change.[12]

The same must be said of the 'Christendom' contribution. It stands somewhat apart from the Christian Socialist Movement, as it did in the 1930s, but it is relevant to this discussion because its latest exponent adopts substantial elements of Marxist economic theory and must therefore be included in a discussion of any form of social-ism.[13] One of the characteristics of the former Christendom Group was to argue that Christian theology leads to a wholly different approach to reality from any other, and therefore to a different social order from either the capitalist or socialist alternatives on offer. The first assumption led it in effect to deny any autonomy to intellectual disciplines like economics, and left it free to take over any purported economic analysis which suited it, without critical examination. In the 1930s it was the Social Credit analysis of how money was supposed to circulate in the economic system, worked out by the engineer Major C. H. Douglas. The second assumption led to the particular proposals which it put forward being so remote from possibility as to remove the Christendom Group from any relevance to the decisions which in fact had to be made. In the 1930s it tended towards a return to a largely rural economy with as little international trade as possible. The Group wrote so confidently about economic issues and so contemptuously of economics that most of the Christian public which read its publication assumed that the members had studied economics and exploded it from within. It never occurred to them that none had studied it.[14]

That kind of thinking faded out, but it is uncanny to find the current Christendom Research Scholar at Lancaster University, John Milbank, reproducing the characteristics of fifty years ago.[15] As with the Christendom Group of the past, there are good insights to be found in his writing, but with respect to the area with which I am now concerned the same defects are there. Milbank argues that the acceptance of Christian doctrine alters the entire intellectual picture so that there cannot be a single, non-controversial description of contemporary secular reality. Therefore there is no point in social theology engaging with so-called experts; instead it should be calling into question the terms on which secular analyses are made.[16] There is some truth here. The assumptions of any discipline or any 'expert', explicit or implicit, need examining in terms of the understanding of the world, and human beings in the world, which they presuppose. But it does not follow that Christian theology requires such peculiar assumptions as to render other disciplines otiose, so that they have to be replaced by Christian ones, Muslim ones, agnostic ones or whatever. If the entire intellectual picture is altered we should have to establish Christian mathematics and Christian engineering: or if the implications of this cause us to draw back, it would certainly involve Christian biology, psychology, sociology and economics.

Instead, however, of producing a Christian economics, Milbank adopts a Marxist one. Because he regards capitalism as a Christian heresy he jumps to the conclusion that Marxism is an ally of Christian orthodoxy. In fact he criticizes Marx's view of the role of religion, and holds that its personalism is ambiguous, and that it probably has not the philosophical resources to sustain it,[17] but he accepts Marxist economics in the form of the writings of the Belgian Marxist economist Ernest Mandel on late capitalism.[18] Mandel says his work is 'based in terms of the basic laws of motion of capitalism discovered by Marx in *Capital*'.[19] He says that the inherent contradictions of capitalism are found in late capitalism. Milbank, following Mandel, writes of the labour theory of value and the theory of surplus value, and argues that the further extension of surplus value leads to a long-run decline of it, because there is less labour from which to expropriate the surplus, and hence to a decline in profits, a diminishing of markets, and so to the collapse of capitalism because of its contradictions. At this point Milbank differs from Marx in thinking that this will not necessarily lead to socialism but maybe to another alienating mode of production.

Milbank, therefore, rejects some fundamental features of Marxism but accepts its economic analysis. In my view this analysis is a fantasy, and the Marxist labour theories of value and surplus value are incorrect. Nor do I think there are laws of motion of capitalism in any sense remotely like the Marxist. The analysis of the present state of 'Western' economies it produces does not seem to me plausible. And *if* capitalism does run into serious trouble I think it will be due to political discontent arising out of injustices which could have been corrected and have not been, not because of inherent contradictions. But the root question is, what entitles Milbank on *theological* grounds (for he is writing a theological paper) to take over a Marxist economic analysis? He shows no signs of having mastered 'bourgeois' economics and thus of being able from within to show that it is fallacious and that Marxist economics is correct. Then he would be an expert, and the rest of us would have to choose between rival expertise in diagnosing the situation today. We are often, as Christians, in this position, and its difficulties cannot be avoided. Decisions continually need expert evidence, but experts often differ, and their claims have to be evaluated to the best of our ability, even though elements of uncertainty often remain even as decisions have to be made. But the decisions cannot be left to them. Medical ethics is an area where this situation has in recent years particularly forced itself on our attention. Discernment derived from Christian faith may well help in evaluating different expert evidence, but it cannot by itself settle the matter.

When it comes to actual recommendations, Milbank bows out by talking of the 'realism of the Cross',[20] and of a creative disengagement from the so-called political realities. This prescinds from any of the choices offered us, and leaves us with all the problems of relating the cross to economic, social and political structures with which social theology has traditionally had to wrestle. The only clue he gives is a reference to 'the new and more genuine socialist policies which may now be emerging';[21] but what they are and from where they are coming we are not told. In my view, in the economic realm new ideas are emerging in left-wing circles which are beginning to take seriously the problems of resource allocation and of innovation, in the light of the abundant evidence from the USSR and Eastern Europe of the failure of the command economies in these respects and the problems they have caused for themselves in consequence. At the same time there are well thought out proposals to deal with the injustices of the social market economies of Western Europe. Whether implementing them would produce a democratic socialist or a social democratic economy is a matter for discussion. The socialist emphasis will continue to lie in the criterion of equality. It is sad that so little attention is paid to these issues by the Christian Socialist Movement.

The problem with the Christendom Group legacy is somewhat different. It purports to have a distinctively Christian diagnosis of our social order, and one which puts it in a position of apparently prophetic witness which is so remote from current decisions that it can carry on indefinitely on the sidelines. It bolsters this diagnosis by adopting dubious economic theories which are not in fact in any way dependent on Christian presuppositions, and which the Christian faith by itself does not provide the criteria to assess. To abandon this habit would require a reassessment of the diagnosis, and perhaps diminish a certain zest for being so distinctive; it would require a greater engagement with the awkward realities of current issues, in a Britain where, as a recent writer in *The Economist* has put it, the future is being designed to belong 'to those who work harder, use their elbows and make more money'. The writer approved of this. I would hope most Christians would judge it unacceptable.

Part III

Ecumenical Social Ethics

8

Fifty Years on from the
Oxford Conference

It was in July 1937 that the ecumenical conference on 'Church, Community and the State' met in Oxford. 'No ecumenically organized reflection on theology and social ethics since Oxford matches it in quality and thoroughness.' This is the verdict of Paul Abrecht.[1] It is a generous one because he himself was the main organizer of the only other ecumenical conference to compare with it, that in Geneva in 1966 on 'Christians in the Technical and Social Revolutions of our Time', which was specifically intended to do for the churches in the 1960s what Oxford had done in the 1930s. By then the churches did not start so far behind as in 1937, so that the advance made in 1966 was more one of consolidation and did not appear so striking.

The Background to the Oxford Conference

Oxford itself, however, did not start entirely from scratch. Its 'Life and Work' predecessor, the Stockholm Conference of 1925, virtually did. That an ecumenical start was made at all was a legacy of the First World War. The scale of it both in the areas of the world involved and the extent of the slaughter, together with the fact that it originated in Western Christendom, the one civilization in which the Christian faith had to some extent moulded the structures of society, made the churches ashamed of their failure. In each country they had been uncritically nationalistic. Moreover they had no sustained tradition of reflection on Christian social ethics, apart from the Roman Catholic Church whose social ethics had made a new start with the encyclical *Rerum Novarum* in 1891, but at this stage its involvement in ecumenical efforts was but a faint hope. The churches were also isolated from one another. Stockholm was a considerable achievement in bringing together official representatives of

Protestant, Anglican and Orthodox churches, in triumphing over surviving tensions on war guilt, and in realizing that it is not enough to
concentrate on individual piety: it is also necessary to allow for the
influence of basic social structures in the nurture of persons. Stockholm did not in fact make much progress in this respect. Attention
was focussed on the tension between a type of other worldly piety,
which had become evident in continental Protestantism, and an optimistic 'social gospel' type of American Liberal Protestantism.

Oxford made a great advance. The external situation had changed
dramatically for the worse. The 1929 Wall Street crash led to a great
economic depression, and the mass unemployment it produced in the
industrialized countries dominated the 1930s, together with the rise
of Nazism, which was made easier by it.[2] The failure of the League
of Nations seemed (rightly) to be leading to a drift towards another
war. In the USSR the ruthless character of Stalin's regime was becoming evident, even to those who had had high hopes of it. Theologically
there was in Protestant circles a new awareness of the centrality for
Christians of the church; previously many doubted whether Jesus ever
intended one, and thought that the heart of his teaching was seen as
an ideal kingdom which was evolving historically and which human
persons would help to build. This revived concern for the church was
not in order to set a totalitarian church over against a totalitarian
state. Rather the totalitarian threat made Christians find some
strength and standing ground in their own tradition against the over-
weening national state, by reference to the universality of the church.
'Let the church be the church' was the call. It was because so many
church leaders had caught a sense of this through the nascent ecumenical movement that they were able to hold together during the 1939–
45 war, and that the WCC could be so firmly established in 1948.
There was no triumphalism behind this slogan. The sense of penitence
for the failures of the churches, particularly in the European heartland, was too strong.

The international situation in 1937 was so menacing that Oxford
had to face the question of war, and that Christians would find
themselves on opposite sides in countries at war with one another.
They had to prepare themselves to live with this tragedy. Oxford
could not resolve the problems of Christians and war, the most
extreme example of the dilemmas posed by living in two kingdoms
at once, church and state, both under God. But it could take the
measure of it and guard against being swept along in a tide of uncritical wartime nationalism. There was to be no repetition among those

touched by the ecumenical movement of the jingoist attitudes of 1914–18.

The bleak economic situation produced some of the best thinking at Oxford. There was a comprehensive review of the economic systems on offer, a critique of them, and the assertion that the church is not tied to any one system. The Christian claims for a capitalist system were discounted and its evils were pointed out. The claims of its ideal socialist opposite (of which there was no working model) were also queried and the evils of the Stalinist system indicated. The report of this section was so much in demand that it had to be printed separately.[3] Much of it is still relevant to industrial societies and, indeed, the 1986 Pastoral Letter of the USA Roman Catholic bishops *Economic Justice for All: Social Teaching and the US Economy* is very similar.

Another emphasis at Oxford was on the role of the laity in their families, their jobs and as citizens. In the long run this was seen as of far more significance than official actions of churches, still less resolutions of synods and such bodies. Slowly, all too slowly, this is beginning to be taken seriously, though in church structures it has a long way to go.[4]

Oxford had 426 delegates, of which 300 came from the USA and the British Commonwealth; 40 were Orthodox; only 30 came from churches of the Third World, and only 16 of these were nationals of the churches they represented; Lutherans from Germany were forbidden by their government to attend. The low Third World attendance was not unreasonable at the time; it reflected the fact that its churches were not as yet much involved in either the Life and Work or the Faith and Order side of the ecumenical movement, being related to one another through the International Missionary Council, which came into the WCC only in 1961, and which in fact held its own Conference in the year after Oxford.

The most enduring legacy of the Oxford Conference to the Ecumenical Movement is its thorough preparation, organized by Dr J. H. Oldham. A preparatory volume, *The Church and its Function in Society* by him and Dr W. A. Visser 't Hooft (who was to become in 1948 the first General Secretary of the WCC) was issued to delegates a month in advance. One of them said to me:[5] 'If the churches get in 25 years to where this book is now they will have done well.' In fact the war of 1939–45 speeded up the process of assimilation. But the book remains relevant, and is probably still the best introduction to the whole ecumenical enterprise of this century towards the unity and renewal of the churches.[6] Oldham had instigated a process of international ecumenical consultation on the themes of the conference. This involved leading theologians, lay as well as clerical, and experts in other fields writing preliminary papers, having them circulated and commented upon by those of other confessional traditions or experience, sometimes discussed in colloquia, and then re-written. Most of these were published in the autumn after the Conference.[7] A number of these papers are of permanent importance, and together they bear witness to a time when theological insight certainly equalled and to some extent outshone that coming from any other contemporary source.

In short, we can say that at Oxford the churches became truly contemporary in issues of social ethics. They did not operate with out-of-date, ill-informed and nostalgic assumptions but really faced the traumatic situation of the 1930s with as accurate a diagnosis as their advisers could muster. Oxford also made it clear that it did not claim to speak *for*, but *to*, the churches. In giving general approval to the reports of its groups it was not giving an *imprimatur* to every word or sentence but saying that in effect 'these are the parameters of our diagnoses; we think that they are probably better based than any one church could have done on its own, and we commend them to your serious considerations'. Those who thought them flawed would be challenged to do better after an equally thorough preparation.

Since Oxford

The Second World War was followed by the era of political de-colonialization. (How far there has been economic de-colonialization is another matter.) This brought churches from Africa, Asia and Latin America into the WCC and greatly altered the balance within it. No longer could 'Western' churches in effect dictate the agenda. Moreover it came at a time of rapid economic and social change with its frustrated hopes for a 'trickle down' of the benefits of economic development. This whole process of change in the Third World with its repercussions on the churches was ironically brought about by the expansion of the influence of 'Western' trade, technology, education and Christian institutions in a way which the 'Westerners' themselves neither intended nor thought of. In effect it created a revolution. Dissatisfaction in the Third World with what was happening, and especially with the inequalities of power, internal as well as external, led to the demand by many for a different kind of revolutionary change (not necessarily violent, but not excluding violence). The Geneva Conference of 1966 was startled to hear this coming from Latin American delegates. Since then its expression with liberation theology has become much more prominent and widely known in ecumenical circles. At the same time Marxism has ceased to be the largely monolithic intellectual and political structure that it was in the 1930s, when dissentients like the Trotskyites were small and ineffective by comparison to Stalin's hosts. Again, within theological circles the era of biblical theology, largely associated with Barthianism, has come and gone with its too easy smoothing over the varied strains in the Bible and its too complete isolation of the Christian faith from all other faiths and philosophies. And a further major change is that in the Roman Catholic Church since the Second Vatican Council 1962–65 in its attitude to the Ecumenical Movement. Though the old and the new lie side by side in the documents of the Council, and a struggle between them has been a feature of the Roman Catholic Church ever since, so that the way of co-operation between the WCC and that church has been cautious and not without difficulty (not least because structurally and ecclesiologically they are such very different bodies), any serious ecumenical work has to take the Roman Catholic Church as a major collaborator, at least to the extent of participant observers.

One of the major differences between the two bodies is the much looser structure of the WCC which enables different sections within it to have much freedom to 'do their own thing'. The effect of this has been marked since 1969, as the WCC has become more involved in action on various fronts, of which the Programme to Combat Racism has attracted most controversy.

On questions of method, the Geneva Conference followed much the same procedure as Oxford, but with a vast agenda. It was the first truly world-wide examination of Christian social responsibilities. Four volumes of essays were published in connection with it, but the process was less smooth and the essays less easy to gear into the work of the Conference itself than was the case at Oxford.[8] Two years later a joint consultation of Church and Society, and Faith and Order in the WCC was held at Zagorsk, near Moscow, to work on the themes of the meaning of revolution, method in Christian social ethics, and ecclesiological issues relating to social ethics. It broadly endorsed the Oldham legacy which had operated from Oxford onwards. No similar consultation has been held since. In view of the dynamic years since 1968 one is overdue. The action-reflection model which has come to the fore since then needs unpacking and relating to the middle level of *church* action which Oldham advocated; middle that is to say between fundamental Christian insights and detailed policies. Discussion on appropriate levels of action was not meant to exclude all church initiatives, such as the Programme to Combat Racism; on the other hand the action-reflection model can mean acting without accurate knowledge of a situation or without considering the likely secondary consequences of actions beyond the obvious immediate ones, and then in reflecting choosing only those sources which support what one has already done. There are issues here which need teasing out.

The 1970s saw a big debate developing in the 'West' on ecological issues. Theologians responded by looking again at the biblical and doctrinal inheritance in the Christian tradition on the themes of creation, humankind and nature. This was intensified by the threats involved in the development of nuclear energy and nuclear weapons. So questions of war and peace, economic development and ecology, and the attitude of natural scientists and the public to the ethos which the technical virtuosity of modern science has shown, all became linked to one another. This was the background of the WCC World Conference on 'Faith, Science and the Future', held at the Massachusetts Institute of Technology in 1979.[9] This was almost but not quite in the succession of Oxford and Geneva because it concentrated much more on the ecological and scientific issues to the relative neglect of the ongoing agenda of economic and political ones; and it did not have much of an ethical-theological overview of what it was doing and how it was doing it. But it was an impressive ecumenical gathering; and for the first time distinguished natural scientists were called upon, and willingly helped, in an ecumenical enquiry.

The Geneva representation was made up of about 400 from over 70 countries, and those from the Third World were there in such numbers that they would not be ignored. It was impossible to discuss simply on a 'Western' basis. Moreover there was a very large lay element. By an immense effort in its own nominations and in its persuasion of member churches in choosing their delegates, the WCC managed to ensure that clergy and ministers did not predominate. In fact some of the Third World churches sent their best lay people from the secular world. I could have written lay *men*, for it was the case at both Oxford and Geneva that there were only a small number of women; the pressure to increase the representation of women came after 1966. At the MIT conference half the participants were natural scientists. However, in all those conference, it proved hard to get economic, industrial, political and military decision-makers to attend; they were all much under-represented.

The Future

It is now fifty years since the Oxford Conference. If we had had another Oxford in 1987 what might have been on the agenda? Indeed what will or should be on the agenda if the planned world conference on 'Justice, Peace and the Integrity of Creation' in 1990 does take place? This theme is the sequel to that of 'The Responsible Society' which lasted from Oxford until after Geneva, and that of 'The Just, Participatory and Sustainable Society' which replaced it in the 1970s. The JPSS was more to the liking of the Third World churches whilst echoing the ecological preoccupations which had begun to worry the First World ones. This theme too was changed, after the Vancouver Assembly of the WCC. The change may have been hasty, in that the previous study had by no means been completed, particularly with respect to the Participatory element, where many problems had hardly begun to be faced. Action-reflection had pre-empted time and resources, and systematic study by comparison had languished. However, in general the new title represents the same preoccupations. The WCC has to attempt to unify its many-sided and potentially fissiparous sections in relation to it, though the new term 'the integrity of creation' needs a lot of clarifying if it is to be intelligible.

There is a huge task if a worthwhile conference is to be achieved in 1990. It is clear from reflection on Oxford onwards that such a conference depends for its success on the input beforehand. It is an expensive occasion; too expensive in time and money to keep together for more than a fortnight, if as long, particularly in the case of the kind of lay folk whose attendance is most wanted and who cannot free themselves for long from their jobs. Once assembled, the conditions under which the conference has to work are intense: plenaries, group meetings, drafting and re-drafting reports. Misunderstanding, apart from disagreements, across confessional and geographical boundaries are a continual hazard, multiplied by problems of translation.[10] Good advance preparatory work of the sort initiated by J. H. Oldham is essential.

A global agenda at a level of generality cannot be avoided. When details are gone into the same problem arises as with Vatican documents.[11] The different worlds whose experience needs to be drawn upon and which need to understand one another are indeed very different. Many of the churches in the Third World are overwhelmed by poverty and refugees. But the Third World itself is not a unity. There are the oil states. There is a newly industrialized country like Korea, facing similar problems to those of Britain in the nineteenth century. There are the sub-Saharan African countries. These are only three examples. In many of them the search for an appropriate technology is coming to the fore when hitherto they have tended to think of it as a 'Western' pre-occupation, with ecology as a device of the 'haves' to keep the 'have nots' at a distance. Appropriate technology, it should be noted, is not the same as a 'small is beautiful' syndrome with which it is often confused. One aspect of the overwhelming presence of poverty is the rapid growth of cities in many parts of the Third World where those displaced from traditional agriculture, where there are now no jobs for them, drift into cities, where there are only a few jobs compared with the numbers seeking them, and live in appallingly squalid conditions. This is likely to present a political problem even greater than an economic one. How can such cities be governed without an explosion? In all this there is no sign of a 'welfare state' hoped to see extended. Instead there has been a backlash among the wealthy against the notion of welfare even in their own states.

The Second World is faced with a dual collapse; the ideology on which it was built is losing its motive force among the people, and the centralized economies of a soviet type have shown up badly compared with the 'social market' economies of the 'West' (leaving aside the ideology of free enterprise which is often associated with them). They have all to consider what kind of economic growth to aim for, since an uncontrolled concentration of growth will lead to ecological disaster. This also applies to the relatively wealthy First World with its technological skills and dynamism, and the economic power which enables it largely to settle the terms of trade with the Third World. These make it hard for the First World to see any self-interest which would require it to take global responsibilities seriously.

If there is to be a major ecumenical conference on social theology in 1990, not only will there need to be careful preparation and choice of delegates; the WCC will need adequate resources from the churches to do the job properly. At the moment whenever the American dollar falls the WCC catches a cold. In addition to being sensitive to evidence from all over the globe the WCC will need greater internal integration. The theoretical questions involved in the method of Christian social ethics, already mentioned, which are part of the challenge of liberation theology, and even more grassroots Minjung Theology from Korea, cut across traditional confessional stances, which themselves were all formed in what were by comparison static situations as compared with our rapid social change. They are only slowly modified by contact with one another in the Ecumenical Movement. The section of the MIT Conference which reflected on 'Towards a New Christian Social Ethic and New Social Policies for the Churches' asked pertinent questions, but its answers for the most part evaded the hard issues. It hardly had time because it was made up of representatives of each of the nine other sections who met only in the last few days. However, it provided a summary of issues from which a start could be made. Moreover, a potentially useful manual to guide action by churches in this area is being worked on, something which Oldham in his concern for the laity did not do. Which problems to tackle? How many? What are the best strategies? How to enlist allies? How to enlist the active support by church members for what synods and the like decide? How to cope with failure, with miscalculation, with unexpected success? How to wean local congregations from taking up only relief type, or 'ambulance', projects?

There is a large quarry of useful material from Oxford onwards. It is hard to believe it has been adequately digested. And the temptation is to overlook it and continually make fresh starts. It is the *tendencies* in the material which are important and have, I think, a good deal of inherent informal authority. The details matter less, especially the resolutions which tend to be both grandiose and vaguely general, exaggerating the influence and practical possibilities open to the WCC in the first instance and after that the churches in general. However where the WCC and the post-Vatican II Roman Catholic Church are showing the same direction in social analysis and diagnosis, as is the case over a wide area, it should be taken seriously. The evidence is patchy. In its original form the material is accessible only to a minority. The WCC is entirely dependent on national Councils of Churches, and after that the churches themselves, to popularize it. On the whole they do not. Moreover the churches work together imperfectly either without a division of labour so that any one does not try to cover the whole field of social ethics, or in looking for further themes on which they can work together. Ecumenical matters tend to come last in time and money when denominational interests have first been attended to. Protestations are fair; actions do not match them. We do well to work harder to both our input from the UK to ecumenical studies and our attention to the output.

9

Critics from Without and from Within

In this article I propose to examine the critics of Church and Society. However, two preliminary remarks are essential. The first is that I have a great admiration for the work of Paul Abrecht. As a serious and ongoing study in practical Christian social ethics, his work is without equal in the World Council of Churches: nothing so comprehensive or complete has been achieved elsewhere. Moreover, it has been accomplished with the minimum of staff and budget resources. Indeed, financial support has been specially raised on several occasions, thus relieving the general budget of the WCC. Paul Abrecht has shown astonishing vitality in maintaining the impetus over the years, and especially in enlisting the co-operation of distinguished collaborators. A number of these had never before been asked for their help by any Christian body, and were often more than ready to assist when asked. It should also be added that anyone who has responsibilities for wide-ranging global commitments of considerable perplexity, involving frequent absences from his base of operations, depends upon an office efficiently and intelligently administered. In this respect Paul has been fortunate over the years, as he has often made clear, in having Christa Stalschus as his secretary.

The second preliminary remark is that criticisms of Church and Society have less and less been confined to it, and more and more directed to the whole social witness and method of the WCC. This is because an expansion of the number of social issues on the agenda has been parallel with the expansion of the WCC itself. Among these issues black theology, feminist theology, the ethical problems of revolutionary action and nation-building in post-colonial political situations, and the uncertain results of scientific and technological development come at once to mind. There has been a diversification of operations within the WCC, and other units have taken over areas which were at one time, or in theory might well have been, the province of Church and Society. For instance economic issues, which at one time figured largely on its agenda, have tended to move elsewhere in recent years. It is not therefore possible strictly to separate criticisms of Church and Society from more general criticisms of the WCC.

Paul Abrecht inherited a method of study which owed much to J. H. Oldham in the formative stages of the ecumenical movement. This process produced some very solid work. The most obvious example is the six volumes issued in connection with the Oxford conference on 'Church, Community and State' in 1937.[1] It is doubtful whether a weightier theological contribution has been made since. In running a special one-year course on ecumenical social ethics in Manchester University in the 1970s, I frequently found that students became excited when introduced to the Oxford conference volumes, and found them still relevant today. Paul Abrecht continued this method, and recently he has brought in a number of highly distinguished natural scientists in connection with the wider and narrower issues raised by nuclear energy and ecology.

The West and the 'Two-Thirds World'

In 1937, and in 1948 when the WCC was finally launched, the context was largely 'Western'. It is just the enlargement of the WCC since then which has produced criticism from 'Western' sources. It is hard for the 'West', the heart of the old Christendom, to find that its viewpoint and priorities are not shared by the 'two-thirds world'. It often leads to bad-tempered criticism. Some of it is based on sheer ignorance of the WCC in general and Church and Society in particular. Some of it is wilful ignorance, exemplified by a recent attack in *Reader's Digest* (USA) which is not worth attention in this chapter. Some of it is based on the old heresy that the church should stick to 'religious' questions and eschew political ones. It is ironic that this is precisely the attitude taken to the church by the authorities in communist countries, whereas those who take it in the 'West' are usually strongly anti-communist. I do not need to expose the fallacy of such an attitude in this essay, though I shall shortly mention two critics, E. R. Norman and Ernest Lefever, who partly exemplify it. Meanwhile how can one explain the disgruntlement expressed in the following passage, except as due to nostalgia for the vanished predominance of the 'West'?

Naturally, the WCC bureaucrats are highly unrepresentative both in their style and their politics: and their ecumenicist assumptions are thoroughly out of tune with the deep-rooted attachments to particular forms and localities found amongst most ordinary Christians. The interests of such bureaucrats lie in canvassing support in the Third World, in problems of racism and the like, and their whole theology and vocabulary has decreasing contact with the home constituency. At one and the same time they bureaucratize and standardize and manage to wield an existentialist-cum-Marxist vocabulary of liberation, dialogue, significant encounters and the like. Feeling their own loss of roots they lean ever more heavily towards third-world politics, condoning whatever is illiberal in the Third World (or indeed in communist countries since they want the prestige deriving from the participation of the Orthodox), while campaigning vigorously against every blot on the social record of their own countries.

This comes from the book *A General Theory of Secularisation*[2] by David Martin, an internationally renowned professor of sociology at the London School of Economics with a special interest in the sociology of religion, and a distinguished lay theologian (who has recently been ordained). His competence in this area is much greater than that of either Norman or Lefever, which makes the whole tone of the passage so sad.

Norman is a history don at Cambridge University and an Anglican priest. His large book, *Church and Society 1770–1970*,[3] which contains much valuable material, becomes increasingly idiosyncratic the nearer it gets to 1970. The only entry concerning the WCC in the index adds 'unsound teachings of', and gives six references. The basis of his attitude becomes more clear in his broadcast Reith Lectures on 'Christianity and the World Order',[4] in which the WCC figures quite largely. It becomes plain that Norman has two unreconciled attitudes. One is that the Christian gospel is basically concerned with the 'ethereal qualities of immortality', and must not be 'politicized', in the sense of equating it with a political option or a secular value like liberation. One can query the first part of this assertion and broadly agree with the second. However, there is also a clear approval of a time when the clergy were influential and sacralized politics from within, and the Christian knowledge of politics served the interests of the church as an institution. No wonder he does not like the extended canvas on which Paul Abrecht in Church and Society has had to work.

Norman is much quoted by Ernest Lefever in his *Amsterdam to Nairobi: the World Council of Churches and the Third World*.[5] Lefever is apparently a much better informed critic, for in the past he has had a good deal of direct contact with the WCC. The book is published by the Ethics and Public Policy Centre, Washington, DC, of which Lefever is President. His formal position is better than that of Norman. The WCC 'should encourage the peaceful and lawful forces that are trying to deal constructively with the problems of poverty, injustice and lack of freedom. There have been, of course, situations so rigid or dangerous that armed violence was the only possible option ... Most crisis are more ambiguous.'[5] When he applies this perspective, however, he finds himself at odds with a great deal of WCC material. This is because his judgments reflect predominant strains in USA opinions, and do not enter at all into those of the rest of the world who are at the receiving end of the enormous power of the USA, and do not see things the same way. The WCC and Church and Society have perforce to hear from a global constituency.

The frequent complaint in the 'West' that the WCC is too sanguine about political violence is overstated in any case, but it hardly makes sense unless it is based on pacifist principles, which it rarely is. The 'Western' critics are using a double standard, one which applies to their world and another which applies to the rest. Similarly, the charge that WCC stances are selective in their condemnations, and especially that they are soft on coercion in communist countries, is again overstated, and ignores the fact that one cannot proceed on a similar issue in all countries in the same way, regardless of whether the Christians are in a small minority, or of the type of government under which they live. South Africa, the USSR and Iran are very different in these respects.

Mixed with these complaints are references to the WCC 'curia', 'bureaucracy', 'centralization' or the 'social action curia'. These pejorative terms are an indication more of prejudice than reasoned criticism. There is however, a grain of truth hidden in them. The permanent staff of any organization always have a good deal of influence, as those involved day by day in its activities, compared with members of committees who meet only occasionally. In the case of the WCC the influence is qualified, real and necessary, although it has to be watched. It is qualified by the need to carry the committees, and by the fact that it is not monolithic, because the staff differ among themselves. Those involved in official assemblies and committees of the WCC are nearly all nominated by the churches, but in study work and consultations and in the appointment of advisers the staff have more influence. A good deal of thought goes to balancing age, sex, nationality, type of experience and confessional tradition. But one phenomenon has been noticed. I have said that much of the criticism comes from the disgruntled 'West', which no longer sets the agenda, and which sees its criteria questioned. Nevertheless there are important stances in the 'Western' tradition which need to be heard. There is a certain tendency to find that those from the 'West' involved in global advisory consultations are persons who respond most fully to critics of their own countries, and are not sufficiently convinced of the value of their own tradition to present it, in addition to paying attention to its critics; and when they ought to call into question simplicities from others, in a truly ecumenical dialogue, they fail to do so.

Moreover, all of us are liable to be swayed by intellectual fashions. No church is exempt from this; neither is the WCC. For a long time it was dominated by what Paul Ramsey in the book mentioned below called 'a truncated Barthianism', though that has now passed. Church and Society was over-influenced for a time by the Club of Rome report of 1972, *The Limits to Growth*.[6] I remember the Church and Society consultation at Cardiff that year. Half of those present were engaged on the theme of 'Violence, Non-violence and the Struggle for Justice', and the other half on economic issues. I myself was so occupied in the former that I had no time to find out what was happening in the latter. However, when I got home I read the papers presented and was astonished at the economic naiveté of many of them, carried away by this first report of the Club of Rome.

Theology and Political Policy

In my view, much the most important criticism of Church and Society was made by Paul Ramsey in his book *Who Speaks for the Church?*[7] which was a direct response to the Geneva conference of 1966 on 'Christians in the Technical and Social Revolutions of Our Time'. In this book he says he is particularly concerned with Christian ethics as an authentic discipline and not simply the religious consecration of strong feelings. Ramsey's complaint is that the Geneva conference rushed to too direct detailed conclusions (on an alleged Christian basis) on political and economic issues. Others have criticized Church and Society at different times, less cogently, for *not* coming to a clear decision for or against, as in the question of nuclear energy. Ramsey is at the other extreme. He makes a sharp separation between a theological statement and one by Christians which comes to a specific decision about an empirical situation. He leaves the latter to 'the magistrates'. It is a strongly 'two realms' doctrine, advanced in this case by a Methodist and not a Lutheran. The most he will grant is a statement in the form: 'If a certain political conclusion is arrived at by the authorities, then a great deal of Christian opinion will support them.' This is in order that, in supporting a specific decision, Christians are made to be clear on the cost of implementing it, and on precisely how one moves from the existing position to the one recommended. However, in his view 'basic-decision and action-oriented principles of ethical and political analysis',[8] which give direction rather than directives, are a better position for Christians to adopt.

This raises questions which I have explored in my Scott Holland lectures, *Church and Society in the Late Twentieth Century*.[9] Suffice it to say here that Ramsey draws attention to real problems, whilst making too sharp a separation between 'the magistrates', or political authorities, and the rest of us. He is also unduly sanguine about the procedures by which Roman Catholic statements on social ethics are made. True, *Gaudium et Spes*, the Pastoral Constitution of Vatican II (1965), is impressive. But Ramsey's praise of 'the concern for the fullness of Christian truth that is attained by the process by which a social encyclical is issued by a pontiff'[10] was written before the encyclical *Humanae Vitae* was promulgated in 1968. There are many questions which arise about the procedures which lie behind the issue of social teaching by the Roman Catholic *magisterium*, and this I have also discussed in the Scott Holland lectures.

To some extent, Ramsey was answered on method in Christian social ethics by the joint consultation of Church and Society and Faith and Order at Zagorsk in 1968.[11] It said clearly that: 'Theology cannot remove the ambiguity of political ethics in revolutionary situation', as against the tendency to moralize in the sense of expecting a clear 'yes' or 'no' as a guide to political action. But other issues remain, and this is the last time that method in Christian social ethics has been explicitly considered by Church and Society. It is due for further attention.

Ramsey has a further criticism that the theory whereby a Church and Society study conference speaks *to* the churches, not *for* them, is 'a situation which invites irresponsible utterances'.[12] Here he is being perverse. It is precisely the right stance. If the WCC does not keep ahead of the churches it is no use to them. Merely to be a post-bag circulating their existing opinions is otiose. They can do that for themselves. Irritating as it is for them, the WCC must push ahead and speak *to* the churches or give its study conferences freedom to do so, presenting the churches with the best work it can do and leaving them to evaluate it.

Ramsey's criticism was more directed at the tendency of a study conference, like Geneva, to pass resolutions addressed to governments on matters of immediate action, which was not its job, and were not and could not be adequately considered. This brings to mind the warning of J. H. Oldham against Christians feeling pleased with themselves after passing a resolution without considering whether they themselves were committed to any action by it. In Church and Society consultations a particular weakness in this respect is the shortage of people from the echelons of government, and indeed from management or trade unions in industry. It is partly because in politics they cannot get away or are subject to instant recall if a critical political vote or crisis arises. This is less true of industry. But neither top level nor middle management has played much part in Church and Society activities, and trade unionists have been almost entirely absent. These are more difficult for church bodies to bring in than are professional and managerial folk, because they are more suspicious, in view of the lack of relation of the church to the labour movement since the Industrial Revolution. However, their absence is a clear defect.

This is connected with a criticism one sometimes hears within the WCC that the whole Church and Society method is too elitist. It pays attention to the professional persons, the expert, the established people in society, and not to the poor. It operates at a rarefied centre and not at the grass-roots. It is *de haut en bas* and not participatory. This is surely a false polarization. It is not that one should be done and the other left undone; both are needed. But there must be some division of labour, though each needs to be alert to what others are doing. In such a self-conscious body as the WCC this is not difficult. The poor and unprivileged need to be heard themselves, and not interpreted by better-off intermediaries. Nevertheless, they do not see the whole. It is impossible to deal with issues of nuclear energy without physicists, or genetic engineering without biologists and medical folk, or unemployment and underdevelopment without economists. None of them have the last word, but they do have a necessary word. Without their contribution good intentions can lead to foolish actions. In mobilizing them Church and Society has done the ecumenical movement an essential service.[13]

10

Convergence and Divergence in Social Theology: The Roman Catholic Church and the World Council of Churches

Convergence

Roman Catholic Social theology was isolated from that of the ecumenical movement until the Second Vatican Council, 1962–65. Indeed the papacy had condemned that movement. One of the most welcome changes brought about by the Council was the decree on ecumenism, *Unitatis Redintegratio*, which acknowledged and welcomed the ecumenical movement and urged Roman Catholics to play their part in it under, of course, the authority of the church. The change with regard to social theology was immediate and striking.

The ecumenical movement had achieved by then a well-developed method in social theology and ethics, largely initiated by J. H. Oldham in the preparatory work for the Oxford conference on 'Church, Community and State in 1937. This was epitomized in the book by W. A. Visser 't Hooft and J. H. Oldham issued just before the conference, *The Church and its Function in Society*. It dealt with the nature and role of the church, how it could relate its doctrine to the rapid social and political changes going on in the world, the relation between the doctrine and the facts of these changes, the level of detail in policies it might be possible to commend, and the necessity of strong lay participation in the process of ecumenical study. It also emphasized the importance of the activities of lay people in economic, social and political affairs in which ninety-nine point five per cent of Christians spend most of their working lives. Oldham's preparatory process for the Oxford conference involved consultations between theologians, experts from other disciplines, and 'lay' practitioners. Papers were written, sometimes in preparation for a colloquium, but in any event circulated for comments quite widely to those of other Christian confessions than the author, and then re-written in the light of comments received before incorporation in the material associated with the conference. Six volumes of these papers were published shortly after it. Oxford proved a pioneer and a model. In this process only one or two Roman Catholics, of which Jacques Maritain was the best-known, made unofficial contributions.

Potential sources of disagreement in social theology between churches and between individual Christians can be due to three factors: (1) disagreements in interpreting the Bible; (2) disagreements in theologies of church and society all claiming to be derived from, or consonant with, the Bible; and (3) disagreements on analyses of the contemporary situation. The first and second are not in principle insurmountable; there is no inherent reason why agreement should not be reached, even though we may think it unlikely when we take into account the protean nature of the phenomenon of the third. Agreement on the third is less likely because of the inherent uncertainties in obtaining and evaluating evidence, and extrapolating from present evidence into the future.

Sources of disagreement between Roman Catholics and others on biblical interpretation have become much less acute since 1943, when the papal encyclical *Divino Afflante Spiritu* gave a blessing to modern biblical study after it had been practically suppressed in the wake of the modernist controversy in the first decade of this century. In terms of theologies of church and society, if we follow Richard Niebuhr's typology in his *Christ and Culture* (1951) the Roman Catholic Church had been associated with a 'Christ over culture' position, which seems implausible in the modern world. But here again the sources of disagreement became much less acute after Vatican II, when a shift to Niebuhr's fifth type 'Christ transforming culture' was clearly discernible.

Moreover, all three sources of disagreement are found within confessional traditions and not only between them. They arise within the World Council of Churches and within the Roman Catholic Church and between them. If they are faced realistically they are not a reason for separation in working in the field of church and society, a point to which I shall return.

It was the Pastoral Constitution on The Church in the Modern World (*Gaudium et Spes*) which marked the change in social theology. This theme was not on the agenda when the Council met. It was added largely due to the influence of Cardinal Suenens of Brussels.

Work on it had to be fast and intense, and it was promulgated only on the penultimate day of the Council. It is characterized by four important features which have remained of central importance in relation to co-operation between the World Council of Churches and the Roman Catholic Church in social theology.

1. It is not 'churchy' in tone, but stresses both the dignity of the human person and the community of humankind. It argues for a fuller achievement of human rights, with Christians working with all men and women of good will to that end. Justice is the norm and love is to be the driving force. The church has been too conservative in the past and should be the servant of the truly human.

2. It adopts a more flexible theology to cope with rapid social change. In particular it sees that a blanket condemnation of atheism is inadequate, including a blind anti-communism. John XXIII's opening to a Marxist-Christian dialogue in his 1963 encyclical *Pacem in Terris* paved the way for this.

3. The theology is less individualistic and more corporate in its concern for the universal common good and the structures of social life. The social rather than the individual nature of property is stressed, and the freedom of individuals and groups found more in the principle of subsidiarity than in private property.

There is a new respect for the autonomy of the secular; of ethics, of the social sciences and of the natural sciences. The church has not all the answers. 'Let the layman not imagine that his pastors are always such experts that to every problem which arises, however complicated, they can readily give him a concrete solution, or even that such is their mission' (para. 43). Laymen should keep the laws proper to each discipline, and labour to equip themselves with genuine expertise in their various fields, gladly working with men seeking the same goals. This point was later to be developed by Paul VI in his Apostolic Letter to Cardinal Roy *Octogesima Adveniens* (1971), where he points out that in widely differing situations in the world it is difficult for Rome to propound 'solutions' which have universal validity. It is 'up to Christian communities to analyse the situation which is proper to their own country . . . and to draw principles of reflection, norms of judgment and directives for action from the social teaching of the Church' (par 4). This should be done in dialogue with other Christians and all men of good will.

The Geneva conference of 1966 on 'Christians in the Technical and Social Revolutions of our Time', designed as a successor to Oxford, had active Roman Catholic participant observers, several of whom had been involved in the background work for *Gaudium et Spes*. This registered the new atmosphere which had so rapidly developed. It seemed that resources of good will and a desire for co-operation which had been latent now gushed out. The line taken by *Gaudium et Spes* was so similar to that which had been developed in the Ecumenical Movement that there was no difficulty in Roman Catholics incorporating themselves in the work of the Geneva conference, and it was no surprise that the thought which emerged from it was very similar to that of the Pastoral Constitution. Moreover there was an impressive convergence in their diagnosis of the contemporary situation, and in the general directions in which they thought the church should use its influence. This broad convergence has continued, and it is noteworthy that such a wide spectrum of responsible church reflection should be at variance with the backlash which has developed in the last ten years in some countries, often characterized by some such term as 'the new Right'.

In the years after 1966 there was much collaboration. The Encyclical *Populorum Progressio* was in accord with the thinking in World Council of Churches circles on the economic and political relationships that should exist between the wealthy first world and the two-thirds economically poor world. It led to the setting up of Sodepax, the joint agency of the World Council of Churches and the Pontifical Commission Justice and Peace, on Society, Development and Peace. This sponsored consultations at Beirut in 1968 and at Montreal in 1969 on this theme, and one on a theology of development at Cartigny in Switzerland, also in 1969. A similar initiative with regard to peace was held in 1970 at Baden in Austria.

It was at Geneva in 1966 that the world of ecumenical consultation first heard the demand for drastic social change coming from Latin America, sufficiently drastic for the term revolutionary to be used of it, not necessarily implying that violence would be involved but not ruling it out. It was maintained that all other avenues of reforming economically blatantly unjust and politically repressive regimes were blocked. This was the first encounter with liberation theology which within a decade was to be a major preoccupation far beyond Latin America.

The question of theology and revolution was examined more systematically at a joint Consultation of Church and Society and Faith and Order in 1968 at Zagorsk, near Moscow. This was paralleled in Roman Catholic circles at the second conference of Latin American bishops at Medellín in Columbia in the same year. There had also been Roman Catholic participants at Zagorsk. The theme has remained on the agenda ever since. The Synod of Roman Catholic bishops in Rome in 1971 produced a document, *Justice in the World*, which had a new stress on collective as well as individual sin, and on oppressive and dehumanizing structures. The theme was continued at the third meeting of Latin American bishops at Puebla in 1979 which, despite what many expected, stayed broadly with what had been said at Medellín. As is well known the World Council of Churches has been dominated by this emphasis.

However, Zagorsk had other tasks. It produced systematic work on method in Christian social ethics and on ecclesiology and social ethics. This clarified the procedures which had developed in the ecumenical movement since the work of J. H. Oldham. It is the last systematic reflection within the World Council of Churches on these issues and a new effort is overdue. Moreover there have been examples since Vatican II of the Roman Catholic Church following a similar procedure in social ethics. Paul VI's letter to Cardinal Roy has already been mentioned. It was a *letter* and not an encyclical. It referred to the difficulty of giving universal guidance and instruction. In addition there is the problem of knowing in the case of encyclicals from where the input behind them has come. *Quadragesimo Anno* (1931) was drafted by one man, and he came subsequently to think of it as an irresponsible procedure. The noted moral theologian Bernard Haring put this cogently in his *Morality is for Persons* (1971):

> The authority of the magisterium will be greater ... if it is really based on a wide range of thinking and discussion. If the Pope relies on only a handful of advisers belonging to one school of thought, then the 'authority' when teaching about the natural law will inevitably suffer ... as has been the case with such matters as usury, torture, the burning of witches, the castration of choirboys (who sang in the Sistine Chapel) and the like.

For this reason, the method of the recent initiatives of the Roman Catholic episcopate in the USA is timely. It has used two weighty Pastoral Letters, of some 70,000 words each, the first *The Challenge of Peace: God's Providence and our Response* (1983), and the second *Justice for All: Catholic Social Teaching and the US Economy* (1986). It has taken the point made by *Octogesima Adveniens* more seriously than the Vatican itself has done. The procedure of the American bishops has been (1) to hear evidence from a wide variety of witnesses,

Catholic, Protestant and secular; (2) to issue two preparatory drafts for public discussion and comment, saying in effect 'this is what we are thinking of saying and we should be glad to receive your reactions before we finalise it'; (3) carefully to clarify the claim to authority made by different elements in it, and to invite further reflection; and (4) to quote extensively from Vatican documents wherever they are useful and appropriate.

Divergence

So much for convergence. There have been difficulties since 1965–66 which are due to divergences. The first concerns population questions. The encyclical *Humanae Vitae* (1968) argues against contraception, and although this concerns personal rather than social morality, in so far as a distinction can be made between the two, it had a direct bearing on public policy concerning population questions. The furore it aroused within Roman Catholic circles is well known. Nevertheless, the Vatican is officially committed to it, so that where co-operation between the World Council of Churches and the Vatican is concerned it has been necessary to avoid any areas where this issue could arise, for the Vatican would not favour any joint document in which more than one opinion on it is given some church endorsement as if it were open to discussion. This avoidance was the case with Sodepax. And it is surprising in how many contexts population questions arise in which this issue lies in the background.

Then the World Council of Churches and the Roman Catholic Church are very different in their role, their relations to their constituencies, and their internal ways of working. Both need sociological examination lest ecclesiological theories do not take account of actual practice. Although the World Council of Churches has had to define the very limited sense in which it has authority *vis-à-vis* its member churches it has nothing like the centralization of, nor the claims to authority emanating from, the Vatican. There is nothing in the World Council of Churches resembling preoccupation with the shades of demarcation within the authority of the magisterium which characterizes the Roman Catholic Church. The preoccupation arises because there is a wide margin between maximum and minimum claims made for it. Where the weight lies at any time is related to power structures within the church, and in particular within the Vatican, which keep Vatican-watchers busy with their interpretations. It was difficulties with the semi-independent role of Sodepax in moving ahead in social-theological exploration instead of merely propagating what was handed to it that led to its demise.

Moreover, since 1969 the World Council of Churches had developed a much stronger action stance. The Programme to Combat Racism has aroused most controversy in this respect. This stance has produced problems within the World Council of Churches itself. Parts of its constituency have been uneasy. At times in some sections the emphasis has been so much more on action first and reflection afterwards as to be one-sided, in that the reflection has tended merely to justify the action and to be selective in its sources to achieve this. The level of quality in study bequeathed by J. H. Oldham has not always been maintained. There is no reason why these differing methods cannot be creatively handled. To have problems is endemic in the whole World Council of Churches enterprise. But it makes the Vatican nervous of what it might let itself in for in co-operating with the World Council of Churches.

Connected with this is the challenge of liberation theology. This has come from the overwhelmingly Roman Catholic area of Latin America, where it is advocated with great power by a minority in the church, albeit a substantial minority; and also by a much smaller minority within the Protestant churches. These are the ecumenically minded Protestants; most are pietistic and indifferent or hostile to the World Council of Churches. While the World Council of Churches has been taking liberation theology very seriously the Vatican has issued two Instructions which are cool towards it: the first, *Certain Aspects of the Theology of Liberation* (1984), and the second, *Christian Freedom and Liberation* (1986). They came from the Sacred Congregation for the Defence of the Faith which of its very nature is backward-looking, and regards repeating the past as the proper teaching for the present. Innovation is against its nature. It thinks of theology as a pure deposit existing in a social, political and cultural vacuum. It cannot easily cope with structured sin and its effect on thought. It finds it hard to think of church as the pilgrim people of God. Formally it accepts Vatican II, as indeed it must, but it finds it hard to take on board the new emphases which led to the flowering of co-operation with the World Council of Churches in the mid 1960s.

Both bodies face the problem of achieving a social theology and method in ethics adequate to deal with a rapidly changing world. There is a spectrum of views within both bodies. But Rome officially finds it hard to accept this because of its centralization and the power of the Curia. What was in origin a civil service has become a powerful body for policy-formation within the authority of the *magisterium*, and it has its own 'pecking order' of power within itself. So does the World Council of Churches, but there it is more open. The Curia plays no part in Roman Catholic ecclesiology. It is not mentioned in the documents of Vatican II. No sociological study of it has been made. Yet the implementation of the impetus of the Council at the official level largely depends upon it. In the World Council of Churches the faintly parallel situation is the influence of the staff by the very fact of being continuously on the job. This puts them in a much stronger position than the members of the Central Committee, still more of the assembly, who meet occasionally for short periods and are scattered over the globe. The staff can have great influence over priorities, the way they are carried out, and who are brought in as advisers and consultants. There is nothing necessarily sinister in this, provided it is acknowledged and allowed for.

Within the Roman Catholic Church there is an intense debate which has a bearing on co-operation or lack of it with the World Council of Churches. It is concerned with method in moral theology or Christian ethics. As far as specific examples go, it is largely concerned with sexual ethics. But method in one area cannot be isolated from method in other areas, and the debate has in fact gone on in respect of issues of nuclear war, with the intriguing result that the more conservative in sexual ethics have proved more radical on nuclear issues. The debate is largely about the understanding of the human person and, as we have seen, it was precisely the stand of *Gaudium et Spes* on this that was one of the two factors which led to the breakthrough in co-operation in social ethics with the World Council of Churches.

Traditional moral theology operated within a fixed idea of nature, including human nature. The human body was divided into various faculties, each of them studied in isolation. On this basis detailed ethical conclusions were deduced which were fixed and timeless. Thus the sexual organs were seen as intended by nature for procreation, so that any use of them which deliberately tries to prevent this is unnatural. It was also preoccupied with the limits of obligation to follow the moral law. Cases of conscience were argued in terms that seemed to be concerned with the minimum level which must be observed to be free from mortal sin. Traditional manuals of moral theology in their preoccupation with law had little mention of Christ or central Christian doctrines and indeed little reference to the Bible. Vatican II vastly hastened the reaction against this. The old manuals have been cast aside. What is human is still a central point, but a dynamic view is taken of the human person and the dignity of personhood; and not only of what humans have in common, but also the importance of the exercise of conscientious judgment by each person in all the varieties of personhood and personal situations.

It is within this new framework that the lively debate has been taking place. The focus of it has been two related questions. (1) The autonomy of ethics: that is to say whether there is any *content* to Christian ethics (apart from the duty to worship God) beyond what applies to all men and women; whether the Christian faith rather provides a distinctive *ground* for following detailed ethical conclusions which others may, and probably should, come to on their own grounds. (2) Whether there are absolute moral rules which are always to be followed, or whether the moral rules found in the Bible or elaborated in Christian tradition in terms of natural law are historical and contextual in character; in that case there is no absolute moral rule independent of circumstances. Moral judgment is an art rather than a science, and *prudence* is the essential quality needed in exercising it. Living in the fellowship of Christian thought and worship is a school of moral discernment or wisdom; in it conscience is educated, so that our moral decisions in the uncertainties and ambiguities of life will show discernment. The root question will then be not whether we are obedient to a fixed moral rule but whether our 'fundamental option' (to quote a phrase of Karl Rahner) is for the mind of Christ as we conscientiously try to discern it. This applies of course to the whole range of ethical issues, from the more personal to the collective where we are bound together in structures with others.

In this debate the more conservative, and that includes the Sacred Congregation for the Defence of the Faith, think a-historically and provide defences on either biblical or natural law grounds, or both, for traditional conclusions held before the reformation of moral theology. This has been noteworthy in various Instructions from the SCDF on sexual issues – for instance homosexuality and *in-vitro* fertilization – and, as already noted, on liberation theology. Moreover, moral theologians not connected with the SCDF and not confined to the Roman Catholic Church (Paul Ramsey, for one) argue that there are basic human goods which are characteristic of human beings and which give a basic fixity to human nature. In his magisterial book *Natural Law and Natural Rights* (1980) the Roman Catholic John Finnis, Reader in Law in Oxford University, lists seven such goods: life, knowledge, play, aesthetic experience, friendship, practical reasonableness and religion. Others have put forward lists which are similar. I do not think there would be much disagreement among Christians about them. How far they carry agreement in non-Western cultures is one that has continually to be explored. But the crux of the argument is the next step, and it is here that the issue of divergence from what is generally thought in World Council of Churches circles arises. It is argued that these goods are incommensurable. There is no common denominator which would enable us to weigh one against another. So they must all be equally respected. We must never damage or destroy an instance of any one human good in desiring another. Hence we arrive at moral absolutes.

Those who do not agree with this think that the argument about incommensurability is contrary to common sense. In fact we do continually make comparisons between values in particular situations; nor can we rank them in a fixed hierarchy of importance, for that too varies with different situations. Their position in its cautious form is that we must not do evil directly or indirectly, but we may allow evil to occur if, and only if, there is proportionate reason to do so. Put more broadly, faced with difficult decisions and conflicting values we should decide on an action which in our conscientious judgment is likely to produce the greatest harvest of values and the minimum of disvalues in the circumstances. Those who take the first view hold that there is no situation in which there is a conflict between human goods such that there is no action possible which respects all of them. Those who take the second view hold that life does throw up such situations of conflicts of interest in which some have to be sacrificed in favour of others.

The problem within the Roman Catholic Church is not just that the SCDF takes the first view, but that it is maintaining that all those who hold 'official' teaching positions in Roman Catholic institutions must take it too. This is the basic issue in the case of Charles Curran. In fact very many Roman Catholic moral theologians take the second view (my guess is that in the English-speaking world, of which I know more, it is a majority). The SCDF is not finding it easy to win general assent. As its Instructions appear they are not uniformly accepted and welcome, but subject to detailed and widespread, but respectful, criticism.

This whole debate has obvious affinities with the situation ethics debate which raged, largely in Protestant circles, from about 1960–75, and then petered out. The World Council of Churches had its own Humanum Study (1969–75) which might have been expected to engage with this Roman Catholic debate, but it went off in a different direction and it, too, has petered out. The intriguing point to note is that the Roman Catholic debate does not depend upon any peculiar Roman Catholic doctrine (though the weight of tradition is in the background), but is an argument about the rational basis of morality which anyone can enter and no one can avoid. One must admire the way in which some of the best minds in the Roman Catholic Church persist in working away at clarifying and resolving the issues. Protestants do not exhibit the same staying power, but tend to tire and chase the next new slant that emerges.

Those in Protestant circles who on biblical or confessional grounds are disposed to take a position somewhat similar to that of the SCDF are mostly not ecumenically minded. They are either minorities within the churches which are members of the World Council of Churches, or belong to churches which will not join it. So within its Protestant constituency the World Council of Churches encounters this debate in only a minor way. It is another matter with respect to the Orthodox. In general they have not yet met the full force of questions which moral theology has not been able to avoid. When they do they will have to go beyond patristics and the first eight centuries to cope with them. But this article is not focussed on the Orthodox situation.

Prospects for Co-operation

To what conclusions does this survey of convergences and divergence between the social thought of the World Council of Churches and the Roman Catholic Church point with respect to future co-operation? I do not think an unambiguous answer is possible. It is obviously easier if the fact of a spectrum of positions within confessional traditions is acknowledged and even welcomed, in the sense that there is a resolve to handle the resulting tensions creatively. It is more difficult if the authorities in one particular church or confession will only officially recognise one position, as the SCDF is doing. But the World Council of Churches has lived with the restrictions imposed by this situation, as far as population questions go, since *Humanae Vitae*, and there seems no reason why it cannot continue to do so in other areas where it may apply. The World Council of Churches cannot directly affect the internal debate with the Roman Catholic Church (unless invited to, as observers were at Vatican II), but the more Roman Catholics are associated with the work of the World Council of Churches the more it will contribute indirectly.

Different interpretations of the Bible, different social theologies, different factual analyses of the contemporary scene are not fixed and immovable, but are likely to exist in some form until the parousia. Convergences and divergences will vary. Stockholm thought that doctrine divides but service (action) unites. On the other hand the Programme to Combat Racism showed that service can divide when doctrine unites. Yet again, after the war there was much division within ecumenical circles between those who were Barthian in theology and those who were not, yet their diagnosis of the direction in which church influence should be exerted in social and political issues was much the same, and this gave a great impetus to the witness of the World Council of Churches in its early days. So did the very similar lines of the Roman Catholic Church and the World Council of Churches after Vatican II. There is nothing in the sources of divergences which precludes co-operation. It depends on whether there is a will to work together. The challenge to the churches of the Lund Faith and Order conference of 1952 to do together all that conscience does not require them to do separately remains. In so far as the leadership of the churches is truly committed to unity and renewal they will find ways of co-operating.

It is with the level of leadership that this article is concerned. I do not doubt that at other levels, less official and more local, more and more co-operation will take place. Roman Catholics and others, separated from one another by centuries of polemics, have come in the last thirty years to meet, to know and to like one another. I do not think anyone will be able to stop them thinking and doing more together. Immense ecclesiological and psychological barriers are being broken down.

At the official level in so far as the Roman Catholic Church follows the line of *Unitatis Redintegratio* co-operation will continue and develop. As far as the World Council of Churches is concerned greater precision, clarity and cohesion within its own units would benefit itself and make official Roman Catholic co-operation easier. Some things may take more time, and some sections may not be able to go so much out on a limb if the Roman Catholic Church is seriously engaged, for instance in the 'Justice, Peace and Integrity of Creation' programme. But the result would be more worthwhile. The fact is that in the plural societies which characterize the old Christendom the churches can hardly get attention unless the main confessions work together. And in countries where Christians have never been other than a small minority the necessity of working together is equally great.

On the question of methodology, apart from carrying on from the Zagorsk consultation the internal Roman Catholic debate would benefit if put in a larger ecumenical setting. As to the immediate agenda the JPIC programme is enormous and potentially fissiparous. It would greatly benefit from Roman Catholic co-operation at every level. Some background questions which need clarification include:

1. What do we mean today by prophecy as distinct from biblical times? How far can the churches, sociologically considered, be agents of social change?

2. How far can analyses of the current situation by church-related groups overcome ideological differences?

3. What are the parameters of proper church commitments in areas of social ethics, as distinct from the role of the lay person as citizen?

4. What is the role of symbolic actions by churches and by individual Christians (e.g. covenanting), as distinct from the search for effective and appropriate actions for social change?

Then there is the empirical task of analysing the facts and the trends, global and regional, and the process of checking and counter-checking in the course of seeing how far an ecumenical consensus emerges from the churches to commend to their constituency and to all persons of good will. This is particularly appropriate if it can be achieved, at the middle level between general diagnoses and detailed policies. The scope has become wider and more complex since J. H. Oldham's day, but the need for ecumenical co-operative work of the highest quality remains as great as ever. Nothing short of excellence will do. In 1937 the churches achieved this. Roman Catholic co-operation is an almost indispensable factor in achieving it now. The Roman Catholic Church and the World Council of Churches may go it alone, but each will be much impoverished if they do.

Humanity, Nature and the Integrity of Creation

The World Council of Churches is to hold a world convocation on 'Justice, Peace and the Integrity of Creation' at Seoul, Korea, in March 1990. The theme is a massive one. The new element in it is the concept of 'the integrity of creation' and this requires special attention. I have worked through the preparatory study material on it issued at the end of 1988. Some dominant characteristics cause me disquiet. This article arises from the reading of that material, especially that from the Sub-unit on Church and Society.[1] I spell Nature with a capital N and Creation with a capital C to do justice to the elevated way in which they are referred. And I use the terms interchangeably.

The JPIC theme is a successor to 'The Just, Participatory and Sustainable Society'.[2] Justice remains and, like peace, has always been a preoccupation. In an attempt to unify the WCC study programme Peace has taken the place of Participatory whilst the Integrity of Creation has taken the place of Sustainable. Whatever the meaning of the new term, and that is something I discuss later, it certainly reflects a growing concern of this decade all over the world and it is one to which the churches do well to address themselves. A well thought-out theological contribution to the complex ecological, environmental and economic issues involved needs to be made.

The WCC faces a danger and a difficulty in tackling the JPIC theme. The danger is not building on studies of recent decades; for example on the significance of the personal, the Humanum study, and that on humans 'come of age' in relation to the secularization issue.[3] The difficulty is that of internal integration. In a recent article Paul Abrecht identifies three tendencies at present influential in the WCC.[4] (1) A stress, going back to Stockholm 1925, behind the 'theological realism' of the Oxford conference of 1937 to a simpler understanding of the expression of an ethic of *agape* in the social order. (2) A populist, participatory ethic with an over-riding concern for those oppressed on grounds of race, religion or sex. (3) Liberation theology with its broad stress on Marxism as a 'science' to guide praxis on the side of and with the poor. All of these sympathize with 'a preferential option for the poor', and all three have their difficulties, but none fits easily into a preoccupation with the Integrity of Creation. When the difficulties of this conception are added the extent of the task faced by the WCC for 1990 is clear.[5]

Assessing the Data

A vast amount of data and comment is now accumulating on ecological and environmental issues. Problems arise in assessing it. Up to a point there is agreement on the picture of Nature, but divisions soon arise between those who stress progress in understanding and influencing it by breaking it down by investigations into simpler elements, and those who stress considering it as an overall entity, Nature with a capital N. This partly corresponds to those who see possibilities of controlling nature and improving the human situation, and those who fear that the consequences of this will produce, or have already produced, a crisis of the biosphere, and have a homeostatic view of Nature with which human beings should not interfere. In the WCC material there is a marked tendency towards the latter position. I find this unconvincing for reasons I now indicate.

There is clearly a unity in Nature. All living things are united in a common chemical structure and process. All molecules are combinations of the same ninety-two chemical elements. The fundamental forces of gravitation, electro-magnetism and nuclear reactions apply universally. Everything is connected with everything else. Yet there seems an unpredictability at the heart of things (first brought to our notice by Heisenberg), with at the same time a propensity towards order; that is to say a chaos which contains a curious sort of order. This uncertainty suggests prudence on the part of humans in dealing with Nature, but not passivity. The fact that we cannot be certain in advance of all the effects of our 'interference' with Nature would not suggest that humans should cease from 'interfering'. Humans have known for centuries, for instance, how to use micro-organisms to produce bread, cheese and alcoholic beverages, and how to select desirable strains in grain and livestock in terms of human benefit, and they have altered evolution by selective breeding.

Alarm bells ring at the thought of going beyond what can be

achieved 'naturally'. Images of Auschwitz are even conjured up. It is rightly pointed out that technology should be a servant of humans and not an idol, and that whereas natural science has incorporated much self-criticism into its procedures – not entirely successfully, but its failures get publicized fairly soon – technology has no such inbuilt self-criticism. Human hubris tends to rush into doing whatever is technically feasible. The further assertion, however, that technology is now more a curse than a blessing to humanity is so disputable as to make a classic subject for a debating society. Certainly the economic growth of the one-third (affluent) world since the end of the Second World War has led to a brash over-confidence. Humans have blundered about in the universe in a careless way which is now being sharply questioned. However, our monitoring powers have increased as the ecological and environmental issues have increased. The stakes are higher. The speed of change is greater. We can accelerate more quickly out of trouble or into more trouble. It does not follow that we should call a halt and make preservation and a steady state our aim. That could be a loss of nerve. Talk of the ecological death of Nature and the ecological suicide of the human race may be necessary to alert indifferent humanity to possible perils, though it is in danger of being counter-productive in obscuring the parameters of the decisions that need to be made.

There seems no good reason for not moving beyond 'natural' processes. Varied examples include fixing nitrogen in the soil, identifying the genetical basis of a particular trait in a species and transferring it to an unrelated one and using bacteria to produce human insulin. Modern genetics is bringing home to us the genetic interchange of all life. Recombinant DNA and molecular genetics are leading us in ways we can only partially foresee. New approaches are being made to cancer, AIDS, tropical diseases and genetically based diseases. Human gene therapy can make it possible to cure a specific disease in a body tissue, for instance to alter a specific gene in a fertilized egg in order to correct a genetic defect leading to sickle cell anaemia. Such examples of what is often called 'genetic engineering' make some people shudder. Perhaps it is the term 'engineering' with its sense of less than human interference with the personal. But should they shudder? It is certainly changing the human relation to Nature by increasing the power, speed and accuracy of the human reaction within it. Is it clear that this should be shunned? It obviously requires prudence. But, to anticipate later sections of the article, are we to think of Nature as fixed? Or are we to think of humans as co-creators, or perhaps participants, or even co-explorers with God in creation?

As to the past and long-term future of our earth and universe, it seems that many earthly species have gone and are going the way of the dinosaurs, and that all living entities will eventually do the same, including *homo sapiens*. It will be too hot or too cold for humans. It is estimated that between five and ten million species share our planet of which one thousand disappear annually. It is not easy to assess the significance of this. How far does the extinction of the dodo matter? In the long-term our sun will die; in a few billion years. Eventually our galaxy, the Milky Way, will do so too. Perhaps our universe will. Perhaps there are or may be other universes. We do not know. The WCC studies do not relate the biblical material, the theme of our next section, to these matters.

Nor do they do much to relate them to the economic aspects of the ecological and environmental issues which were part of the theme of Sustainability. Here the Bruntland report of 1987, *Our Common Future*, is important. It is the third of a trio of UN reports, the first being the Brandt report *North-South* (1980) and its sequel *Common Crisis* (1983); and the second the Palme report *Common Security* (1985). The Bruntland report is a careful piece of work which deals with major problems like the greenhouse effect, deforestation and soil loss, the debt crisis, the global commons and the explosion of cities. It is on the side of those seeking approximate and possible ways of dealing with the issues, and not on that of those who demand either a halt to, or a reversal of, economic and technological developments, though it places considerable stress on regional differences and responsibilities, especially as between the affluent countries and the rest. Ethically it stands for (1) meeting the needs of the present without compromising the ability of future generations to meet their needs; (2) creating a sustainable situation for all countries; (3) a concern for equity within and between generations, not just physical sustainability. It is a serious omission that it plays next to no part in the WCC material.[6]

The Bruntland report does not argue a basis for its ethical concern. Clearly it is a form of secular humanism which is consonant with a Christian view of the person even if in a Christian view less securely based. The Brandt report tried to move opinion by appealing as much as it could to long-term self-interest. This is not to be despised as a weapon in the political forum, but more than that is needed. A more searching ethic is one which is based on the acknowledgment that humans are rational and purposive agents who should recognize the same trait in other humans, and affirms therefore that these others are entitled to the same respect that they have for themselves. Christians do not deny this but would claim that they have a stronger basis for an ethical stress on the personal. But should they make this stress? Here we come upon an emphasis in the WCC studies that Christianity has been too human-centred. The demand is for a biocentrism instead of an anthropocentrism. Sentient beings have their own interest; they have a good of their own, and a moral standing independent of the interests of humanity. This applies both to the bluebottle and the slug on which it is feeding.

It is against this criticism that we must turn to an appraisal of the biblical material on the relation of humanity to Nature, for this must in some way or other be a prime source for any Christian contribution to an understanding of the Integrity of Creation, and it naturally has a key place in the WCC studies on that theme.

Assessing the Biblical Material

In using the biblical material there is a continual temptation to misuse it by seeking to find in it unified normative timeless teaching on matters which are not the focus of its concern. The controlling concern in the selection of writings which form the canonical scriptures is that of the Covenant and the Election of a people of God. The implications of this for daily living are expressed in several different types of literature, to be set against the changing milieu out of which they came. In addition the Bible also *presupposes,* without elaborating, some basic realities such as the central importance of human beings making moral judgments and that they have the capacity as made in God's image to make them.

So the first thing to point out is the very varied nature of the material of Nature in relation to God and humanity. There is no one single worked-out doctrine in the matter, any more than there is on other features of human life, such as marriage or the state. There are building bricks out of which such doctrines may be arrived at in the Christian community. There are likely to be different emphases within these doctrines in different centuries and in different parts of the world. Richard Niebuhr's *Christ and Culture* (1951) is a classic demonstration of five typical attitudes to that theme which have persisted down the centuries, and all based on the same biblical material. Christians have to bring this material alongside the data of their own time, evaluating its use in the church in the past, and letting the biblical material and the empirical data illuminate one another. In doing so they need to be consistent in the use of the Bible as between one issue and another. (At present we are seeing attempts by those who would no longer defend slavery by quoting the many biblical texts which presuppose or support it, to use its texts in a similar way to condemn homosexuality.)

It is necessary to make these provisos because of a tendency to stress some passages on Nature and humanity and ignore others according to the predispositions of the selector. The stress on human dominion over Nature, according to the myths of Genesis 1 and 2, has been replaced by a tendency to ignore them and stress other biblical material. To point out that they have often been misused in a triumphalist anthropocentric way does not justify this. All biblical and doctrinal formulations are subject to abuse, and have been abused in Christian history. The lesson of this is not to denigrate or ignore the material, but to make proper use of it.

It is not possible to refer to all the material in the Bible on this theme. It must suffice to pick out some of the different types which are of most significance. We begin with election and covenant as fundamental. In the Mosaic covenant God's gracious initiative requires a joyful persona and corporate response from the covenant people in worship and life. The covenant had basic moral implications and was conditional on them being fulfilled. The inability of those elected to fulfil their side of the Covenant led to the thought of a new covenant (e.g. Jer.31.31ff.), taken up in the New Testament, by which God would find a way of restoration for those whose sins had flown in the face of the basic moral demands which could not but be made upon God's covenant people.

A covenant with Nature on the other hand must be *un*conditional, for Nature cannot make moral choices. And so it is in the myth of Genesis 9. God rules out any future dramatic interference by a flood to clear up the mess humans have made of Creation. (Note that it does not say anything about whether it might not gradually peter out which, as already mentioned, seems likely.) The covenant in Genesis 9 is made with humans and living creatures together, but to assume that it puts the two in the same partnership with God as some of the literature does (so modifying Genesis 1 and 2) is reading a lot into the text. In Genesis 1 and 2 human dominion means being a kind of viceroy under God, or a responsible steward, or like a shepherd or a farm manager. Commands are given to humans in a way they cannot be given to less than human species: to procreate, to harness and utilize nature, to labour, to be vegetarians, and not to eat the fruit of one tree (no reason is given). Genesis 9.24 modifies the vegetarianism by allowing Kosher meat. The myth of the fall in Genesis 3 expresses the ambiguity of Nature in relation to humanity; she both sustains humans and is hostile to them.

Some World Council material urges the churches to enter into fellowship with Nature, but it is not easy to see what this means. Jesus teaches God's concern for sparrows (Matt.10.29ff.), and Jesus appreciates grass and lilies (Matt.6.28), but this is hardly fellowship with them. We can understand fellowship only by an analogy with the personal, and see it is a possibility according to the level of personal being in Nature. Some people apparently talk to plants, but what kind of response to the personal can plants make? It is also said that, being on the side of the oppressed, God is on the side of Nature, which has been exploited by humans, who should repent and express their solidarity with nature by becoming servants in a sacrificial relation to it. Without denying the exploitation, the remedy proposed reverses the drift of the biblical material. This line of thinking goes on to suggest that if God is held to suffer with humanity God must suffer with Nature too; if so it must be with its ambiguities, so that when the fox chases the rabbit God is on the side of both.

Are humanity and Nature linked to the future? Does salvation cover the entire world of Nature? Does it, for instance, cover the chimpanzee who can reach the equivalent of a human age of one and a half years? Traditional Christian belief is that human destiny under God transcends the present aeon of space and time. Does this apply to Nature? Process theology, which exerts quite a lot of influence in these studies, suggests that God seeks the whole universe in God's experience, human and sub-human, in a kind of memory; for this is thin gruel compared with traditional Christian hopes for humanity. Apocalyptic language in the Bible is at the opposite pole. In Romans 8.18ff. St Paul writes of Nature being dragged down by human responsibility and as destined for glory with humans; a cosmic fall and a cosmic restoration. In this he echoes a strain in the prophets of the Old Testament (Isa.11.6ff.; Hosea 2.18ff.). Apocalyptic language indeed raises the struggle between good and evil to a cosmic level. A pre-cosmic fall is paralleled with a post-cosmic restoration; Revelation 22 restores the situation of Genesis 1. The goal of Creation is the eternal sabbath involving God, humanity and Nature alike.[7]

What are we to make of apocalyptic language? Many seem to take it literally as a projection of the future. I am doubtful of the significance of the genre of apocalyptic today, though there is increasing stress on it both in popular and scholarly circles. It seems a prime example of where a gulf exists between the categories of the world of the New Testament and our own. I have already mentioned that there may be other universes. We cannot know. Nor, as far as I can see, can we know whether all that has ever existed or will exist in this creation will be restored. Dinosaurs, for example. Nor do we know whether all the species which prey upon and harm one another and also harm humans will be restored to live in harmony in a new heaven and a new earth. No more stinging wasps! But whether it will be so or not, I cannot see that it throws any distinctive light on the ethical decisions we have to make. For this we need to be related to the present scene and its likely trends. Nor should we be tied to the common apocalyptic view that the state of this world can only become worse until God cleans it up and that at best humans can only hang on.

However, if apocalyptic is a dispensable category, eschatology is not. The kingdom of God as inaugurated in the ministry of Jesus and working like yeast in the world towards its fulfilment is central to the New Testament. It presents a radical challenge to our *status quo* and a source of strength in modifying it. But the kingdom of God is not to be taken at Mark 1.15 (as one document implies) as signifying all creation. Not only is there no indication that this is so in the Gospels but also it is specifically denied by St Paul (Rom.14.7; I Cor.15.50).

For the rest, in our survey of aspects of the biblical material we can note the high value set on persons (e.g. Gen.1.26; 9.6; Ps.8; Luke 15). At the same time God's power over nature is celebrated irrespective of its ambiguous relation to humanity. From it the Wisdom Literature can derive moral lessons for humans, for instance the example of the ant (Prov.6.6). God's power and splendour is celebrated in the great poem of Job 38–40. This incorporates predators in chapter 41 (as does Ps.104.21 and 26). So we might say the spider's web celebrates God's splendour. But Job's complaint is not answered. He is silenced by an assertion of power. If there is to be any kind of answer to Job it has to be sought in the New Testament, not the Old Testament; it has to be sought in the cross of Christ. Meanwhile there is a positive side to the relation between humanity and Nature. A blessing is given to the selective breeding of livestock in Genesis 30.25–43. There the Old Testament is responding to existing agricultural technology. God is not only a God of exodus, but is also a God of agriculture in Canaan, and so can be a God of modern technology. It is an instance of the fact that the Bible, incidental to its main theme, draws on aspects of life in the times from which its texts come. Translating this into the new and dynamic kind of civilization brought about by the scientific and technical changes from the late seventeenth century onwards, is a skilled hermeneutical task.

From this varied material I draw four conclusions: (1) Nature is to be respected beyond what is immediately relevant to human beings, but the continuities in nature must not obscure the distinctiveness of the personal; (2) humans are to exercise stewardship over it under God for human purposes (and in doing so not to be brash and idolatrous); (3) it is flawed;[8] (4) we can know little about its ultimate future, but this lack of knowledge is not relevant for ethics.

However, there are two conclusions which are being drawn in many of the WCC study papers which should not be drawn.

1. That Creation is fixed in its basic features and inherent structures, and that attempts to modify it by, for example, genetic engineering, should be ruled out on the ground that it assumes that God's creation lacks sufficient wisdom and is in need of restructuring. This is a version of the old Natural Law argument, and subject to all the difficulties which have led to a drastic reconstruction of Roman Catholic Moral Theology.[9] The Bible can give this impression only because it took fixity for granted, as have all traditional Christian theologies. Today it is impossible to hold to this, especially in view of what we know of the 'groping' process of evolution; in that seemingly chance movements and changes appear to have some purposiveness about them. There is also our experience of rapid technological and social change.

2. That we should not try to overcome chance on behalf of human purposes. This is one of the arguments against contraception in *Humanae Vitae* (though it allows attempts to regularize 'natural' rhythm methods). It is also one of the arguments in favour of the free market and *laissez-faire* by the new right against what is regarded as the 'log rolling' of politics, instead of leaving economic decisions to impersonal chance. This is false and dangerous. Human creativity is bound to want to free humans from chance in matters vital to their well-being, if it can be done without unacceptable side effects. The challenge is to do this without hubris.

The Category of the Personal

For most of this century there has been a concentration in theology and the philosophy of religion on the significance of the personal. It has led to a good deal of reconstruction of classical Christian doctrine, because the modern understanding of the person is so different from the connotation of the term 'person' in the Greek metaphysics under-lying trinitarian formulations. Influential thinkers have included such very diverse figures as Maritain, Macmurray, Mounier, Berdyaev, and those influenced especially by the rediscovered Kierkegaard. The existentialist stress of the last-named also strongly influenced secular philosophy where it was not dominated by the positivist legacy of the Vienna Circle.

This personalist emphasis had a great influence on the Second Vati-can Council, especially on the Pastoral Constitution *Gaudium et Spes*. One of the results of this personalist emphasis, which is only a second-ary concern of this article, was to bring out the fact that persons are constituted by the mutuality of their relationships; the independent individual, the isolated self is an illusion, a non-entity. The unit of human life is not the 'I' alone.[10] Another result of the personalist emphasis is the concern to relate persons to Nature, since the human world is built upon the organic as the organic is on the inorganic. There is one world, but with many ambiguities. Human understand-ing of it, 'personalists' hold, must perforce move from what is more plainly known to us as personal being (even though much remains mysterious) to the less than personal. We have no access to the inner life of animals and plants. We cannot interrogate them and they can make no explicit revelation to us. So we are bound to be tentative and uncertain with respect to them. We can see in aspects of Nature an apparent likeness to life as we know it in our own experience: a kind of continuity through change, a response to changing environ-ments, and the undertaking of what seems purposive action. Investi-gations of animals suggest that in varying degrees they are capable of rational thought, of playing games, of family and community care (as is a pack of wolves), and of having a nervous breakdown.[11] House-hold pets almost become honorary members of the family. There is a twilight zone between the animal and the human as there is between light and darkness.

How does the difference in humans show itself? At first we might think there has been a jolt to the distinctive understanding of the human, especially to the traditional stress on rationality as the distinctive human trait, by the development of artificial intelligences. However, these are concerned with modelling computationally single human skills, and no exhaustive account of human personality can be given in computational terms. Rather it leaves us marvelling at the complexity of human mental processes and the mystery of the human person. This goes far beyond noting particular characteristics of humans like cooking their food, looking at their faeces after defecation, burying their dead, committing suicide. Humans can create an identity not inherent in inborn instructions. They have a sense of history. They can think of themselves as having a past and a future, and can think ahead of their death. They can conceive of universes, they are metaphor-makers and producers of symbols. They are aware of a gulf between what morally *is* and what *ought* to be the case in their lives; that is to say, they can sin. They can say one thing when they really mean something else, and know that they are being understood by someone else who knows that they know. In short they can live untruths. On the other hand they can respond to Nature (Creation), in wonder, awe, piety, love and joy, and make or refuse to make a response as co-creators. Of humans, when we talk of human rights we can require duties (though not completely, as in the case of infants and of the mentally ill and handicapped) which we cannot of animals, plants and the inorganic.

Although, as already mentioned, we have good reason to suppose our universe will persist long after humans have died out, it is not vulgar 'speciesism' for humans to stress the crucial category of the personal,[12] and to see in theological terms the penultimate end of the universe as to serve humanity, as its ultimate end is to express the glorious creativity of God. But this does not mean that every entity of God's creation must have an eternal future. Nor, as far as humans are concerned, does it mean that the creation is infinitely malleable. Humans should seek out and respect its limits; but this will be a never-ending quest because the limits are not fixed, and increasing human powers will reveal new possibilities and new dangers if the powers are misused.

The Personal and the Integrity of Creation

How does the category of the personal relate to the theme of the Integrity of Creation? What does the term mean? A good deal of the WCC material denies any special significance to the dimension of the personal, though some admits it incidentally. But there is little reflection on it. The stress is overwhelmingly on Nature (Creation).[13] Much of it so stresses Creation as a seamless web as to blur any significant distinction between the personal and the less than personal. Process theology does not necessarily lead to this conclusion, but it is brought in on occasion, together with quantum mechanics, to stress the fact of relationship and consciousness in the entire universe. Matter is not utterly inert but possesses the power of purposive activity. Degrees of being are not always admitted in the WCC material, though it is usually admitted that since plants have no nervous system their intrinsic value is slight. It is held that animals have a nervous system, have a fundamental urge to live, and are oppressed by humans who do not respect it. All creatures have an interest which humans should respect, and they have a 'right' to share in the kind of fulfilment appropriate to their own interest; an ant, for instance. However, it is clear that Nature itself in its ambiguities respects such an interest, but this is not discussed.

Charles Birch has provided an illustration which sharply questions humans in their attitudes, though not Nature in its attitude. He posits a company called Disposa Pup Ltd, which, capitalizing on the attractiveness to humans of the young of animals, offers to provide families with a pup every year and painlessly destroy it at the end of the year.[14] To ask ourselves why this would not be morally acceptable is to go a good way into an ethic which respects Creation. It clearly involves more than not being cruel to living creatures. But it does not go so far as assenting to the equality of all living species. Still less does it support the further assertion that freedom is indivisible, so that unless all creatures are free to be themselves the freedom of humans to be themselves will not be maintained, because those who want to master Nature soon want to master human beings.

The conclusions on Nature (Creation) I draw from the evidence, which need to be put alongside those I drew in the second section from the biblical-Christian tradition, are six:

1. It is ordered, intelligible and open to rational investigation.

2. It is inter-related, from fundamental particles upward.

3. It is not static but has an inbuilt creativity which proceeds through chance within the laws of physics and chemistry in what I have described as a 'groping' of what we might say is a 'do it yourself' manner.

4. There is a conflict in Nature: both an ecological balance and a death of old forms.

5. Humans are the crown of the process with the greatest self-awareness, the greatest possibility of suffering, and with the possibility of modifying the ongoing process of Nature for good or ill.

6. It is ultimately mysterious; at a basic level quarks are, and at the highest level so are persons.

So what meaning can be attached to the term 'the Integrity of Creation'? It cannot be criticized merely because it is not a biblical term. The Bible cannot be expected to provide all the concepts needed to grapple with contemporary evidence down the centuries. Even in doctrine the church has to go outside the Bible to cope with the Arians at Nicea. Sustainability was not a biblical term either. So the question is, how useful is the term? At this stage the evidence is not clear. The danger of the term is that it can easily be taken to mean that Nature/Creation is static, and a harmony with which it is impious for humans to 'interfere'. A monism which subsumes humans in nature is socially disastrous and the tool of a vicious conservatism. Eastern religions are prone to it. On the other hand it may mean that Nature/Creation is to be respected as of value to God, not solely because of humanity, but that it is coherent and worthy of investigation. But this is no new thought. It does not _require_ a new term. The best interpretation I can give it so far is that it affirms that Nature (Creation) as we have come to know it, with all its ambiguities, is what God intends for humans, with in turn all their ambiguities, to exercise responsible and thankful stewardship.[15]

The Perspective and the Agenda

To what conclusions does this survey lead? Clearly there is no special _method_ for dealing with the ethical issues that arise as distinct from ethical issues in other areas. It is beyond the scope of this article to consider what I think is the best procedure. The best perspective within which to proceed is to follow Rosemary Radford Ruether when she points out that there is no linear process in history, either revolutionary or evolutionary, leading to some salvation and point. There was no paradise in the historical past and there is not one in the historical future. Ethically there is the ever to be renewed ongoing task to achieve a workable balance free from 'the tyranny of impossible expectations'.[16]

The specific ethical issues involved include, for example: (1) The introduction of new techniques: technology can be a source of gratitude and delight, as is the case with new techniques for educating the blind, or the joys of water skiing. What are we to think, for instance, of *in vitro* fertilization, the patenting of life forms, and research into the possibilities of nuclear fusion? (2) Environmental issues: do these all present only threats, like the destruction of tropical rain forests, and the dispersal of nuclear waste, or are there beneficial possibilities? (3) The treatment of animals in teaching, pure and applied research, 'factory farming', and zoos. (4) Responsibility for future generations, as far as we can reasonably foresee, so that we do not foreclose options for them unnecessarily. Behind these issues lies the need for examining the ethics of risk. Quite a large secular literature is emerging on this but there is little from theology. It was much discussed in past centuries in moral theology, one upshot of which was that a 'safety first' method of living (Tutiorism), of always taking the safest course, was condemned as a feeble kind of Christian living. That is why the demand for caution in dealing with issues raised by the JPIC study needs to be handled with care. Prudence is the virtue needed. It needs to be thought out in terms of current dilemmas highlighted by the JPIC study. So far the WCC literature is silent on the subject of risk taking.

Ethical issues lead in turn to the need for a spirituality which can respond with discernment, within which a pro-worldly ethic may be developed. This is particularly needed by the affluent because they have most power, and need the consciousness that basic human needs are the same the world over to prevent them off-loading their ecological and environmental problems on to the Third World. This brings us back to Justice and Peace, and their connection with the Integrity of Creation. However, everything cannot be dealt with in one article and the new term, the Integrity of Creation, certainly warrants separate attention.[17]

Facts and Fables in Ecology and the Integrity of Creation[1]

The Integrity of Creation is a powerful phrase. It entered the vocabulary of the World Council of Churches at the Vancouver Assembly in 1983. Its origin is obscure but it may have begun within the World Alliance of Reformed Churches. Considering the dominant influence it has had in the WCC since 1983, it is surprising that it played so small a part at the Vancouver Assembly. It did not figure in the debates and there is only one explicit reference to it in the book of the Assembly, *Gathered for Life*.[2]

From the Nairobi Assembly of 1976 until the Vancouver Assembly the programme on what we may call the Life and Work side of the WCC had been under the heading, 'The Just, Participatory and Sustainable Society', which had gathered momentum by 1983. It takes some years for such a theme to register among the 300 or more member churches of the WCC, and more work needed to be done on it. particularly in connection with the term Participatory, as well as ongoing work on Just and Sustainable. After Vancouver the theme became Justice, Peace and the Integrity of Creation, a suggestion which came from a Programme Committee meeting during the Assembly. This is an interesting case study of how quite a small group of people who have a clear ideology can influence a large and fairly loosely structured organization.

The new Programme dominated the 1980s and built up to a major Convocation at Seoul in 1990. After the Canberra Assembly in 1991 the theme became incorporated under the heading, 'The Theology of Life: Justice, Peace and Creation'. The word Integrity has disappeared from the title, but the dominance of it remains. The result of the study will be presented to the Harare Assembly in December 1998.

Sustainability has not dropped out. It has been more oriented towards questions of economic growth, whilst the Integrity of Creation is more oriented towards ecological issues. Environmental questions are involved in both. This paper is to concentrate on the ecological issues that we believe have been distorted in the debate.

Facts and Fables in Ecology

The concept Integrity of Creation as interpreted in writings of the World Council of Churches refers to a view of nature that emphasizes wholeness, unity, connectedness, fragility and the idea that any interference of any part will upset the whole and lead to disorder and chaos. We now ask, Is this good science? In so doing we make a distinction between the facts of the case and what are little more than fables.

  1. *The balance of nature*. The idea that there is a balance of nature is widely held by people who think at all about nature. It is the idea that organisms in a community are harmoniously adjusted to one another so that a state of equilibrium exists. It includes the idea that if one component of the community is destroyed the community will collapse. It also includes the idea that significant changes in numbers of each species occurs only when something upsets the natural 'balance'. It is a view that is perpetuated in popular magazines and nature films and so has become a part of the lore of the man-in-the-street. It is a view which also persists in the minds of some environmentalists and some professional ecologists. It should be added that, in some form or other, the concept has been hotly disputed by ecologists for the past fifty years or so. Some have maintained that the concept is still relevant while others deny that any balance of nature exists. There is no consensus about the balance of nature amongst ecologists but the present trend is against balance. The historian of ecology Donald Worster writes: 'Over the past two decades the field of ecology has pretty well demolished Eugene Odum's portrayal of a world of ecosystems tending toward equilibrium.'[3]

Paul Ehrlich and Charles Birch wrote a paper in 1967 giving arguments against the concept of balance of nature.[4] Both authors still maintain that the arguments in this paper are as valid now as when they were first written. Birch together with co-author Andrewartha wrote two books on population ecology essentially putting an alternative model to the balance of nature concept.[5] The details of their argument need not concern us here. Ehrlich has also recently written strongly against the balance of nature concept. For example, he writes: 'We are properly nervous about having our science distorted – of seeing pronouncements by environmentalists, such as "complexity enhances stability" or references to "the balance of nature" that do not necessarily reflect a current disciplinary consensus.'[6]

Another population biologist Richard Lewontin writes: 'The banner of "Save the Environment" ... assumes that there is such a thing as the balance of nature, that everything is in a balance or harmony that is being destroyed only by the foolishness and greed of humans. There is nothing in our knowledge of the world to suggest that there is any particular balance or harmony. The physical and biological worlds since the beginning of the earth have been in constant state of flux and change, much of which has been far more drastic than anyone can now conceive.'[7] He goes on to point out various features of the history of the Earth that have been in constant state of flux and change, much of which has been far more drastic than anyone can now conceive. Oxygen was not present at all in early stages of the Earth's atmosphere. It was put there by the activity of plants. Animals evolved in a world made for them by the earlier organisms.

The Permian extinction of about 250 million years ago wiped out 90% of all species on Earth. Some 65 million years ago the dinosaurs, which were widespread over the face of the Earth, were wiped out seemingly by the impact of an asteroid. A succession of Ice Ages changed the face of nature on all continents. In the last Ice Age great slabs of ice stretched as far south as London and New York some 20,000 years ago; 100,000 years before that the conditions were similar to today. Some 20,000 years before that another big freeze had come over the Earth. This drastic change from cold to warm and back to cold has been going on for the past million years. There has never been a balance or harmony.

During both the cold and the warm phases countless species found themselves unadapted and became extinct. Fully 99.999% of all species that have ever existed are already extinct and in the end all will become extinct. Indeed life is about half over. The first living organisms appeared on Earth about 3 to 4 billion years ago. Cosmologists promise us another 3 to 4 billion years before everything comes to an end. Considering such a history Lewontin concludes that 'any rational environmental movement must abandon the romantic and totally unfounded ideological commitment to a harmonious and balanced world in which the environment is preserved'.[8]

Michael Soule is another population biologist who argues strongly against the concept of balance of nature. 'Living nature is not equilibr-ial', he says, 'at least not on a scale that is relevant to the persistence of species. In a sense the science of ecology has been hoist on its own petard by maintaining, as many did during the middle of this century, that natural communities tend towards equilibrium. Current ecologi-cal thinking argues that nature at the level of local biotic assemblages has never been homeostatic.'[9]

What, then, has the principle of balance been replaced by? The full answer to this is complex because nature is complex. An alternative answer sees a much more chaotic state in nature than balance sug-gests. It looks at each species in a community of plants and animals as having probability of surviving and reproducing. This may be quite low for some species, in which case the species becomes rare. For others the chance is high which could lead to 'outbreaks' in numbers to huge levels such as is a regular phenomenon in locusts and plague grasshoppers. A species may be kept rare or common by any component in its environment that affects its chances to survive and reproduce. That is what the study of population ecology is all about. Ecologists ask the question, how is it that lions do not completely cause their prey to become extinct, or why wolves don't cause the extinction of Moose in Isle Royale National Park, an island in Lake Superior? Contrary to widespread notions, there is no simple 'balance' relationship between the predator and its prey but a combination of many factors that lead to the survival of both but in anything but a balanced state.[10]

Picket and White argue that until the 1980s the major priority of both theoretical and empirical work in ecology has been dominated by equilibrium perspective.[11] Repudiating that perspective and embracing one of constant change, these authors examine the evi-dence for equilibrium or otherwise in what has been regarded until recently as examples of equilibrium, namely the tropical rain forests of South and Central America and the Everglades of Florida. They reveal instabilities on every hand; a wet green world of constant disturbance and changing patchiness. The message is consistent: the old concept of equilibrium is dead and with it the concept of the ecosystem has receded in usefulness. In its place nature is a landscape of patchiness continually changing through time and space with an increasing barrage of perturbations and change.

Ecologists agree on many things. Virtually without exception they agree that there is an environmental crisis created by humans. How-ever, there is as yet no grand unified theory of ecology that has a consensus. Ecologists tend to think of themselves as either population ecologists, community ecologists, biomedical ecologists, mathematical modelling ecologists and so on.There are schools of thought within these categories.

2. *Ecosystems are fragile.*   The word ecosystem is a metaphor. People refer to a lake as an ecosystem or a coral reef as an ecosystem. The term is meant to include all the plants and animals and other organisms in the lake and as well the water and the mud in the bottom. A problem with the concept is that its boundaries are not at all easy to define. For example, the bird that flies in from outside and leaves its droppings in the lake may have some effect on the organisms in the lake. But it may normally live far away. Ecologists are divided amongst themselves as to the best way to study ecology. There are those who say let us study the lake and everything in it. You might then come up with a tremendous inventory of organisms and minerals and what have you. There are others who say let us study the fish in the lake and what determines their chance to survive and reproduce. There are the population biologists. They would claim that they have more chance of getting answers to questions than the ecosystem students who often are not clear as to what the important questions are.

Environmentalists who set out to save a coral reef from destruction by human activities are tempted to argue to the politicians that the coral reef is a very fragile ecosystem. By this they seem to mean that if you disturb it in any way the system collapses. But, as Ehrlich says, 'It is rare that an ecosystem can usefully be described as "fragile" . . . That wetlands and tropical forests are rapidly disappearing is beyond dispute; whether or not they are normally "fragile" is beside the point.'[12] Ehrlich gives 'fragility' as an example of an outdated concept that can backfire against those well-intentioned greens who invoke it for support. They are unable to document their contention about fragility when pushed by developers.

3. *Nature is benign and harmonious.*   The natural theology of the late eighteenth century saw in the order of nature the perfect design of plants and animals with, in many cases, design for human ends. The bee collected nectar, not for itself, but to make honey for us.

In 1859 Charles Darwin told a very different story. Nature was a 'struggle for existence'. Nine years before the publication of *The Origin of Species*, Tennyson described nature as 'red in tooth and claw'. That is indeed one aspect of nature. Lions hunt and kill antelopes. Wasps hunt caterpillars into which they lay their eggs so that their larvae survive at the expense of caterpillars. Darwin devoted a whole chapter in *The Origin of Species* to the struggle for existence. He borrowed the phrase from Thomas Malthus' *Essay on Population* and made it clear that the phrase was a metaphor and included much more than predation of one organism on another. He wrote 'Two canine animals in time of dearth, may be truly said to struggle with each other which shall get the food and live. But a plant on the edge of a desert is said to struggle for life against drought, though more properly it should be said to be dependent on the moisture. A plant which annually produces a thousand seeds, for which only one on the average comes to maturity, may be more truly said to struggle with the plants of the same and other kinds which already clothe the ground.'[13] The gist of the argument is that far more individuals, be they plants or animals, are born into the world that can survive to reproduce. This is the struggle for existence. Hence Whitehead said 'life is robbery'.[14] He added the metaphysical comment that 'The robber requires justification.'

Darwin was fully aware that plants and animals had other relations that were co-operative such as the bees that pollinate plants, yet none escapes its own struggle for existence. Population biologist Michael Soule takes up a timely criticism of worn out views of ecology parading as modern ecology when he writes:

> The real biological world little resembles the rose-tinted television portrayal. Certainly the idea that species live in integrated communities is a myth. So-called biotic communities, a misleading term, are constantly changing membership. The species occurring in any particular place are rarely convivial neighbours; their co-existence in certain places is better explained by individual physiological tolerances ... Though in some cases the finer details of spatial distribution may be influenced by positive interspecies interactions, the much more common kinds of interaction are competition, predation, parasitism and disease ... The idea that living nature comprises co-operative communities replete with altruistic, mutualistic symbioses has been overstated.[15]

4. *The world of nature is completed and fine-tuned.* The phrase 'integrity of creation' used by the World Council of Churches suggests wholeness and completeness. In the previous section we indicated how nature is ever changing both in the numbers of individuals and in the number of species. As to completeness, the creative process is not complete. It never has been. It is ever evolving. Central to that

process is the continuous production of mutant genes, most of which are deleterious but some few add to the adaptiveness of the species and are incorporated in the genetic composition of the species. It is now known that genes that confer resistance of insects to insecticides such as DDT were being produced even before DDT existed. But they did not persist in the population because they did not confer any advantage until DDT arrived. This happened when DDT was invented by humans and used as an insecticide. DDT resistant mutants which were wiped out before DDT became part of the insects' environment now survived. When DDT arrived the insects that carried mutant genes conferring resistance to the poison survived. Central to this process is the idea of chance variation and the selection of those variants that confer benefit on the species. It is an order of nature very different from that of a design made by some outside omnipotent creator which was a common idea prior to Darwin. We have to take seriously the role of chance.

5. Complexity enhances stability. A much-contested proposition amongst ecologists is the thesis that diversity of species in a community enhances stability in the sense that the number of individuals and the number of species in a community are kept more or less constant. There is so much dispute amongst ecologists based on mathematical models and observations in nature that it is unwise at this stage to place much credence on this and related propositions.

Two leading evolutionists, Levins and Lewontin, maintain that virtually every modern theorist of evolution, especially evolutionary ecologists, has claimed that complexity results in stability. Complexity in turn is thought of as a strong interaction between elements with different functions. It has been supposed that a community with many different predators, competitors, decomposers and primary food sources is the most resistant to change in the environment. Hence the proposition that evolution leads to greater and greater diversity, complexity, homeostasis and stability in the living world. But heed what these two leading evolutionists say about this thesis. Levins and Lewontin state 'The extraordinary feature of this conceptual structure is that it has no apparent basis either in fact or in theory.'[16]

Whatever we think about stability and complexity, it makes no difference whatsoever to the programme of conservationists to maintain biodiversity. There are other arguments for maintaining diversity of species. A cogent one is that diversity of organisms is required to maintain the life-support systems of the Earth, that is those cycles in nature that help to maintain the constancy of the composition of the atmosphere, the water cycle and the cycle of nutrients; a diversity of organisms is involved in the detoxification and decomposition of wastes. Ecologists do not know enough about these processes to be able to pinpoint all the organisms that are involved. Lack of information suggests a precautionary policy of conservation.

Because there is no consensus about the stability-complexity argument, it is inappropriate to include it in an environmental ethic as was done in Aldo Leopold's so-called land ethic. An environmental ethic needs to be informed by science. What is important is that the science which is taken into account in an environmental ethic is valid science.

6. *The Earth is a super-organism.* The idea of the Earth as a homeostatic super-organism was brought to life in 1972 in the so-called 'Gaia hypothesis' of James Lovelock. The hypothesis was named after the Greek Earth goddess. The hypothesis considers the Earth to be a linked system of physical, chemical and biological processes, interacting in a self-regulating way to maintain the conditions necessary for life. The Gaia hypothesis has aroused controversy amongst the scientific community from its beginning. It has been accused of being poorly defined and impossible to subject to any falsification test. Worst of all, Gaia received an extra mystical flavour when it was adopted by the New Age movement. What is established is that there are cycles in nature such as the nitrogen cycle, the phosphorus cycle and the carbon cycle which involve feed-back processes that result in the composition of the atmosphere or of the oceans remaining remarkably constant, except for major interventions by humans such as the increase of carbon dioxide in the atmosphere since the industrial revolution. A conservative assessment of the Gaia hypothesis is that what is true in it has been mostly known for years, such as the feed-back cycles involved in the maintenance of the components of the sea and the atmosphere, and what is new is questionable. The Earth is not an organism, not even a super-organism. Gaia and homeostasis are hazardous models of nature as they can give a false sense of security. If nature is self-regulating it will care for itself. The notion can lead to a theory of wildlife management known as benign neglect.

7. *The duality of the natural and the artificial.* There is not a continent that has not been invaded by species of plants, animals and micro-organisms that were previously foreign to these places. Natural communities, so called, are full of invaders. The most common mammals in Australia are rabbits, cats, mice and goats that came from

Europe. All the mammals in New Zealand are from Australia and Europe. In so far as the invaders have survived and continue to reproduce they are part of the present scene of nature. Probably more ecological studies have been made on invaders than on endemic species because of their economic importance. European rabbits destroy farmlands in Australia. Australian possums in New Zealand destroy forests. Other invaders, such as many species of birds, are common but of little, if any, economic importance. There may be no such thing as a community of plants and animals in the world today that is without its invaders. The point is that there is no valid distinction between natural communities and so called artificial ones. All are natural.

8. *Indigenous people are superior conservationists.* It is right and proper that we should learn what we can from indigenous people who have lived with nature far longer than most other human communities. Some of what we learn is positive and constructive. On the other hand indigenous people have been responsible for much devastation of nature. We can learn from that also.

Some tribes of Australian aborigines kept sacred areas free from hunting which, whatever its purpose, had the effect of conserving in these areas native species of plants and animals. On the other hand Australian aborigines have been credited with the extinction of the large mammals that once roamed the continent. Some sixty species of large marsupials were killed off after aborigines arrived in Australia 40,000 or more years ago. Furthermore, their use of fire to aid in hunting caused dramatic changes to huge tracts of country. In those National Parks in Australia that are today under aboriginal control, the aboriginal inhabitants are free to live off the land as their predecessors did. As a result, according to some reports, many species of animals have become rare in these parks.

Some tribes in New Guinea are notable for having practised a sustainable agriculture for countless years. On the other hand Diamond claims that in thirty years of visiting native peoples on the three islands of New Guinea, he has failed to come across a single example of indigenous New Guineans showing friendly response to wild animals or consciously managing habitats to enhance wildlife. A consequence has been the depleting or extermination of susceptible species. Diamond seeks to dispel what he sees as a myth of native peoples as 'environmentally minded paragons of conservation, living in a Golden Age of harmony with nature, in which living things are revered, harvested only as needed and carefully monitored to avoid depletion of breeding stocks'.[17] The role of the modern American Indian in affecting wild nature has been widely discussed and remains controversial.[18]

At the end of the Pleistocene epoch some 12,000 years ago, about two-thirds of the large mammal species in North America became extinct. Included were several species of huge mammoths, giant ground sloths and sabre-toothed cats. Similar losses of large mammals occurred on other continents. The dates of these extinctions more or less coincided with the arrival of the first *homo sapiens* in the Western Hemisphere. This has led to the theory of 'Pleistocene over-kill'. The idea is that the relative poverty today of the Earth's megafauna (animals weighing over five hundred kilograms) is due primarily to over-exploitation of relatively defenceless large animals by ever-increasing numbers of skilful hunters. There are various lines of evidence that make it seem likely that human beings got an early start in the process of extinction.[19]

9. *Ethics can be derived from nature.* The great protagonist of Darwinism, Thomas Henry Huxley, was deeply concerned that Darwinism, with its concept of the struggle for existence and survival of the fittest, might be converted into a social doctrine for humans, as indeed it was by some who saw in the struggle for existence a doctrine to apply to human behaviour. Social Darwinism has been used to support economic and political competition in the belief that this will lead to the survival and increase of the best and strongest. Social Darwinism appealed so much to Karl Marx that he wanted to dedicate *Das Kapital* to Charles Darwin. Darwin refused. Nearer to our time Mussolini invoked social Darwinism to justify the invasion of Abyssinia. Because it is 'natural' it is therefore right is no basis for ethics. Thomas Henry Huxley should be recognized as having given the knock-out blow to the doctrine of Social Darwinism in his Romanes Lecture in the Sheldonian Theatre in Oxford in 1893. He argued that human cultural progress reverses the biological Darwinism of survival of the fittest. Social evolution is not to be achieved by a struggle for existence in which the weak go to the wall. The law of the jungle is not the law of civilization. Humans came of age, he argued, when they ceased emulating nature. He was correct. Nevertheless his contention has often been challenged, not least by his grandson Julian Huxley who gave the Romanes lecture fifty years later under the same title, 'Evolution and Ethics'. Julian Huxley contended that our task was to find out the direction of evolution and join the natural stream. The discussion has never died down and has its present resurgence

in the modern doctrine of socio-biology. Thomas Henry Huxley was clearer headed than Julian and others like him. His basic position stands.

The Ecologically Sustainable Society

The World Council of Churches made a lasting global contribution to the understanding of the environmental crisis when it introduced the important concept of the ecologically sustainable society. This concept had its birth at the conference of Church and Society in Bucharest in 1974 entitled 'Science and Technology and Human Development'. The concept of the ecologically sustainable society was the outcome of a discussion of limits to growth. It means the society that could persist indefinitely into the future because it sustains the ecological base on which society is utterly dependent. The concept was accepted by the Nairobi Assembly of the WCC in 1975 in its programme 'The Just Participatory and Sustainable Society' (JPSS). The concept of the ecologically sustainable society quickly caught on around the secular world in quite an extraordinary way. Its time had come. Lester Brown, Director of the Worldwatch Institute in Washington, wrote his book *Building a Sustainable Society* in 1981. This book diagnosed the present state of global unsustainability and suggested paths to sustainability. The first *State of the World Report* of the Worldwatch Institute in 1984 had the subtitle 'Progress toward a Sustainable Society'. A report has been produced annually ever since. Each issue has retained the subtitle 'Progress toward a Sustainable Society'.

The 1998 State of the World Report analysed many situations throughout the world where ecological sustainability is threatened. Once the sustainable yield threshold of a natural system such as an oceanic fishery is crossed, growth in consumption can continue only by consuming the resource base itself. When the amount of fish caught surpasses the sustainable yield of a fishery, fish stocks begin to shrink. If fishing continues the fishery collapses and may never recover. A similar situation exists with forests. Once the demand for forest products exceeds the sustainable yield of the forest, it begins to shrink. As excess of demand over sustainable yield widens, deforestation accelerates. Within scarcely a generation countries such as Mauritania, Ethiopia and Haiti have been almost entirely deforested, largely because of local unrelenting demand for firewood. If the growing demand for water exceeds the sustainable yield of an aquifer, the water table begins to fall. When the aquifer is depleted the rate of recharge falls to the rate of pumping. If it falls below this further cutbacks are necessary.

The UN Food and Agriculture Organization who monitor oceanic fisheries report that nearly all fisheries are now being fished beyond the capacity for replacement. Water tables are falling on every continent. Water use has tripled since mid-century which has led to massive over-pumping. This has led to curtailment of irrigation. In many countries water diversion from rivers has reached the point where some of them no longer make it to the sea. The Colorado, the major river in south-western United States, rarely reaches the Gulf of Mexico where it used to enter the sea. Rangelands on all continents are being overgrazed making them less and less sustainable with resultant soil erosion. Over half of all the rangelands in Australia have such serious soil erosion that they no longer support the herds of animals they once did. The world consumption of grain has tripled since mid-century. As a result, farmers have extended agriculture to marginal lands where continuous cropping is unsustainable. Soil erosion on agricultural lands in Africa has reduced African's total grain harvest by 8%. This is climbing towards double that amount in the next decade if steps are not taken to reverse the trend. Further example of ecologically unsustainable practices can be found in the State of the World report for 1998. The destruction of resources below the sustainable level can only be changed by a change in human practices. The same can be said of the extinction of species of plants and animals in the world today. The main cause of extinction is destruction of habitats such as the tropical rain forests of Brazil and South East Asia.

The recognition of the need for ecologically sustainable practices is one of the most striking examples of a clear-cut practical concept that has had a global appeal both because the phrase itself has an appeal that has caught on and because it leads to clear cut change in practices that are realistic. No matter what the rubric of our environmental programme, whether it be JPSS or Integrity of Creation, our main task is to preserve habitats around the world from rivers and oceans to deserts and rain forests. We don't need romance ecology to make it work.

The Integrity of Creation

In adopting the term the WCC responded to a growing concern beginning in the 'West', but now more global; its origins can be almost precisely dated to the publication in the USA in 1962 of Rachel Carson's *The Silent Spring*. By the 1970s this concern was strong. Some of the drastic economic forecasts were already shown to be mistaken, but the drastic ecological forecasts seemed well founded. No one doubts that there are ecological problems, and the WCC was rightly concerned with what guidance the churches could offer to their members, and in the public forum in dealing wisely with them.

There is nothing new in the churches being faced with new ethical problems. Three examples in this century are; contraception; nuclear fission and the implications of the cracking of the DNA code. In dealing with such new issues the churches have three tasks: (1) to sift the evidence; (2) to see what light can be thrown on it by the Bible and the tradition based on it in the past 2,000 years; (3) in the light of the first two to illuminate the choices that humans have to make today. To sift the evidence is not easy. It depends on the evidence of experts in the field in question. Sometimes the evidence is clear. But in most areas of study, experts differ and there are schools of thought. There can be both corporate and personal intellectual vested interests; and the evidence may be inherently ambiguous. In the end the 'lay' person or 'lay' groups have to decide. In this paper we have examined the ecological evidence. Now we examine how the WCC has dealt with the theological and biblical issues when using the term Integrity of Creation.

That term has certainly had a powerful resonance. Pope John Paul II used it in paragraph 26 of his social Encyclical *Sollicitudo Rei Socialis* (1987) and again in a statement of 1990. It has appeared in UN documents and is now quite widely used. Creation is a theological term, not a scientific one. The scientific term is Nature. Our knowledge of Nature has expanded enormously and goes on expanding. The creation sagas (or myths) of Genesis 1 and 2 tell us of creation that it is good in God's eyes and that human beings are stewards of it under God. From Genesis 3 onwards we learn that creation is flawed because of human sin (the myth of the Fall). What is meant by referring to its Integrity? Strangely enough, although WCC documents are full of it prior to the Seoul Convocation and after it, there has been no organized ecumenical theological critique of it.[20] Since 1992, with the setting up of Unit III to pursue the theme Theology of Life; Justice, Peace and Creation, its Moderator, Professor Larry Rasmussen of Union Theological Seminary, New York, has written extensively on this theme, most succinctly in a lecture to the American Society for Christian Ethics in 1995; this is greatly expanded in a book published a year later.[21]

However, the only specific group effort to elucidate the meaning of the term was that of a very small group which met at Amsterdam in 1981 and produced a booklet *Reintegrating Creation* (WCC) in which the substantial theological contribution was by Professor Douglas John Hall of McGill University, Montreal. He was later given the task of writing the entry on the term in the *Dictionary of the Ecumenical Movement* (1991), which is in a sense an official publication in its selection of entries and writers; so it is useful to consider what he says.

The overwhelming note is that of a radical change in Christian thinking after about 1970. Taking a longer perspective than Hall's article, in earlier years of this century, and particularly after the struggle against political totalitarianism, the emphasis had been on the category of the personal. One thinks of men like Maritain, Mounier, Buber, Berdyaev, Macmurray, Bultmann and (in a sense) Brunner and Barth. Existentialist philosophy and its influence on theology through the discovery of Kierkegaard pointed the same way.

Roman Catholic theology at Vatican II celebrated the dignity of the person, particularly *Gaudium et Spes*, the Pastoral Constitution. In the 1960s, with its enormous economic and technological expansion, the effort was to recover the category of the secular from its bad connotation in Christian tradition. The secular was seen as an area of human liberation under God. One aspect of Bonhoeffer's thought, that humans had 'come of age' in the universe, was influential. There was no suggestion that humans had been morally re-made, but that they had been given responsibility for running the world under God. No longer should they be content to be passive, accepting human ills as the will of God, but should set to work to alleviate them, by organized scientific and political effort. This was not to be impious, or 'playing God', but responsibly using power given by God, now seen to be more extensive than hitherto thought. Nature had been de-sacralized. It was not static but dynamic.

Hall's article is very different. He refers to a much quoted article of 1967 by an American historian, Lynn White, that Christian theology is largely responsible for an ecological and environmental crisis, because of its stress on the human domination of Nature. Modern secularity and Western technology have been celebrated in a simplistic way. Hall criticizes the work of the Geneva Conference on Church and society of 1966 on Christians and the Technical and Social Revolution of our time. It said: 'The traditional Christian doctrine of creation teaches that nature is to be dominated by man and is to be offered to man's contemplation and awe. Nature is both under the providence of God and the mastery of men. It is the de-deification and de-sacralization of nature which is one basic starting point of true science and of its results in technology. God gives no limit upon man's dominion or control over nature except that it has to be fulfilled under God's "lordship". Man is responsible to use his stewardship of nature to make possible a fuller human life for mankind.'

Hall goes on to point out that in the light of the ecological and environmental crisis the Vancouver Assembly resolved 'to engage the churches in a conciliar process of mutual commitment (covenant) to justice, peace and the integrity of creation'. He refers to the small meeting at Amsterdam and says its report assumes the solidarity of the human steward with all the creatures for whom the steward is responsible. The language of human mastery bypasses human accountability, and the attribution of human pretensions to sovereignty amounts to rank sin and disobedience.

Later a much bigger consultation than the Amsterdam one at Granvollen in Norway in 1988 reached the same conclusions. 'For the first time in any consistent manner such documents demonstrated the church's readiness to consider the creation for its own sake and not only as a setting for the human drama. *Creation possesses an inner coherence and goodness . . . every creature and the whole creation in chorus bears witness to the glorious unity and harmony with which the creation is endowed*' (our italics). Hall concludes: 'In a context comprising enormous threats to the future of the planet the hope of the gospel must be articulated as the redemption of creation itself. By the choice of the term the Integrity of Creation, the WCC has demonstrated its intention to do just that.' So much for Hall's article.

The WCC's work in the field since 1983 reveals the overwhelming influence of this outlook. Nature is seen as oppressed by humanity and so is included in the call for dedication to the cause of the marginalized. The tables are turned. Instead of humans being the masters of nature they are called to be servants of it. We should read the Bible from the perspective of birds, trees and plants and learn to think like mountains. One exaggeration is being counterbalanced by another. That humans are to be stewards under God is a better way of expressing human responsibility for nature.

Involved in these thoughts is a picture of unity and harmony in nature in which each species has a right to flourish. The term 'Integrity of Creation' suggests a certain wholeness and completeness as well as harmony. A kind of homeostatic situation is being suggested in which everything in nature is so related to everything else, that to 'interfere' with it at any point is to upset the whole and create disorder; it is an expression of the hubris and anthropocentricity of twentieth-century humans. Rasmussen says that science has now discovered what theology already affirmed, that nature is a glorious harmony and unity, and that we need a morality based on nature. This certainly accords with the picture which has been presented by some ecologists, and one quite widely taken up in some 'Western' intellectual circles. We have given clear reasons for challenging this as good science.

Questions also need to be asked about the theology. Has not the reaction against the theology of the 1960s gone much too far? It is true that the Christian tradition has often overstressed human dominion or stewardship, especially in relation to animals, and a critique of that is healthy. But the unsatisfactory interpretation of a doctrine does not overthrow it, as has often been shown in Christian history. It must be asked whether the criticism of previous ecumenical thought in Hall's article does justice to its importance. Questions need to be asked about what is enthusiastically replacing it. Is this a well-founded view of the evidence? Nature is clearly not the unambiguous harmony that is alleged. Is it a suitable basis for morality? T. H. Huxley, the great pioneering teacher of evolution showed, as we have seen, conclusively that it isn't.

We have considered the theology of creation as exemplified in recent work within the WCC. A brief word needs to be said about its use of the Bible (which lies behind tradition).

Spurred by the assumption of an ecological and environmental crisis, the Bible has been ransacked to find texts which support the attitude to nature we have described. The creation sagas, which hitherto have loomed large, are underplayed because the word 'dominion' given in them to humans over nature, from which the doctrine of stewardship is derived, is in the Hebrew a very strong one. (The dominion is under the lordship of God.) The Mosaic covenant, which had tended to be stressed as the foundation of the story of God's people of Israel, leading in the Christian view to a major modification with the new creation in Christ (II Cor.5.17), is under-played by comparison with the Noachian covenant with humans and Nature. The Wisdom literature, including the Psalms, is ransacked for favourable references to nature. Any texts from the New Testament in a similar vein that can be found are stressed. In fact the Bible points both ways; nature is both a friend and an enemy to humans. Nature is both a harmony and subject to internal struggle within itself. This is not surprising. The Bible reflects the many attitudes to nature which human life *vis-à-vis* Nature suggested and they are very similar to those experienced today. The texts are building blocks out of which a doctrine of creation can be arrived at. What is clear is that humans are rooted in nature but transcend it decisively. What this means for ethics and human attitudes to nature is what a contemporary doctrine of creation must deal with. Our purpose has been to examine whether the recent discussions have been prompted by a well-founded reading of ecological evidence.

Five Concluding Points

1. The WCC made a notable contribution to global environmental issues when, following a conference at Bucharest in 1974, it formu-lated the concept of the Just Participatory and Sustainable Society (JPSS). Sustainability was relevant to the secular world and was widely taken up. To some extent also the call for a theology of nature and an ecological ethic was responded to by the churches.

2. The concept of the JPSS was replaced by the Integrity of Creation as a more theological expression. But is the theology of the Integrity of Creation good theology? If it continues to be used it needs theological clarification. Those who developed it have an ideological interpret-ation of it in relation to nature which is not based on good science. This has been pushed by the WCC and its chosen experts.

3. The WCC should be aware of adopting one school of thought in a natural science like ecology as the basis of its study work, and in effect propagating it, without examining others in the light of scholarly opinions.

4. In this paper we separate facts from fables by examining how ecological studies today deal with these issues. We find a concept of nature that: has its close inter-relationships but is nevertheless in all probability without balance; has a certain resilience as distinct from fragility; is ever changing as distinct from stable; besides having co-operative features is one of struggle and cruelty as contrasted with

being benign and harmonious; is incomplete; is seemingly wasteful; is ever changing and has evolved and is evolving by a kind of groping process with chaotic features.

5. We call for a more realistic understanding of ecological concepts and ask how a realistic view of nature relates to the Christian doctrine of creation. It has always been a problem for Christian theology to reconcile its understanding of God's love for the world with evil and suffering in it that it is not attributable to human sin. If the whole universe is to be seen as a kind of sacrament of God it is a flawed one. The problem of evil and suffering has not been removed by modern scientific views of nature. It cannot be avoided by resorting to romantic ecological myths.

Part IV

Roman Catholic Social Ethics

13

Laborem Exercens: Pope John Paul II on Work

Laborem Exercens was issued on 14 September 1981. The Pope had intended to issue it on 15 May, the ninetieth anniversary of the first of the modern papal social encyclicals, Leo XIII's *Rerum Novarum*, but it was delayed by his recovery from the attack on his life. It is thus consciously in the sequence of *Quadragesimo Anno* (1931), *Mater et Magistra* (1961), *Octogesima Adveniens* (1971), with *Populorum Progressio* (1967) also being drawn upon.

It is safe to say that no previous Pope had worked in a stone quarry attached to a chemical factory, as Karol Wojtyla did at Krakow from September 1940 to August 1944, and this adds interest to the theme of the encyclical.[1] Work is the single theme, unlike *Populorum Progressio* or *Quadragesimo Anno* which have many, and the encyclical reads like a philosophical-theological position paper put forward as a basis for reflection. The frequent words and phrases italicized appear to reflect a personal style, reminiscent of Queen Victoria's letters.

The English text divides the encyclical into five sections. (i) Introduction; (ii) Work and Man; (iii) Conflict between Labour and Capital in the present stage of history; (iv) Rights of Workers; (v) Elements for a Spirituality of Work. I pick out some basic points. Work is fundamental to man's existence. This is largely established on the basis of the Genesis creation myths, together with the witness of the Gospels to Jesus as a manual worker and one who took the world of work for granted in his teaching.[2] The Pope seems to hold that the Genesis passages bear witness in an 'archaic' way to truths about the fundamental nature of work for man discovered by the human sciences. The question at once comes to mind, if the human sciences had come to, or do in the future come to, a different conclusion what would be their status *vis-à-vis* the archaisms of Genesis?[3]

Work, then, is fundamental. Leisure is not mentioned until page 87 (out of 99), where rest is seen as a foil to work in the case of both God and man (from Hebrews, picking up the thought of Genesis). Work is the key to the social question. Work is meant to make life more human. True, there is an element of toil in it. Toil nevertheless brings out human fulfilment, and it is also the means by which man shares a small part of the sufferings of Christ. Work is meant for man, not man for work. Man is not just one among other factors of production, as in liberal capitalism. Man has priority over things. The church has always taught the priority of labour over capital,[4] labour being a primary and efficient cause and capital an instrumental one.

Developments since *Rerum Novarum* and *Quadragesimo Anno* are mentioned, notably the world scale on which the subject has now to be discussed. There is also increasing technological change (though technology is to be seen as an ally), and the increasing solidarity of workers.[5]

The Pope holds that intellectuals are being 'proletarianized' because of unemployment among them.[6] Conflicts between capital and labour have become one of Liberalism versus Marxism with its class struggle.[7] In the church's teaching, the right to private property is subordinated to the right to common use. Whether property is privately or publicly owned it should serve labour, and with this in mind adaptations in the rights of ownership in the means of production are needed. 'Rigid' capitalism is unacceptable. Socialization of certain means of production cannot be excluded. State collectivism, however, is by no means equivalent to socialism. Each worker needs to consider himself part owner 'of the great workbench at which he is working'. He needs to know that even 'on something that is owned in common, he is working "for himself"'. This is the principal reason for the private ownership of the means of production. A wide range of intermediate bodies is needed to achieve this.[8]

The rights of the workers are stressed. A distinction is made between the direct employer and the indirect employer, the state. The latter must act positively against unemployment by overall planning.[9] A just remuneration would perhaps include family allowances, and sufficient to ensure that a mother should not have to leave home and family in order to work. Trade unions are necessary to protect the rights of workers, but ultimately work does not involve serious conflicts of interest; it unites people. Hence unions should not have too close links with political parties.

I turn now to a critique of the encyclical.

I have already referred to the style of *Laborem Exercens*. In 1971 I raised the question whether we should see a new style of official Roman Catholic teaching on social ethics,[10] reflecting in the light of Vatican II more of the method which had developed in the World Council of Churches. Later in the year *Octogesima Adveniens*, which was a letter to Cardinal Roy, President of the Pontifical Commission for Justice and Peace, seemed further evidence of a new trend. This present encyclical is different again. Interesting as it is as a basis of reflection it hardly seems suitable to carry such a weight of authority. It is hard to fit it in with categories of infallibility (unclear as these are). The latest statement known to me bearing on the matter is that of *Lumen Gentium* (para. 25) which says, 'This religious submission of will and of mind must be shown in a special way to the authentic teaching authority of the Roman Pontiff, even when he is not speaking *ex cathedra*. That is, it must be shown in such a way that his supreme *magisterium* is acknowledged with reverence, the judgments made by him are sincerely adhered to, according to his manifest mind and will.' One hopes this will not be the last statement on the matter. Certainly the final ARCIC Report strikes a different note, and perhaps that is why the Congregation for the Defence of the Faith has received it so coldly. In any event the attitude prescribed by *Lumen Gentium* seems inappropriate to the tone and style of *Laborem Exercens*.

There are problems in trying to give universal teaching on these matters. Paul VI disavowed the task. In *Octogesima Adveniens* (para. 4) he says, 'In the face of such widely varying situations it is difficult for us to utter a unified message and to put forward a solution which has universal validity. Such is not our ambition, nor is it our mission.' John Paul II is more ambitious, but in several respects the universal frame of reference of the teaching needs qualifying.

His stress is clearly on manual work. He hardly faces up to the growing disappearance in advanced industrial societies of the routine physical and menial jobs by which at least half of the working population have hitherto earned their living. They are increasingly becoming service societies, a process which needs to go much further if the long-term structural unemployment which we face is to be tackled. This requires a new philosophy of society, for services need to be paid for, and it will mean more communal and less private consumption. There are also implications for leisure which it is now hard to discuss apart from work, as this Encyclical does. Nor does management fit in easily to John Paul's scheme, as his brief references show. In his labour-capital division management is clearly work (labour), but it is also part of capital.[11]

The Polish political situation seems to condition what John Paul says about trade unions. He thinks that political activity will mean that they will lose their chance to fulfil the role of standing for the just rights of workers. But can there be a clear distinction between industrial and political activity, especially when the government is the employer? Should unions in Britain shed their links with the Labour party? It is arguable that they should, but far from obvious.

The Roman Catholic Church is hampered by the traditional teaching on private property in providing an alternative between free capitalism and collectivist socialism. It is a pity it does not feel more free to situate that teaching more closely to its mediaeval context, and to re-think the concept of property in the light of the technical and social developments of the last two centuries.[12] The result is vagueness where greater precision is needed. For one thing it prevents the Pope from considering whether the market may not be a useful mechanism for human good in its due place. He thinks it involves 'materialism' and 'economism' unworthy of man. There are in fact shifts in the emphasis of papal teaching. In *Rerum Novarum* private property is almost a metaphysical right; Leo XIII seems to be thinking largely of peasant proprietors and pre-industrial guilds. In *Quadragesimo Anno* no one can be a sincere Catholic and a true socialist; it seems to favour a corporate state.[13] The Popes from John XXIII have clearly moved some distance from this, as has their attitude to Marxism. John Paul II would appear to favour some form of Workers' or Producers' Co-operatives.[14] These do not solve all problems because they represent the vested interest of one group as against that of other producers (when there are relatively scarce economic means with alternative uses), and of the whole body of consumers. However, Catholic thought has tended to deny (as John Paul II does) that there is any fundamental conflict of interest in society, and this is a weakness in it.

The method of papal social ethics has also shifted to some extent. *Rerum Novarum* was deductive; there is no place in it for scientists, nor indeed for the contribution of lay persons other than as learners. *Quadragesimo Anno* was still teaching deductions from universal principles as a third way between liberal capitalism and socialism, but with a greater emphasis on an historical element in applying principles to practice. *Mater et Magistra* and *Populorum Progressio* (after Vatican II's Pastoral Constitution *Gaudium et Spes*) follow a more inductive method. There is no longer deductive reasoning from immutable Natural Law, but a scrutiny of present reality in the light of the gospel. Lay persons have a share in this scrutiny and in the construction of social teaching.[15] *Octogesima Adveniens* says it is up to Christian communities 'in dialogue with other Christian brethren and all men of goodwill to discern the options and commitments which are called for in order to bring about the social, political and economic changes seen in many cases to be urgently needed' (para. 4). In *Laborem Exercens* John Paul II, in referring to the social changes taking place says, 'It is not for the Church to analyse scientifically the consequences that these changes may have on human society,' but it is for her 'to help to guide the above-mentioned changes so as to ensure authentic progress by man and society'. *Octogesima Anno* reflects exactly the kind of inter-confessional, inter-disciplinary group work which is needed in social ethics, and is more adequate than *Laborem Exercens*. John Paul II's statement makes too sharp a break between 'science' and church teaching; in group work they will react reciprocally upon one another.

I tend to take up church documents in this sphere not expecting to find anything new but to find out how far they have caught up with the best (as I judge) Christian and secular thought of the time. I do not think *Laborem Exercens* takes us any further than the flurry of Christian writing on the subject of work which followed the 1939–45 war,[16] if as far; or the work that has begun to come from the years of Industrial Mission since the war. On the other hand it is clearly in touch with the realities of our day. I applaud its stand for social justice, and its insistence on fullness of life for persons as the criterion for dealing with the industrial and economic order. The wrongness of regarding labour as merely one factor of production among others cannot be stressed too often. As a personal *tour de force* it warrants our careful reflection; as official teaching it would have benefitted from widespread group work prior to publication, both in content and as a means of communication.

14

Sollicitudo Rei Socialis: Twenty Years after *Populorum Progressio*

The encyclical *Sollicitudo Rei Socialis*, which I shall subsequently refer to as SRS, seems to be known in the UK as *The Social Concern of the Church* which are its first six words. 'Concern' is an indefinite word as compared with 'doctrine' or 'theology' or 'teaching'. One of the questions it raises is how far it is expressing a more formal position than 'concern'. It seems clear that to a considerable extent it does. Further questions are the nature and cogency of its teaching and the authority it carries.

The Occasion

Issued to commemorate the twentieth anniversary of *Populorum Progressio* (1967) SRS is the latest in a sequence of papal documents which began with *Rerum Novarum* (1891) and is building up a body of social teaching. (What happened before 1891 under Pius IX, and before that, seems to have been banished to a lumber room where there is to be found traditional teaching on usury, slavery and religious liberty, to mention three themes; and one would like to have clearly stated what were the elements in the new start in 1891.) Since 1891 there has been *Quadragesimo Anno* (1931), *Mater et Magistra* (1961), and the letter *Octogesima Adveniens* (1971), and *Laborem Exercens* (1981). Presumably we are likely to see a major document in the centenary year 1991. To these must be added *Pacem in Terris* (1963). Apart from papal documents there is the Pastoral Constitution of Vatican II *Gaudium et Spes* (1965) and two Instructions from the Sacred Congregation for the Doctrine of the Faith, on *Certain Aspects of the Theology of Liberation* (1984) and *Christian Freedom and Liberation* (1986). Also I think important the Report of the Second Plenary Assembly of Roman Catholic Bishops, *Justice in the World* (1971), though under the influence of the SCDF the significance of episcopal gatherings is now being downplayed.

The Question of Continuity and Renewal

SRS begins with the theme of continuity and renewal in church social teaching. Continuity is obviously important when so much weight is put upon the authority of the teaching. SRS has ninety-two references, almost all to scripture, or previous papal or conciliar documents. (Continuity also stands out in the sexist language which obtrudes.) Renewal presents more difficulties. In a restricted sense it could mean that unchanged doctrine, which in part is claimed to go back to our Lord himself, is brought to bear on changing circumstances. SRS mentions three tools for doing this, the Bible, rational reflection and the human sciences. This is not, of course, a new position in Roman Catholic documents, but the methodology involved is never spelled out. How is the Bible to be used? What happens when rational reflection is brought to bear on it, as in the critical studies of the last two hundred years? What status have the human sciences? In what sense is 'science' used of them? Have they to some degree an autonomy from theology? How far may one's understanding of the human person affect one's estimate of the significance of the data they disclose or even what are to be regarded as data? Questions such as these are not raised. The aura of magisterial authority is given to whatever mixture emerges in the document, and the contribution of the three tools is not clarified.

The next question therefore is, what are the sources of the analysis of the changing circumstances since 1967? Apart from two references to United Nations documents no information is given. This is common in such Vatican documents, and is in contrast with the recent documents issued by the RC Bishops of the USA, on war and peace and on the economy, where there are abundant references to sources and lists of those who gave evidence, besides preliminary drafts of the final text. In the case of SRS we know nothing of the written sources of who was consulted. Magisterial authority has to cover its reading or the empirical evidence of the last twenty years.

I do not propose to go through it in detail. As far as the 'Western' world is concerned it accords with what most 'progressive' readers of quality newspapers would think, but will not commend itself to advocates of 'Reaganism' and 'Thatcherism'. It ranges over the north-south gap, neo-colonialism, international debt, the wastage of resources on arms, refugees, terrorism, and the super-development of the affluent countries who at the same time tolerate large-scale unemployment and bad housing.

In a less restricted sense, renewal might mean a change of balance and emphasis in church social teaching, or even new insights, as when slavery came to be condemned and religious liberty approved. SRS does not say so but it does bring in at least two new elements in papal documents, the notion of structural sin and ecological issues. I do not include a preferential option for the poor because this is recent but not new. Since the newness of the two themes is not pointed out there is no reference to the sources from which they came.

Structures of sin are referred to briefly in paragraph 36 but the force of it is largely taken away by relating them quickly to the perennial sins of individuals. There is a long footnote, quoting from an Apostolic Exhortation *Reconciliatio et Paenitentia* (1984) which concludes that a structure is not in itself the subject of moral acts. The immediate but unavowed source of this reference to structures of sin is liberation theology. In Protestant theology, however, the theme has been thoroughly explored in this century from the Social Gospel movement (Rauschenbusch) onwards. Persons can mould structures but structures also mould persons (from infancy, before they have the possibility, which later as adults they have, of being aware of it). Bad structures put 'good' people in positions where they cannot avoid 'bad' acts. The Pope relies on a call for a moral awakening to will changes in power structures. But changes in structures are also needed to enable good wills more scope to develop. These considerations lead more directly into the political realm, which is less easy for churches than staying at the hortatory level of urging conversions of the will. If they are to enter this realm, churches need a clear method in moving into the area where the theological and empirical mix. No church finds this easy. (The latest method which is getting some support in ecumenical circles is to turn an issue into a *status confessionis*, but in my judgment this is of very limited use, and I think the badly named 'middle axiom' method is the least bad option.)

The other new element, the ecological, appears in paragraph 26 with a brief reference to 'the need to respect the integrity of cycles of nature'. This is expanded in paragraph 34 which speaks of a growing awareness of the fact that 'one cannot use with impunity the different categories of beings whether live or inanimate – animals, plants, the natural elements – simply as one wishes according to one's own economic needs. On the contrary, one must take into account the nature of each being and of its mutual connections in an ordered system which is precisely the 'cosmos'. Behind this lies the growing ecological concern which began unsteadily with the 'Limits to Growth' controversy in the 1970s and, recovering from the inadequacies of that, has greatly developed in this decade. It is closely related to the post-Vancouver Assembly theme of the World Council of Churches, 'Justice, Peace and the Integrity of Creation'. No mention is made in SRS of either of these. Much background material is now coming from the WCC and the discussion is in danger of getting out of hand in trying to connect everything with everything else. In particular the term 'the Integrity of Creation', or 'Nature' (with a capital N), is an awkward phrase and a theological minefield. The WCC is intending to stage an international Consultation on the theme at Seoul in Korea in 1990. The Vatican has refused to co-sponsor it, but is seconding one person to work on it. SRS sheds no light on it, and the words of paragraph 34 realize issues which need exploration. In particular, the demand for an ecological theology which is not anthropocentric and for a respectful human dominion in nature is a reasonable aim but does not give any help in dealing with the problems of achieving it.

SRS talks of offering principles of reflection, criteria of judgment and directions for action (para. 3). However it does not systematically specify what these are. In this respect again it is unlike the document of the USA bishops on the economy which makes very clear what are its guidelines and from where they have come, so that one has the evidence in weighing their plausibility. In SRS 'the dignity of the human person' is explicitly one principle, criterion of judgment and direction for action. SRS refers back to *Octogesima Adveniens* but appears to draw the opposite conclusion. That letter, the best in my opinion of the documents under discussion, talks very cogently of the widely varying situations in the world and of the difficulty of uttering a unified message or putting forward universal solutions. It calls upon Christian communities in their own countries to draw up principles, norms and directives. SRS, however, clearly thinks of these as being laid down by itself and to be acted upon locally. The move is subtly done. It sets an example of the increasingly centralized tendency in the Roman Catholic Church in the last decade. It also shows how closely these documents need to be read in order to capture the nuances in them, rather like reading an editorial in *Pravda*.

Reading the Events of History

In general, SRS produces a pessimistic survey of the years since 1967. The 'development is the new name for peace' of *Populorum Progressio* has run up against the geo-political rivalries of the superpowers, and against the super-development of the rich world as against the miseries of those with little or nothing. It was always a bland slogan. The Indian economist, the late S. L. Parmar, remarked that it would be more accurate to say that revolutionary change is the new name for peace, meaning change that is rapid and decisive, not necessarily violent. In the long run SRS is optimistic about humans and their history. The text does not share the apocalyptic gloom which is about in some quarters. It speaks forthrightly against what it calls Liberal capitalism and Marxist collectivism; both are hostile to authentic human development. The treatment of Marxism is perfunctory. It says nothing that has not been said for years and pays no attention to the pluralism in Marxism, even more evident since 1967. *Glasnost* and *perestroika* have not affected the text although they have been with us since 1985. There is no hint of the possibilities opened up by John XXIII in *Pacem in Terris*.

The discussion of Liberal capitalism is much more extensive in its analysis of the last twenty years, but in the end it fudges the issue. It criticizes the 'consuming desire for profit' and the 'thirst for power' (rightly seeing some link between the two), but it does not cope with the outlook of the New Right which has had an ideological resurgence in the last decade, any more than with the introduction of elements of a market economy in China and Russia. Since competition and profits are essential to a market and neither are to be condemned on Christian grounds (and I do not think they should be), the areas where they are to operate and the social framework which sets the bounds where they are not to operate, needs indicating. This takes us back again to the political realm. A market implies the effort to maximize relatively scarce resources. It cannot do what it is meant to do if people are not trying (lawfully) to do this. Individuals or firms can not be urged to be less eager in this respect if less tender-hearted competitors are under no such restraint. Modifications to the market system must be matters of public policy involving such issues as social services, provision of open spaces, basic income provisions as well as the commonly acknowledged defence, law and order. This lack of following through an analysis also characterized Pope John Paul's first social encyclical *Laborem Exercens*. There he stressed the priority of labour over capital (which SRS also presumes) without developing its further implications. This affirms the socialist criticism of capitalism which is that it treats labour, land and capital on the same footing as factors of production, thus treating persons (labour) as things (land and capital). This is what a market does. That is why if its usefulness to humans is to be harnessed and its potential hazards neutralized it must not become the basis of an entire philosophy of human relations (as the libertarians of the New Right think). It must be put in a social framework – which makes it a servant of, and not the master over, human well-being. Failure to analyse such issues precisely leaves SRS to escape too easily into the hortatory.

No third way between Liberal capitalism and Marxist collectivism is indicated. The only detailed positive suggestion is the establishment of free trade regional co-operatives to share services, banking and monetary policies as an antidote to those of the rival super-powers; there are echoes here of the non-aligned movement. The difficulties of Third World countries in agreeing together in UNCTAD are not referred to. There is also in paragraph 43 a list of general suggestions about reform of the international trading system.

For the rest there is a good deal of what perhaps might a little unkindly be called moralism. Nations are addressed as if they could behave as individuals. (The categories of nation, state and peoples are undifferentiated.) There is a good deal on solidarity; and the responsibility of all for all is finely stressed. There is a little on the perennial conflicts which arise between groups and which cannot be neatly resolved, or how they can be handled within a concern for the common good.

The Church

What of the role of the church itself? Like many church documents it is self-congratulatory, except on one point. In discussing the duty of the church to relieve miseries and sufferings it says (para. 31): 'Faced by cases of need one cannot ignore them in favour of superfluous church ornaments and costly furnishings for divine worship; on the contrary it would be obligatory to sell these goods in order to provide food, drink, clothing and shelter for those who lack these things.' This is thinking at the level of 'ambulance work', but that is not to decry it for such work is always necessary, even if we have to go further and tackle underlying causes. But whether the alternatives present themselves in this stark way, and what are to be thought of as superfluous, are questions which suggest the challenge to the church should be more precisely posed if it is to be taken seriously. What, for example, is the Pope expecting the church of the First World to do? Is there any sign that it is doing anything of this kind? How far would it be an effective strategy if it did?

For the rest there is the usual assumption in papal documents, and often in those from other churches, that the church stands in an independent principled position apart from the causes and struggles which divide humanity. There is no recognition that it has a keen nose for its own self-interest as an institution, and therefore no exploration of how this happens and how it might be modified. We know that for centuries churches identified themselves with the kingdom of God in the New Testament. Modern biblical scholarship makes this no longer possible, but the convenient habit of thought remains. It is not easy for the church to think of herself as a 'service organization' of the people of God. A more self-critical reflection on the extent to which the church is herself part of the structures she deplores would increase her credibility. Moreover, the stress on human participation and emancipation needs to be brought to bear by the church on her own structures. There has been justified alarm in this respect in the last twenty years. No hint of these matters occurs in SRS.

Inherent Authority versus Ecclesiological Status

SRS seems to have aroused little comment in the UK. *Populorum Progressio* when first issued led to much more. Why is this? It provides a check list of most of the social issues at least as they impinge on the 'Western' world. The mood of the UK may not be disposed to attend to them. On the other hand it is not 'a good read'. It is wordy, repetitive and diffuse. At times the papal 'I' carries more force than an impersonal manner of writing; at others it becomes imprecise and hortatory at crucial points. It is hard to see how this kind of writing can fit in with the assent to non-infallible teaching of the magisterium which the CDF has recently been requiring in accordance with the position most recently stated in the Dogmatic Constitution on the Church of Vatican II, *Lumen Gentium* (para. 25), which says, 'This religious submission of will and mind must be shown in a special way to be the authentic teaching of the Roman Pontiff, even when he is not speaking *ex cathedra*. That is, it must be shown in such a way that his supreme *magisterium* is acknowledged with reverence and the judgments made by him sincerely adhered to, according to his manifest mind and will.' We recall that it was in such terms that Monsignor Lambruschini introduced *Humanae Vitae* to the world.

I do not myself think that the process behind the production of such encyclicals as SRS is a suitable way to arrive at and express church social teaching; that of the USA bishops is far better, and more in accord with *Octogesima Adveniens*. But if a way such as led to SRS is pursued, I find it hard to see how a document whose strength is in its exploratory character can be accepted in the spirit *Lumen Gentium* requires. Perhaps, as often in church history, practice does not coincide with ecclesiological theories, whereas in official church presentations it is assumed that it does.

15

Centesimus Annus: An Appraisal

This is in many ways a notable encyclical. There is too much in it for every element to be considered in this appraisal. Since it is explicitly a commemoration of the centenary of *Rerum Novarum* in May 1891, it is necessary to begin with some reference to the background and content of that encyclical. After that I give a broad conspectus of CA,[1] looking in particular at some of the basic issues it raises, before in the third section considering some further underlying issues in Christian social theology. Upon analysis CA can be seen as a discursive and somewhat repetitive document, and this may be reflected in this appraisal.

RN, as its title implies, was in many respects a new start in papal social teaching. Throughout the nineteenth century the Roman Catholic Church had been reacting against the French Revolution and its aftermath. It had seemed like a beleaguered fortress. Leo XIII was the first Pope not to have lived through those tumultuous years. Meanwhile old teaching continued, as on slavery and usury, but had no influence. A new kind of civilization based on industry was rapidly taking shape in Western Europe, a new phenomenon in human history. A new and vigorous wealth-creating class was growing which challenged the traditional, landed, hierarchical society with which the Church was allied. Status came from land, not money. Leo XIII was close to the conservative, aristocratic elements in society. How did he come to produce what is often known as the 'Workers' Charter'? One of the chief influences on him was an annual meeting of the Fribourg Union from 1885, a largely lay body which was alert to the alienation of the new working class from the church. They and he brought to their analytical task a Thomist social philosophy and theology (which Leo had recently declared official), whose hierarchical corporation and emphasis on duties rather than rights was quite opposed to the philosophical and economic individualism which accompanied tendencies to a *laissez-faire* economy. It is not cynical to say that it was because Leo was so mediaeval in outlook that he saw through the individualism of the new 'Western' culture before the leaders of any other mainstream churches. Unfortunately, however, the intellectual isolation of the papacy meant that in bringing his critique to bear on nineteenth-century capitalism he had not the necessary tools to understand precisely how it worked, a weakness which has dogged papal social and economic teaching until quite recently. A conference of economists was called at the Vatican before the issue of CA. It shows.

Nevertheless, Leo's reaction against capitalist ideology which was content to treat labour as a thing, as inert a factor of production as land and capital, as a commodity and no more, was a valid insight. It has meant that papal teaching has never accepted the philosophy of capitalism, even if its criticism has had an archaic and anachronistic air, compounded by its antipathy to socialism. I shall return to this point. In the British situation a comparable illustration is the chaotic and heterogeneous Chartist movement. One element in it was the support by some traditional élites, who were the more alert to the inhumanities of the new industrialism in its attitude to workers because the new entrepreneurial bourgeoisie were undermining their position; but they had no alternative to offer except an impractical archaism. Leo, however, took a step forward in recognizing the need for workers to organize in trade unions, since they could no longer rely on traditional élites whose duties included (at least in theory) that of protecting them.

According to Pawlikowski the main features of RN are: (1) an affirmation of the rights of private property; (2) a denial of the class struggle; (3) hostility to socialism; (4) no unqualified endorsement of capitalism; (5) a stress on the need for workers to unionize; (6) an attack on Protestantism for its individualism and undermining of political authority.[2] I make a comment on each of these here, though I shall have later to return to some of them.

1. *Private property*. Leo was particularly fearful because of the attacks on church property from the time of the French revolution, and because of the loss of the Papal States in Italy. It was perhaps because of this that he added to the traditional defence of private property in Aquinas an argument taken from John Locke, a labour theory of the appropriation of private property which makes it an absolute and untouchable right, beyond the power of the state to modify.[3] It is in fact expressed in a more extreme form by Leo than

by Locke. This has now been dropped, so that in LE John Paul II can blandly say that the Christian tradition has never [*sic*] held the rights of private property to be absolute and untouchable. This is repeated in CA.[4]

2. *The class struggle*. CA says that the denial of class struggle does not mean to deny the existence of every form of social conflict, but those in the Marxist sense of the term which exclude reasonable compromise (para. 14)

3. *Socialism*. This has been equated with Marxist socialism, what CA calls 'real Socialism'. The Vatican has not shown awareness of any other.

4. *Capitalism*. CA has come nearest to an endorsement of capitalism, partly because it shows a better understanding of the free market as an institution, but not without strong criticisms of the ideology of capitalism.

5. *Trade unions*. Support of them has been consistent, but at times it has been accompanied by an unreal separation of their industrial and political functions, disapproving of the latter. This is particularly unreal when the state is the employer.

6. *Protestantism*. This criticism has disappeared in a more ecumenical age.

What of the other features of papal social teaching between RN and CA? QA introduced explicitly the concept of 'subsidiarity'. Industrial units and economic concentrations of power had become much greater since 1891. It said that economic and political decisions should be made at the lowest level practicable for good administration. For some time many treated this with reserve, partly because as expressed in QA it seemed to support Mussolini's corporate Fascist state, with which the Vatican had recently made the Lateran Treaty.

QA's corporatism, with capital and labour joining in self-governing groups, as expressed in Italy, was controlled by the Fascist party. Subsidiarity has also been thought to be too ambiguous a concept. The Right has interpreted it as anti-socialist, and an attack on the welfare state, and on state intervention in economy, whilst the Left has preferred the term 'participation' which, indeed, is what is positively implied by subsidiarity. However, there may still be mileage in the term.

By the time of MM Vatican concern had spread far beyond that of the Western working class into a global frame of reference, and especially conditions in the Third World. The 'common good' was now seen as more fundamental than the rights of private property.

PT includes a deft reference to possible important features in Marxism despite its false philosophy (p. 58 in the CTS edition; paragraphs not numbered). PP was still more restrictive in its attitude to private property, allowing for its expropriation in certain circumstances (para. 24).[5] LE, which is unusual in style as an existentialist personalist philosophical-theological reflection on work as central to the fulfilment of the person, who through it shares in God's creativeness, stresses the priority of labour over capital (para. 12). This is what the modern Christian socialist tradition (of which the papacy has shown no awareness) has always said. CA drops this. LE goes far beyond the traditional stress on the just wage into brief references to profit-sharing, co-management and co-ownership. SRS and CA are much more concretely orientated. The market economy is the force of CA. There is a certain backtracking on the role of the state as compared with LE, in particular a distinctly negative section on the welfare state (para. 48), oddly out of keeping with the rest. I shall return to this. In addition, new themes come into SRS and CA, such as ecological issues and militarism.

Of course there is a consistency in the century 1891–1991, and the texts themselves strongly emphasize continuity in the *magisterium*. All the more interesting, therefore, are the (often subtle) changes. But perhaps the most important one is that after QA the church no longer claims to offer an alternative model of social order to capitalism and socialism; rather it offers 'an indispensable and ideal orientation' (para. 43).

I now pick out some significant features in the text of CA.

Introduction. This says that in addition to looking back on the 'new things' of RN it intends to look at what new things need to be considered today. In doing so it distinguishes between principles enunciated by Leo XIII 'which belong to the church's doctrinal patrimony and as such, involves the exercise of her teaching authority', and an analysis of current events which 'is not meant to pass definite judgments since this does not fall within the *magisterium*'s specific domain' (para. 3). This shows a caution which was not evident in 1891, but which was noticeably expressed in QA and had come out clearly in *Gaudium et Spes* (the Pastoral Constitution of Vatican II). However there are problems in this distinction to which I shall return in the third section.

Ch. 1: Characteristics of RN. CA continues the practice begun by John XXIII of including 'all men and women of good will' among those to whom it is addressed. What are we to make, then, of the statement that 'there can be no genuine solution of the "social question" apart from the gospel' (para. 5)? If by 'genuine' is meant 'ultimate', *sub specie aeternitatis*, the Christian will agree. But, as the Pope knows very well, this world must hold together in less than ultimate ways, on a basis that believers in various humanist religions and ethnic faiths can affirm. Indeed at the end of CA the hope is expressed that 'many people who profess no religion will also contribute to providing the social question with the necessary ethical foundation' (para. 60). In this setting the exclusive claim for the gospel seems a piece of thoughtless rhetoric.

On private property we have seen that CA contradicts RN, without saying so, but it does realize that Leo was influenced by landed property, and thus shows a willingness to put RN in context and not treat it as a source of timeless, authoritatively proclaimed wisdom. However, it has its own absolute statement (not a new one) when it says that the rights of the human being precede his or her incorporation into political society (para. 7); and that the individual, the family and society are prior to the state (para. 11). In my view the person cannot be isolated from the family (which CA might admit), but neither from the economic and social order nor from the state, which are all divinely instituted as the necessary structures for human flourishing, and reciprocally related to one another. The person is at first profoundly conditioned (not determined) by the structures into which he or she is born, and later becomes able in principle to exercise in turn some influence over them. The effect of the Pope's teaching is to underplay the role of the state. Nevertheless the chapter ends with the robust statement that man [sic] has 'rights which do not correspond to any work that he performs but which flow from his essential dignity as a person'. This sets the Pope firmly against 'unbridled capitalism' (para. 8) which denies what he affirms.

Ch. 2: Towards the 'New Things' of Today.   Leo is said to have arrived at the crux of the problem in defining the nature of socialism as the suppression of private property (para. 12). This is false. Socialism can mean many things, but its essence is a particular, but not exclusive, concern for equality for the sake of fraternity. CA continues the caricature of socialism, blaming it on atheism and a rationalism born of the Enlightenment. (Militarism is also blamed on atheism, showing a remarkable selectivity when one thinks of various modern states.) Of course it is 'real' or Marxist socialism that is in mind, but even so this is slipshod treatment. I have no special brief for Marxism but there is clearly more to Marxist theories than has been appropriated by CA. There is no sense in it of how Marx has transformed our way of looking at the world (as have others, of course, like Darwin and Freud).

This chapter ranges widely: war and peace, the national security state, transnational corporations, de-colonization, the consumer society, a stable currency, without having anything particularly striking to say. It does, however, maintain that the state should protect the worker against the nightmare of unemployment (para. 15; repeated para. 48), without apparently realizing how far this departs from the pure theory of the market. Paragraph 19 approves what is in effect a social market economy, modifying a free market by a public control which upholds 'the principle of the common (or universal) destination of material goods'. This is explained at the beginning of chapter 4 and seems to be a way of saying that private property must be subordinate to the common good. I am not sure.[6]

Ch. 3: The Year 1989.   The dramatic events of this year presumably overtook the drafting of CA. It rather blandly refers to the recovery by the Eastern Europeans of the 'religious roots of their national cultures' (para. 24). There is no reference to the evils of nationalism through which Europe has provoked two world wars in this century, nor of the way in which churches have found that the easiest way to be popular is by sacralizing nationalism in each country, nor to the antisemitism they have often encouraged.

In this chapter are two strong statements which could have come almost anywhere. The first is on the need to 'abandon a mentality in which the poor as individuals or as peoples are considered as a burden, as irksome intruders trying to consume what others have produced' (para. 28). The second is on sin. The doctrine of original sin 'reminds us that Man [*sic*] tends towards good, but he is also capable of evil. He can transcend his immediate interest and still remain bound to it. The social order will be all the more stable the more it takes this fact into account and does not place in opposition personal interests and the interests of society as a whole, but rather seeks to bring them into a fruitful harmony' (para. 25). This reminds me of the pungent remark of William Temple that 'the art of government in fact is the art of so ordering life that self-interest prompts what justice demands'.[7] William Temple, however, better integrated this into his social theology than CA does its thought into its social theology. It plays little part in the rest of the encyclical, except for a reference to 'structural sin' in paragraph 38.

Ch. 4: Private Property and the Universal Destination of Material Goods. There are some key passages in this chapter. It faces the fact that, globally, perhaps the majority of people are 'if not actually exploited [they] are to a great extent marginalized, economic development takes place over their heads, so to speak, when it does not actually reduce the narrow scope of their old subsistence economies' (para. 33). Nevertheless CA wisely says (contrary to much Christian opinion among international aid workers and others) that 'they should not isolate themselves from the world market and try to be self-sufficient'. But that means 'getting fair access to the international market' (para. 33), and CA does not spell out what a challenge this is to the First World, which may talk of a free market but is apt to protect itself against trade with the Third World.

On the free market CA says it is the most efficient instrument for utilizing resources and effectively responding to needs. But that is true only for those needs which are 'solvent (in so far as they are endorsed with purchasing power . . . but there are many human needs which find no place in the market. It is a strict duty of justice and truth not to allow fundamental human needs to remain unsatisfied . . .' (para. 34). The next paragraph says that the market 'needs to be appropriately controlled by the forces of society and the state so as to guarantee that the basic needs of the whole of society are satisfied. The Church acknowledges the legitimacy of profit . . . but profitability is not the only indicator of a firm's condition.' So it is 'unacceptable to say that the defeat of so-called "Real Socialism" leaves capitalism as the only form of economic organization' (para. 35). Indeed there is 'a risk that a radical capitalist ideology could spread', which 'blandly entrusts their solution [*sc.* economic problems] to the free development of market forces' (para. 42). 'Hence the answer to how to think of capitalism as the victorious economic system is complex.' If by capitalism 'is meant an economic system which recognizes the fundamental and positive role of business, the market, private property and the resulting responsibility for the means of production as well as for free human creativity in the economic sphere, then the answer is certainly in the affirmative . . . but if by capitalism is meant a system in which freedom in the economic sphere is not circumscribed with a strong juridical framework which places it in the service of human freedom in its totality . . . the roots of which are ethical and religious, then the reply is certainly negative' (para. 42). Economic freedom is only one element of human freedom (para. 39); and in this chapter CA discusses the family as the first and fundamental structure of 'human ecology'.

Ch. 5: The State and Culture.   This chapter opens with a robust endorsement of political democracy (as understood in the West): 'The Church values the democratic system in as much as it ensures the participation of citizens in making political decisions, guarantees to the governed the possibility both of electing and holding accountable those who govern them, and of replacing them through peaceful means when appropriate' (para. 46). This is as big a change from nineteenth-century teaching as was that of Vatican II on religious liberty; for in Pius IX's *Syllabus of Errors* (1863) it was said that the Church could not endorse democracy. CA goes on to say that democracy needs 'to situate particular interests within the framework of the common good. The latter is not simply the sum total of particular interests, rather it involves an assessment of integration of those interests on the basis of a balanced hierarchy of values' (para. 47). Nothing further is said about this hierarchy.

In this chapter is a strange section on 'the so-called Welfare State'. It is said that 'excesses and abuses especially in recent years, have provoked very harsh criticisms of the Welfare State, dubbed the "Social Assistance state". By intervening directly and depriving society of its responsibility, the Social Assistance State leads to a loss of human energies and an inordinate increase in public agencies . . . which are accompanied by an enormous increase in spending' (para. 46). The grain of truth in this is far outweighed by its superficiality. It is out of keeping with the rest of CA, for the welfare state seems to express precisely what the main body of CA demands.[8] This passage seems to be by a different hand. One can only surmise why it is here. My guess is that the Church wants to appear impartial in the controversies of the day by criticizing all sides. The idea of the New Right on capitalism having been so strongly criticized, a section is included which echoes its views; many wealthy and important Roman Catholics share them, particularly in the USA.

However, the chapter ends on a different note. 'To cope with the poverty of the Third World involves sacrificing the positions of income and power enjoyed by the developed economies. This may mean making important changes in established lifestyles' (para. 52). These crucial words, which surely need some filling out with suggested examples, are left in the air. SRS was just as vague.

Ch. 6: Man is the Way of the Church.   This curious title covers the claim that the Church's social teaching in the century has not been 'in order to recover former privileges or to impose her own vision' (a partly disingenuous claim), but out of concern for man [*sic*] who is 'the only creature on earth which God willed for its own sake, and for which God has his plan, that is a share in eternal life' (para. 53). I am in sympathy with this, but it is so contrary to powerful theological trends today which in one way or another subsume humans in nature that I am sorry they are ignored and the point not argued for. The chapter returns to the need, if marginalized or excluded people are to be brought into the sphere of economic and human development, for 'a change in lifestyle, modes of production and consumption, and of the established structures of power which today govern societies' (para. 58). For this to happen, 'it is necessary that there be increased co-ordination among the more powerful countries, and that in international agencies the interests of the whole human family be equally represented' (para.58). This, without an analysis of how international relations and structures of power actually work, is no more than pious talk; as if to say that if everyone behaves in a different and more radically moral way from what in human history they have always done, our problems will be solved. It is a constant temptation of the preacher to speak like this, and to imagine that he has produced thereby the Christian solution to the world's problems.

CA reflects within its continuities different philosophical and ethical approaches 1891–1991, due partly to the different personal outlooks and approaches of different popes.[9] The change in tone since 1891 is very great. The horizon is vaster, the historical consciousness greater, and the Church less triumphalist. The competence in analysis is also greater. If there are two voices, the old and the new, lying side by side in places and unreconciled (like J, E, D and P in the Pentateuch), this is the same as in many of the documents of Vatican II. No one can ignore traditional teachings, but an excessive respect for them is a hindrance to the total effect of CA. Of new things it has accepted from Vatican II are religious liberty, a greater stress on freedom and equality, and a new emphasis on participation. Its greatest weakness is its absurdly utopian picture of a new world economic order. In this respect it is the same as much recent work coming from the World Council of Churches. The two need to get together and work out more clearly the steps towards a more just and yet viable economic order, after the collapse of the Soviet-style economies with particular reference to the Third World. I am not thinking of detailed policies, but as a middle level between these noble generalities and such details.

Mentioning the WCC makes me note the lack of ecumenical input in these encyclicals. The habit of quoting only previous Popes, other documents of the *magisterium*, the Fathers, and now the occasional United Nations document, prevents an inclusion of ecumenical work. There has been a lot of it, of varying quality, and there has been considerable co-operation with Rome, especially in the decade following Vatican II, but less since then. Certain WCC themes connected with ecological issues and creation theology have been introduced into SRS and CA but are poorly integrated into the whole. It is difficult not to think that both might get on better if they worked more together.

Allied with this is the lack of criticism of the church itself. For instance, the 1971 Synod of Bishops in Rome was the first occasion on which the need for justice in the Church itself was mentioned. I do not think it has appeared since. It is vital to move away from the view of the Church as the impartial teacher of humanity, immune from any vested interests, and able to administer friendly correction from a superior stance to all.

Is CA too European-orientated ? Clearly the events of 1989 have dominated the preparation of it. In May 1991 the Justice and Peace Commission held a conference in Rome to celebrate the centenary of RN and launch CA. Those from the Third World tended to criticize it as irrelevant to their problems of an economic order as do the de-Sovietized countries and those of the wealthy West. This is strikingly the case in Latin American countries, as they are being liberated from 'National Security' authoritarian governments. What the Third World chiefly needs is more economic power. CA sees this, but says no more.

The more scriptural approach to social theology since Vatican II as against a 'natural law' approach has advantages and disadvantages. In practice, it seems to have added to the confusion between speaking to all men and women of good will and making an exclusive claim for the gospel. It need not. It depends on how the gospel is read. But certainly an approach to the world on the basis of the challenge of *human* (which is a better natural law approach) appears to be the more promising one.

In conclusion I return to the difference between authoritative principles propounded by the magisterium and the concrete analysis it offers without claiming a special authority for them (para. 3). There is also the statement near the end of CA that the authoritative teaching 'enters into dialogue with the various disciplines concerned with man [*sic*]. It assimilates what these disciplines have to contribute and helps them to open themselves to a broader horizon' (para. 59). Is not this a little simple? What are the principles? The one most often quoted is 'the dignity of man', or of the 'person'. (Sinfulness, as we have seen, comes in one important passage, not integrated in the rest.) This dignity is a corollary of Christian theology, but it is shared by others, on less deep grounds; but fortunately so, or the world would find it hard to hold together at all. This needs exploring. Also it now needs to be related to the theologies of nature at present being advanced. Another principle appears to be 'the common destination of materials goods'. What is its meaning and how far is it, too, shared by others?

There is also the further point that one cannot simply assimilate the work of the various disciplines concerned with 'man'. SRS made the same assumption, that the work of human sciences would fit in with what the Church teaches. But behind every study of the human are basic assumptions about the nature and destiny of persons in the light of which 'facts' are seen and assessed. Sometimes these assumptions are 'secular' in a non-Christian sense, and it is necessary to be alert to this. But this does not mean that we need to have a separate Christian economics or sociology or political philosophy or whatever, which others could not accept. Fortunately Christian beliefs about persons can be held on less than Christian grounds. The fact that Christians affirm that Christ died for us gives a deeper weight to what can be affirmed by others. Moreover it is possible that work in the human sciences may call in question elements of a traditional Christian understanding of the person (homosexuality is an example). Traditional theology was reluctant to allow a certain autonomy to first the natural, and then the human, sciences. Modern theology, having allowed this, must not endorse what they say without scrutinizing their assumptions. Getting the balance right is not easy, and it is more complex than SRS and CA allow for.

16

Veritatis Splendor: A Comment

I write with some diffidence and sadness. I write with diffidence because the encyclical is directed towards a conflict which has divided the Roman Catholic Church for more than thirty years, and in which highly skilled theologians and philosophers have been engaged; as an outsider I tread warily, conscious of running the risk of being faulted, a risk which I must take. I write with sadness because many outstanding Roman Catholic moral theologians, some of them valued friends, from whom I have learned much over the years, are now having the weight of papal authority employed against them.

Intellectual argument in theology and other disciplines does not take place in a vacuum. In this case it has been related to an internal power struggle involving the position of the Curia, and externally to the negative attitude of the official Roman Catholic authority to other churches. This encyclical is an attempt to recover from the disaster of *Humanae Vitae* and, although contraception is mentioned only twice in it (47,80), it cannot be understood without reference to the background of that encyclical and its reception. It is here I must begin.

Before Vatican II there had been growing pressure in the church for a revision of traditional teaching on contraception. At the Council John XXIII removed it from the agenda in March 1963 and appointed a papal commission to deal with it. In March 1965 a majority voted in favour of a change (15–4). The minority said it could not defend the traditional teaching on natural law arguments, but held it should be maintained on the authority of tradition focussed in the papacy. In May 1966 the minority produced a crucial Working Paper which included these words. 'If contraception were not declared intrinsically evil, in honesty it would have to be acknowledged that the Holy Spirit in 1930, in 1951 and 1958, assisted Protestant churches, and that for half a century Pius XI, Pius XII and a great part of the Catholic hierarchy did not protest against a very serious error, one most pernicious to souls, for it would be suggested that they condemned most imprudently, on the pain of eternal punishment, thousands upon thousands of human acts which are now approved.' It went on to point out that the Encyclical *Casti Connubii* was solemnly issued in 1930 against the report of the Lambeth Conference of Anglican bishops that year in its reference to contraception, and said, 'Is it nevertheless now to be admitted that the Church erred in this its work and that the Holy Spirit now assists the Anglican Church?' It added that the traditional teaching could not be changed because of changing historical conditions, for the Anglican Church was teaching precisely that, and for the very reasons which the Catholic Church solemnly denied.[1]

When I read this I realized that the Roman Catholic Church would not officially alter its teaching. True, authoritative papal teaching has been subsequently changed, for instance on slavery, or freedom of conscience, but in this case Rome would not bring themselves to face a change, and so it proved. I hoped that there would be a delay, that the issue would be left unresolved for the present and nothing said officially. Not so. The Pope rejected the report of his Commission, and *Humanae Vitae* maintained on papal authority the traditional teaching (whilst making an important change in upgrading the relational aspect of marriage with respect to the procreational). When introducing the encyclical to the press, Monsignor Lambruschini said that while it was not infallible 'there is also loyal and full assent, interior and not only exterior, to an authentic pronouncement of the *magisterium* in proportion to the level of authority from which it emanates – which in this case is the supreme authority of the Supreme Pontiff – and its object, which is most weighty . . .', and that 'the authentic pronouncement of the *Humanae Vitae* encyclical prevents the forming of a probable opinion, that is to say an opinion acting on the moral plane, in contrast with the pronouncement itself . . .'. In spite of this there was a widespread explosion of dissent within the church, as is well known, and it has shown no signs of abating. Its central conclusion did not follow from the arguments advanced. They depended on papal authority. *Veritatis Splendor* is the long awaited attempt to recover the official position. The upshot is the same; the official position depends on papal authority. I will refer in a moment to the dispute at the level of practical reasoning. At the level of authority it concerns that of the ordinary, non-infallible *magisterium*. The doctrine of the infallible *magisterium*, which at first seems clear and definite, becomes hazy on closer inspection. There has never been an infallible statement on a moral matter, and perhaps there never will be. So many authoritative statements on moral matters in the past have been abandoned. (Two have already been mentioned. Others include: usury; that all heathens, Jews and heretics and schismatics go to hell unless converted to Catholicism; that the burning of heretics is in accordance with the Holy Spirit; and that co-education is erroneous and pernicious.) Most of these would come within Mgr Lambruschini's category of weighty.

The authority of the ordinary *magisterium* is being strongly stressed. Huge claims for it are made in *Veritatis Splendor*, such that dissent from it is practically ruled out. Moreover, this *magisterium* is being confined to the Pope and his advisers and not to the bishops as a whole (113). This encyclical is addressed to the bishops. This goes against much in Vatican II. The encyclical says that in it the *magisterium* is setting forth for the first time in detail the fundamental elements of Christian moral teaching, restated with the authority of the successor of St Peter (115).

I leave this aside, as an internal issue for the Roman Catholic Church, and turn to the general moral reasoning within *Veritatis Splendor*, with which its authoritative tendency is buttressed. This focusses on intrinsically evil acts, which are always wrong, apart from intention and circumstances, on account of their object (115). I think it fails in four respects.

1. The examples it gives (80) of intrinsically evil acts from *Gaudium et Spes* are unconvincing; mostly they do not define acts in the abstract, but with the circumstances or conditions which make them evil. (And slavery is included which, as already mentioned, Popes approved for centuries, until well into the last.)

2. The New Testament texts it chiefly relies on, Romans 3.8 and I Corinthians 6.9ff., do not require the interpretation the Pope puts on them. Also its stress on universal exceptionless negative prohibitions ignores Matthew 5.34 on swearing. So, far from regarding this as intrinsically evil, the church has required it.

3. Since there is nothing in Revelation about contraception, apart from papal authority, there is only practical reason to call upon; it comes within natural law thinking because we can reason about it. Here St Thomas Aquinas does not, as I see it, support the Pope, as is claimed. The ten commandments are unalterably right about what is just, but what can alter are the criteria which decide in particular cases whether this or that is murder, adultery or theft. (S.T.1-2, qu.100,ad.8).

4. The Pope misunderstands the position of two main opposing positions which he attacks.

(i) He says proportionalists maintain that a good intention can justify an evil act. In fact they ask *whether* an act is morally wrong, considering all the circumstances.

(ii) He says that those who talk of a person's 'fundamental option' for or against God, maintain that this could be wholly independent of their moral choices. In fact, because they were uneasy with the traditional teaching that one unrepented mortal sin could result in eternal damnation, those who write of the 'fundamental option' have been concerned with the fundamental stance of the person, seen as a process towards or away from God, not based on a single act but not wholly divorced from it either.

It is hard to see how a timeless, a-historical act can be adequately described and established as intrinsically evil on the basis of practical reason. One can think of acts which are virtually prohibited without exception (and contraception is not one of them) but that is different from an intrinsically evil act. So the authority of the ordinary *magisterium* is brought in to enforce the conclusion. 'While recognizing the possible limitations of the human arguments employed by the *magisterium* . . .', moral theologians are required to give it loyal assent, both internal and external (110). This is the core position of the encyclical.

In it the Pope has other and easier targets; for example, against those who say that God has not revealed to us any moral requirements (37); against social scientists who say that moral values and the decisions of individuals are no more than the product of different cultures (33); against those who say that a statistical study of human behaviour and moral beliefs is an adequate ground for morality (46). He begins with a sermon on Jesus and the rich young man. But these are ancillary to the main target. In these parts the Pope makes fundamental claims for Christian faith and ethics, and delineates the parlous state of modern humans without it, which would come better if there were an acknowledgment of the serious evils which have flourished under the aegis of the church, such as antisemitism, slavery, the oppression of women, colonialism, and arrogance towards other faiths.

Veritatis Splendor will not end the debate. Those who are not Roman Catholics will not accept the inflated claims for the ordinary *magisterium* which are a considerable hindrance ecumenically. But large numbers of Roman Catholics will also not accept it. I hope the debate will continue in public. After the publication of *Humani Generis* in 1950 many eminent Roman Catholic theologians, like Congar, were silenced, and then subsequently rehabilitated at Vatican II, even becoming advisers to it. This time I hope dissentients are far too numerous to be silenced.

17

Theology and the Economy: The Roman Catholic Bishops in the USA

The Reagan and Thatcher administrations are so similar in their ideology that a major statement on the economy of the USA by the Roman Catholic bishops of that country is of interest in the UK. It is also of wider significance because of the manner of its production and because of its method.

The Canadian Roman Catholic bishops had issued a short statement in 1982 on the economy of that country,[1] whilst in the USA the bishops, who had already decided to prepare one, postponed it until they had completed in 1983 another major pastoral letter, on issues of war and peace in the nuclear age.[2] The first draft of the economic letter was published in November 1984 and the final draft in November 1986.[3] It is entitled *Economic Justice For All: Catholic Social Teaching and the US Economy*, runs to about 53,000 words divided into 365 paragraphs, and concludes with eight pages of detailed references to church documents and secular sources. The drafting committee of five bishops, chaired by Archbishop Weakland of Milwaukee, had 32 days of hearings involving over 200 witnesses from different confessional traditions and of different experience and expertise. A three-year follow-up plan has been agreed upon to propagate its message.

What is the nature and authority of the document? The basis of the teaching is held to be in line with the general approach of Roman Catholic social teaching, especially since the encyclical *Rerum Novarum* of 1891.[4] On the other hand, it says that the movement from principles to policy is complex and difficult, and that the particular analysis of the US economy and the recommendations are to be taken as at the level of prudential teaching; their soundness will depend on the accuracy of the information and the validity of the assumptions which lie behind the text (para. 134). Archbishop Weakland has expressed the hope that it will be a catalyst for a longer process of reflection together on the meaning of discipleship today, using the resources available through modern means of communication, and adding that it has enabled the bishops to perform their role as moral teachers in a unique way.[5]

This point is important. The method that the bishops have adopted in preparing this and their previous statement is a new and welcome one in the Roman Catholic Church. It takes seriously the point made by Pope Paul VI in the Apostolic Letter *Octogesima Adveniens* that in widely varied situations in the world it is difficult to issue from Rome 'solutions' which have universal validity, and that it is 'up to the Christian communities to analyse the situation which is proper to their own country – and to draw principles of reflection, norms of judgment and directives for action from the social teaching of the Church'.[6] Indeed it takes the point more seriously than the Vatican itself has done since 1971. The procedure of the American bishops has been (1) to hear relevant evidence; (2) to issue drafts for public discussion and comment, saying in effect 'This is what we are thinking of saying and we shall be glad to receive reactions before we finalize it'; and (3) in the final version carefully to clarify the extent of the claims to authority made by it, and invite ongoing reflection. Whether it is wise, or necessary in the Roman Catholic context, to confine the drafting to bishops is a further question, but for them it is an open and hard-working way by which to exercise leadership.

The internal method of the document itself is of general significance. There are four steps; it begins from the Bible, goes on to moral philosophy and then to traditional church social teaching, and fourthly engages in rational reflection on the current situation.

1. Beginning from the Bible is relatively new in Roman Catholic documents and is a sign of the ecumenical times, but raises problems in a document which is intended to appeal to all persons of goodwill (para. 27), but which are eased for the bishops by an assumption which will be mentioned under point two. It is better than bringing in odd texts of the Bible, often taken out of context, to support positions arrived at on other grounds. The question of *how* to use the Bible is not explicitly discussed, but we are left to understand how the bishops think it should be done by the way they do it. It is possible to query a point here and there but I do not think they can be seriously faulted. From the Bible they arrive at a basic criterion for assessing economic life, the dignity of the human person in

community with others. They spell this out in more detail under three headings, Creation, Covenant and Community, in the following way:

(1) Creation in the Old Testament leads to the concept of stewardship, and in relation to a Covenant people which, beginning with Israel, expanded after the Exile and in the New Testament to include all peoples.

(2) New Creation in the New Testament means a new Covenant with a new Community, and the note of solidarity.

(3) Solidarity leads to a concern for the neighbour, and the concern must include justice for him or her.

(4) Justice is measured especially by the treatment of the poor and powerless; in the Old Testament the prophets were on their side and in the New Testament Jesus is. The conclusion is drawn that the church should show the same solidarity with the disadvantaged, and in doing so confront *structural and institutional injustice* (my italics).

2. The bishops say that in the Bible justice is more comprehensive than in subsequent philosophical definitions (para. 39).[7] They discuss justice in the familiar categories of moral philosophy and add the term *contributive* justice (para. 71). By this they mean that all should make a contribution to the common good but in order to do so they must be put in a position by the community where they have the means to do so. The bishops can make this smooth transition from the Bible to moral philosophy because they assume that what the Bible and the Christian church teach conform to what human wisdom independently arrives at. This is, of course, a common assumption in Catholic ethics but it is open to question. There is a note of radical eschatological paradox in the most distinctive strain in Jesus' teaching on the kingdom of God and the ethics appropriate to it which is not what common-sense ethical and philosophical reflection would arrive at. The church has had so much difficulty with this that she has found various ways of domesticating it. What difference would an awareness of it have made to the specific recommendations of the bishops? I am not sure, but later I make one point in this connection.

3. The bishops remark that the tradition of Catholic social thought is dynamic and growing (para. 26). It is an important point when there is often a tendency to stress how unchanging and perpetually adequate it has been. The bishops give extensive references to support their claim, and in particular the influence of the meetings of the Latin American episcopate at Medellin in 1968 and Puebla in 1979 is clearly seen. From the tradition the bishops draw in particular two concepts:

(1) The Common Good. This is defined as 'the sum of those conditions of social life which allow social groups and their individual members relatively thorough and ready access to their own fulfilment'.[8]

(2) Subsidiarity, according to which it is 'an injustice ... for a larger and higher association to arrogate to itself functions which can be performed efficiently by smaller and lower societies' (para. 99).[9] They point out that this does *not* mean that a government which governs least governs best (para. 121). The Bishops also want to draw upon Protestant social teaching, remarking that it has a strong emphasis 'on the vocation of lay people in the world'; and also upon ecumenical efforts 'to develop an economic ethic that addresses newly emergent problems' (para. 59). Unfortunately they give no references to either point.

4. On the rational reflection on general desiderata in the economic order, as distinct from detailed recommendations, I give some examples of the approach of the document.

(1) There is a section on human rights, not confined to civil and political rights but including economic and welfare ones as well. These include the right to life, food, clothing, shelter, rest, medical care, basic education, healthful working conditions, the possibility of property ownership, and a wage in keeping with human dignity (para. 80).

(2) Positive action is required to create social and political institutions that enable all persons to become active members of society (para. 82).

(3) The economy is not a machine that operates according to its own inexorable laws, and persons are not mere objects tossed about by economic forces (para. 96).

(4) Collectivism is rejected, in the sense of a centralized statism, and so is the notion that the free market automatically produces justice; the socialization of certain means of production cannot be excluded, as Pope John Paul II said in his Encyclical *Laborem Exercens* (para. 155).

(5) The way society responds to the needs of the poor through its public policies is the litmus test of its justice or injustice (para. 120).

(6) Full employment is the foundation of a just economy (para. 136).

(7) Stress on the inescapably social and political nature of the economy (para. 313).

(8) The need for overall economic planning, but not in highly centralized structures (para. 315).

Armed with these teachings the bishops subject major aspects of the US economy – employment, poverty, food and agriculture, and the relation of the economy to that of the developing nations – to a detailed investigation which I do not pursue here. Apart from the fact that the US economy is very much more powerful than that of the UK, the general picture is similar to what analysis of the UK situation would produce. To take two examples, (1) it is shown that one in seven of Americans are poor by the Government's own definition of poverty, and (2) 50% of the financial assets of the country are held by 2% of the families. The bishops state that an unemployment rate of 7–8% is quite unacceptable; in the UK where in 1979 one million unemployed was thought to be intolerable it is now being seen by some as a triumph for the Government if by various policies and statistical devices it can get the total to just below three million, or some 11–13%. In their first draft the bishops set a target of 3–4%, very similar to what Beveridge in 1942 envisaged for the UK, but in later texts they have not specified a precise figure.

The particular economic criteria the bishops arrive at from their biblical-philosophical-traditional church teaching basis, and in the light of which they assess the US economy, lead them to stress the active participation of all citizens in economic and social institutions, and that if this is to be achieved particular attention has to be given to the basic needs of the marginalized, especially in respect of investment and employment policies. These should be designed to ensure that no one is hungry, homeless or unemployed. So long as any one is, there is a presumption against existing inequalities of wealth and income.

Archbishop Weakland sums up the general tenor of the document in the words: 'Our document could be called "reformist" in that it suggests that we should stimulate the best energies of the capitalist system but also continue to transform it for the benefit of all.'[10]

Critical reaction has come largely from the 'New Right'. The political Left has generally welcomed it. It has in fact criticized the document for ignoring the problems of population growth in many parts of the world; but, apart from the pros and cons of the issue, Vatican official policy is so tied to the position taken up in the encyclical *Humanae Vitae* that the US bishops could hardly go against it even if some, or many, would privately like to do so. Those who oppose it have to find other means of minimizing or undermining it. Apart from this, criticisms from the Left are that it does not go as far as *Laborem Exercens* (which is true); or, and naively, that it does not advocate the replacement of the profit motive, or denounce capitalism as 'inherently exploitive'.[11]

Critics on the Right have been numerous, beginning with an unofficial Lay Commission on *Catholic Social Thought and the US Economy*, which was co-chaired by William Smith, a former Secretary of the Treasury. It was made up of 27 conservatively inclined members, 17 of them chief executives of major business corporations. It tried to upstage the first draft of the bishops' letter by publishing its report one day ahead. Several of its members had given evidence to the bishops. Their report draws upon the same tradition of Catholic social thought but to arrive at broadly 'New right' conclusions.

Since then a number of reasoned criticisms of the bishops' document have appeared. For those I have seen I have analysed the main points of criticism.[12] The general line is that what the bishops advocate is a rehash of failed policies which are inherently unworkable. Behind this is a disagreement on the criteria by which the Bishops work, as being inimical to the freedom of the individual which is taken to be the supreme value; for instance the concept of the common good is said to be an infringement of individuality. Five main lines of criticism emerge.

1. What the bishops purport to draw from the Bible, and especially the gospels, is really drawn from the secular Enlightenment. In any case the Bible operates with a family model which provides no model for an economic order. This is more of a Protestant criticism, especially from a Lutheran background which tends to make a sharp separation between the two kingdoms, of church and of political authority. To my mind the biblical exegesis basically holds. However, it is true that it was a long time before the church interpreted its biblical heritage in quite this way, and that post-Enlightenment influences have helped it to be aware of aspects to which it previously had given too little attention or ignored. Yet the bishops deliberately do not derive a model economic order from the Bible. If they had emphasized more the radically eschatological element in New Testament ethics, as I mentioned earlier, this might have been clearer to the critics.

2. Government is fundamentally coercive. It must be limited to abstract and impersonal rules; otherwise it becomes prey to special interest groups. It should be realized that governments cannot solve all social problems; and that they themselves can be a threat to human

dignity. This criticism draws heavily upon the thought of Mises, Hayek, Nozick and Friedman. I have recently discussed it elsewhere[13] and will not repeat myself here. The danger of the totalitarian state has proved a real one in this century, and there is a strong legacy of ecumenical social thought on the matter dating from the era of Fascism, Nazism and Stalinism and best expressed in the Oxford Conference of 1937 on *Church, Community and State*.

3. Justice is involved in procedures and not in outcomes. Otherwise we shall be driven to a minutely detailed centrally-planned economy. An open society with private property and markets is a better realization of the Christian gospel of freedom than a coerced morality. The bishops' proposals will not achieve what they want and will generate problems more serious than the ones they are addressing. However, to set up a free market and a totally planned economy as polar opposites and to maintain that we must have one or the other is absurd. The stages in between are untidy as compared with the unambiguity of the extremes, but it is precisely the in-between area which politics in Western democracies is concerned with. To take just one example, a study of the Swedish economy is instructive. In any case the Christian gospel is not one of individual freedom but of *koinonia*, the New Testament word for freedom-in-community.

4. The bishops do not understand the role of the market, with its relative process, in providing the information necessary for the working of an efficient economy. They think capitalism is a selfish struggle and socialism a mutual sharing. Also they are preoccupied with the distribution of wealth and ignore the need to create it. This criticism sets up economic efficiency as the key value, an assumption that needs challenging, as I shall shortly mention. The bishops are in fact saying that capitalism unchecked can produce a selfish struggle. They do not discuss socialism, except to repudiate centralized collectivism. Their point about wealth applies to whatever level there is of it in society;[14] and they show themselves well aware of the creativity of the US economy.

5. Church teaching should remain at the level of ends and not get embroiled in means. That there are problems here is not to be denied. But churches are driven to try to get beyond ethical generalizations so lacking in specificity that no one can object to them because they have no bite. Hence the need to study the possibility of arriving at some middle level of ethical recommendation, between the general and the detailed, indicating the directions in which in a particular context policies should aim. In most cases detailed recommendations

are subject to so many uncertainties that they are unlikely to command general assent and are not suitable for 'official' church teaching. This is another theme I have discussed elsewhere.[15]

Explicit in many of these criticisms is an idealization of the free market. Economic efficiency, in the sense of maximizing the output of relatively scarce resources, is set up as the supreme value, and then it is maintained that any modification of the structure which prevents each citizen of working age from individually following the haggling of the market will produce less than maximum efficiency. Hence it is alleged that any such interference is inherently contradictory. Moreover it will end in a totally centralized economy. Indeed in this literature the free market is referred to as an immutable principle, like the law of gravity. One writer sees the hand of God at work in it as an invisible hand in the 'pure, pristine beauty of the market place'. This is accompanied by a hostile attitude to politics, if seen as the arena where who gets what, when, and how is decided. It is not seen as a fundamental area of human responsibility, where the complex mixture of conflicting human ideals and interests have to engage in give and take in the public forum, and establish provisionally tolerable policies which enable the political-economic process to continue within the parameter of the criterion of justice as fairness.

On the economic side the free market should I think be seen as an 'ideal type', a concept made familiar to us in the early years of this century by the sociologist Max Weber. The market is a very useful human construction for certain human purposes but there is nothing immutable about it. In its pure theoretical form it is a highly artificial concept, depending upon a series of assumptions which are rarely, if ever, completely fulfilled. It ignores the organic relations between human beings in its unrealistic, atomistic individualism. It also ignores the fact that economic and power relationships are closely connected, and that politically the owners and managers of capital will always be trying to bend the free market to their interests, and are pretty successful in doing so, with or without the collusion of government. The individual owners of labour who are much less powerful, will do likewise if they can organize themselves collectively to do so. Professional associations do the same.

It is depressing that this unreal picture of the free market should be brought out as the latest wisdom. The reality and the rhetoric of it are very different, whether in Reagan's USA or Thatcher's UK. One wonders how much in the case of its advocates is deception and how much self-deception. Theologically speaking, when conceived ideologically it is contrary to the doctrine of person-in-community, both in creation and in the new creation in Christ. The basic starting point of the US bishops is quite right.[16]

On two points I wish the bishops had gone further. They could have examined more closely the model of the human person in society latent in the philosophy of capitalism and compared it with their own. And I wish they had examined the problem of bringing rational thought to bear on a political and economic analysis of society. They do not indicate how hard it is to overcome ideological influences and achieve objectivity. It is as hard for Christians as it is for others, though Christians should be alert to it. This means that the achieving of even a broad consensus, let alone a detailed one, is not easy. In British political terms it means that the bishops' letter can be broadly acceptable, though in different degrees, and bring illumination to a spectrum from Tory 'wets' leftwards, but not to Tory 'drys'. In the USA the latter will be a much more numerous element in the population than in the UK, and many of them will be Christians, and indeed Roman Catholics. The bishops could have sharpened thought under the umbrella of Roman Catholic social teaching by asking questions put to each side of these two positions by proponents of the other. Then working with the one they adopt they could have brought out more clearly the economic implications or trade-offs of the line of policy they recommend, in terms of hard choices and structures. They do at times tend to take refuge in the need for changing personal attitudes; necessary as this is it is only half the problem.

The bishops have produced a noble document. The ecumenical consensus of those in the churches who have most intensively and competently studied these issues is strongly with them and against the New Right. It is not hard to confute the latter theologically; at the level of economic and political analysis different arguments are needed to refute the charge that what the bishops propose is inherently unworkable. It is a pity that in their final text they do not explicitly anticipate this charge, make use of expert evidence, advance boldly into the economic-political field, and address themselves to it.

Part V

Christianity and Political and Economic Issues

18

The Common Good

The Common Good is a phrase which trips lightly off the tongue. It has deep roots in the Classical-Christian culture of European thought. It is referred to in the United Nations Declaration of Human Rights of 1948, where Article 14, Sections 1 and 2 guarantees private property and the rights of inheritance, whilst saying its use should serve the common good. It occurs in the suggested form of intercessions at the eucharist in the Alternative Service Book of the Church of England (1980), 'give wisdom to all in authority, and direct this and every nation in the ways of justice and of peace, that men [sic] may know one another and seek the common good'. It figures in the titles of a number of theological and philosophical books in this century, such as Jacques Maritain's *The Person and the Common Good* (1943). Until recently I had rather easily taken it for granted, though I knew of course that it had been questioned, particularly in the Marxist tradition, according to which there can be no common good, only class interests, prior to the communist utopia. But as I consider Marxist theories to be seriously flawed, they did not disturb my easy acceptance of the concept. What shook me was the negative attitude to it taken by my friend John Atherton in his recent study, *Christianity and the Market* (1993). Since reading it I have felt the need to clear my mind on the matter, and the invitation to give this year's Hartley Lecture has provided me with an occasion to do so, for which I am grateful.

It is clear that the concept has many other critics besides John Atherton. It is a fundamental question whether the concept of the common good points to a profound necessity for the flourishing of human society, or a bland notion which Christians and others have too glibly accepted. Christians have often had a *penchant* for assuming that an ideal concept can be realized in the structures of society if only everyone behaves with good will to everyone else. Countless sermons reflect this attitude. Since there is no society in which this has happened, and we have good reason to suppose it never will, the concept in this exposition never touches reality. So is the common good a profound and necessary concept or little more than pious waffle? That is my theme. I turn now to three challenges to the concept, beginning with John Atherton.

The main theme of John Atherton's book is to stress the importance of the market in the economic order, which he argues (rightly in my opinion) has been underplayed and misunderstood in much Christian social theology since the seminal work of Adam Smith on it on the one side and Frederick Denison Maurice on the other. Here are some of the points he makes. Much Christian social thought has been suspicious of the market and in favour of the common good because the market exalts selfishness. (Here he rightly is drawing attention to much confusion in Christian thinking on the place of self interest in human life.) Yet the common good stifles the dynamics of the market, a dynamic which is necessary if human beings are to flourish in making best use of their relatively scarce resources in producing goods and services. 'The commitment to the common good overrides legitimate claims of self interest, and reduces the potential for dynamic change, reducing the market to the position of a servant mechanism' (p. 199). He quotes some words of Reinhold Niebuhr (as quoted by Michael Novak), 'There is no one society good or wise enough finally to determine how the individual's capacities had best be used for the common good' (p. 220). Atherton says that the Christian stress on communitarian values and the virtues of interdependence and the common good ignores the vital importance of self-help and individualism without which the common good would be valueless and highly restrictive of personal development (p. 220); he also argues positively that 'market economies promote modern civic virtues through responsible economizing'. Contrary to this 'the common good with its overtones of undue political interference with economic life and private choice may no longer be an appropriate concept for Christian social thought' (p. 250). The individual pursuit of self-chosen ends suggests the encouragement of a plurality of ends which is not (he infers) what the common good fosters (p. 256). It cannot reflect the changing complexities of an increasingly plural world, for it is too static. So the concept 'must be forgone if we are to do justice to the market economy'. The promotion of political and economic liberties does not suggest a homogeneous society expressed through concepts like the common good (p. 274).

I was startled when I read these remarks of Atherton because it had not occurred to me that the concept of the common good was necessarily static and discouraged pluralism. So we need to ask what is meant by it, and how it has been, and can be used. And as one who is an advocate of a market economy (within a firm political framework), I was surprised by the moral claims Atherton makes for it. True, it depends on certain moral stabilities in human life, but it does not directly promote them, and by themselves they are insufficient for wholesome human living. This, however, is not the focus of my present concern. I part company with Atherton when he carries his libertarian thought so far as to give priority to the market over the political authority, and says that to give the political authority priority is to treat the market as a servant mechanism. In my view that is what it is, a human creation for human purposes, depending on a firm framework which must be established by political authority (predominantly the state), without which it will be carried away to inhuman excesses. How extensive that framework should be is a main theme of contemporary political argument. At least we know from the collapse from within of the Soviet economy, that an overwhelmingly political control of the economic order will not do. Yet although we cannot survive without an economic order, a political order is prior. Without it there is anarchy.

I turn now to another attack on the common good, this time from an acute French Reformed theologian, André Dumas in his *Political Theology and the Life of the Church* (1977). He says that the common good appears similar to a biblical social ethic with its stress on the family, and on inter-personal solidarity, and that we need one another and need to break down oppositions and divisions. But the concept is too optimistic in thinking that a given society has a common object which calls for unquestioning obedience. (Notice that the introduction of the word 'unquestioning' is unfortunate, for there is no necessity for the common good to require that.) In fact, says Dumas, it has blessed an hierarchy of functions as a necessity of earthly society, and urges those who suffer from it that earthly troubles need a heavenly remedy from God, who cares for them; the rich should be generous and the poor patient. The common good is an indigestible mixture of courageous and profound spiritual truths with a reverent resignation over natural and social inequalities. It *either* assumes a stable society in this world and retribution in the next, thus justifying the present privileges of conservatives, *or* serves as a slogan for those who want to be middle of the road. At this point I add the comment that this is particularly congenial to churches who, if they do not support the status quo (which has been their general tendency because of their dependence on the absolutely or relatively well-to-do), like to make critical comments to all parties and groups in controversies over current public issues, as if they operate from an entirely independent position *au dessus de la mêlée*. They do this because they fear internal controversies among their congregations (as well as pressures from the powerful among those they may criticize). Dumas concludes that the common good must be seen as the possible outcome of conflicts, not as the prohibition of them, nor as a seal of approval for the status quo. He points out that the Bible is full of conflicts within the fratriarchy with which it deals, and from it we need to learn to live as brothers within the conflicts which arise in both Christian and secular communities. I agree here with Dumas' basic position, and I shall return to it.

A third attack on the common good comes from post-modernist thought, which is so taken by the conditioned and contextual factors in human life and thought that it asserts that humans have no overall language, values or rationality. It says that our various points of view are each based on a language game, which itself is based on a prior commitment. Each language is a closed system of signs. We can never go outside the system of signs. There is nowhere to appeal, no reality to which these languages point. The common good has no intelligible place in human discourse. Indeed even to speak of 'the human' can be labelled as euro-centric! Some Christian theologians and philosophers have accepted the substance of this position and used it to exalt the exclusiveness (as well as the centrality) of the Christian community. Alasdair MacIntyre's *After Virtue* (1981), the first and most extreme of an influential trilogy, maintains that our society has no shared moral first principles (p. 263). He and the theologian Stanley Hauerwas have stressed the vital importance of Christian nurture in church communities, where the vision of the good life, and the virtues of loyalty, honesty and compassion can be taught and incarnated. The stress is on the gulf between these communities and any of the others in which human beings are fostered. Hauerwas pays little attention to Christian civic responsibilities in plural societies. He concentrates on what is distinctively Christian, and would regard a concept like the common good as a relatively unimportant social generality.

It is not possible in the present discussion to consider in any detail the post-modernist position. I regard it as an over-reaction to the static forms of thinking, including theological thinking, and the understanding of the conception of rationality itself, which was endemic in the thinking of the European tradition before Marx taught us to be awake to conditioning factors in human thought. (Marx and Marxism both move uncertainly between conditioning and determining factors; the latter produces self contradictions.) We now know it is always relevant to ask, for example, of any theology, such questions as: 'In whose interest is it taught?' 'What are the interests of those who teach it?' 'Who consumes it and what are their interests?' Such questions do not dissolve it into nothingness, leaving no reminder, but they are capable of throwing light upon it. Yet to carry such questions too far is to cut off the bough on which one is sitting.

There are also positive arguments for the common good, which do not depend on Christianity but are consonant with it. John Rawls advances one in his *A Theory of Justice* (1971). The common good would represent the social arrangements which would be chosen by a rational person in a state of ignorance as to what his position in society would turn out to be, and which, if he were to be among the least privileged, would be in his interests. This is a very individualistic account of the common good. It assumes citizens have no duties to one another except by contract. It is predominantly a procedural understanding of the common good. It covers the rule of law, and defence against aggression, together with what economists call externalities, that is to say costs which apply to everyone but cannot be charged to individuals because their consumption is essentially communal.

However, while I cannot see that Rawls and post-modernism rules out this minimal conception of the common good, it seems to me too thin. It ignores the extent to which human beings are essentially social, so that one might expect them to arrive at some civic obligations beyond merely non-interference with others, some common purposes and common responsibilities for the various foreseeable, as well as for the unforeseen and unintended, events of life. This raises the question whether there is a natural morality common to human beings (which the Christian faith may well transfigure and take further). It is time to turn from attacks on the common good, which I do not think decisive, to an exposition of it.

As I have mentioned, the roots of the conception of the common good go back to both classical Greece, especially Aristotle's teaching that human life is fulfilled in the *polis*; and also, as far as the state goes, to strains in biblical teaching such as that of St Paul, who in

Romans 13.4 enthusiastically endorses the Roman empire on the ground that governments are ordained by God for the common good. Later, St Augustine's exposition of the two cities, the earthly and the heavenly, in his *City of God* explored the relationship between them, and gives a position role to the earthly city as necessary for human well-being. We can say that the notion of the common good has always been present, or latent, in Christian thinking. From the renewal of Roman Catholic social thinking in the encyclical of Leo XIII *Rerum Novarum* (1891), it has played a large part in it. Leo defined it as 'The sum of those conditions of social life which allow social groups and their individual members relatively thorough and regular access to their own fulfilment' (para. 74). Leo himself used it to condemn both individualism and collectivism in favour of an organic hierarchy on the analogy of St Paul's picture in I Corinthians 12 of the one body having various members, all of them necessary for its proper functioning but not all of equal functional importance. The Pastoral Constitution of Vatican 2, *Gaudium et Spes*, defined the common good in almost identical terms to Leo (para. 26), and from Leo to Vatican II Roman Catholic social teaching was largely based on the common good. Vatican II itself was more personal, more dynamic, bringing in human rights as well as human duties, and the importance of personal participation in decision making. Here the influence of Maritain was powerful. He entrusts the individual, who essentially is replaceable, with the person, who transcends the *polis*, but whose personal existence is nevertheless constituted in relation to other persons. The truth in Kant's notion that we are free when we obey what we have laid down for ourselves does not sufficiently allow for the social formation inherent in human growth and development. Before ourselves acting we must be acted upon, by parents or parent substitutes, by school teachers and several other social and cultural influences. All of us are entitled to respect as moral agents. Because of this we can claim the human rights which are necessary to ensure this. It will include basic material rights, and that is why the recent emphasis in much Catholic teaching endorsed by others on 'a preferential option for the poor' does not negate a commitment to the common good. Indeed the purpose of claiming these rights is to share in the common good and not simply to pursue purely private interests.

Since Vatican II there has been a less explicit emphasis on the common good in Roman Catholic social teaching. I think it is because the concept has in many cases been associated with a static, hierarchical view of the social order (as Atherton and Dumas claim), and one also tied to a particular interpretation of the doctrine of Natural Law. Essentially this doctrine is concerned to affirm that recognizing distinctions between good and evil, right and wrong, and making moral choices in changing circumstances in the light of this recognition is natural to, and distinctive of, human beings. However, the doctrine came to be interpreted in terms of a static understanding of nature and fixed norms derived from this. This is exemplified today in the official Roman Catholic teaching on sexual ethics. Also since Vatican II liberation theologians have been questioning received social teaching. Ellacuria has re-defined the common good as 'a coherent set of structural connections that promotes the interests of all members of society' (I quote from an article 'Ethics and Liberation' in the American journal *Theological Studies*, March 1995). This is what I had always taken it to mean. However, though the common good has not played so prominent a part in Roman Catholic social theology since Vatican II because it had been interpreted in too classical and static a fashion, it is still there. The task is to see that it is interpreted in a dynamic fashion. Rapid social change has become endemic since the scientific revolution of the seventeenth century, and the industrial revolution of the eighteenth century. The latter began in this country, and has become global and even more rapid. Any theology which cannot help us to cope with dynamic change is useless.

Elements of the good of each person which the common good would maintain as needful for persons can be enumerated from personal experience. They must include the material conditions of life, for without various obvious basic necessities which each person has access to, those who do not have such access are excluded from participation in the commonly accepted community life: they are marginalized. Mention of participation takes us beyond the material necessities of food, shelter, medical care and education to being part of the decision-making processes in voluntary and statutory groups and structures. If any are excluded from them they are excluded from the common good. Therefore there are many forms of political organizations in human history which have excluded some, many, most or almost all citizens from participation, and therefore from sharing a common good. Western type democracy, if properly implemented, does minister towards the common good, but we must not assume that it is necessary or best for all states or all times. Different participatory structures may be needed in some states, for instance, to overcome tribalism; or in parts of South East Asia where village communities are of central importance.

This raises the question, how far are states the proper agents for the promotion and conserving of the common good? This relates to issues between the person and the collective which are perennial in discussions of political philosophy and political institutions. A thin theory of the common good uses individualistic language in preserving human rights in the cause of self-determination. A thick theory of the common good uses communitarian language. Neither should be pursued without reference to the other.[1] Persons can only be persons in community, and yet the person transcends the community and can oppose it, and can judge on occasion that they must do so. That is why Dr Johnson said to Boswell, referring to Christians in the Roman empire, 'Sir, the state had the right to martyr them and they had the right to be martyred.' Yet individual salvation is no salvation. We must be saved with others if person-in-community is to be fulfilled. That is presumably why the epistle to the Hebrews says of the heroes of faith, 'they did not receive what was promised, since God had provided something better so that they would not, apart from us, be made perfect' (11.39f. NRSV). Translated into political and social terms that is why what we have come to call the welfare state is so important in principle, however much argument there can be about the details. It stands for a corporate recognition of the status of citizens, whether deserving or undeserving (to quote the unfortunate distinction so characteristic of nineteenth-century Britain). Citizenship is characterized by a community of giving and receiving, at times giving more in taxes and in other ways, and at other times in life receiving more in benefits, a mutual exchange through collective agencies through all the stages of life, with its many unforseeable as well as unforeseen ups and downs. To replace it with a system where everyone is urged personally to insure themselves according to the scale of their income against these eventualities so as not to be dependent on others, leaving the state to target those too poor to do so (so that there is a safety net below which they will not be allowed to fall), is better than leaving them to the vagaries of private charity, but is no substitute for the welfare state as worked for during the first half of this century and established half way through it. That is why the present dismantling of it is so serious.[2] However I cannot now pursue the details of current controversies for it is time to sum up the case for the common good in five steps.

1. Any static picture of the common good must be given up. It can only be worked out in relation to changing social conditions;

and it must inspire hope for a re-direction of whatever forms of social justice we have achieved into new forms which cannot be known beforehand (though they may be adumbrated), and which will be held to less statically than many past forms of the common good have been.

2. The social virtues already mentioned need fostering at every level of social groups and institutions, with the state at the top of the pyramid. It cannot be left to the sole operation of market forces to foster them by an invisible hand. They do not foster them and, by neglect, undermine them. Once this is granted then individual-personal autonomy and self-responsibility has a vital place. Adam Smith would agree with this. His *Theory of Moral Sentiments* preceded *The Wealth of Nations*. He assumes that the moral force of the community would check individual excesses, but he had a more specific place for social policies than is often realized and, in my judgment, if he were writing now it would be a larger one, in the light of global developments of the economic order than in his day.

3. An understanding of the common good must allow for conflicts within the social order, together with the reality of power relationships. We must not step into a sentimental theology which says that if everyone will co-operate with everyone else and love them as themselves the common good will be realized. To the contrary, we all see partially, both personally and collectively. We see life through spectacles which highlight our own interests, and our perspectives clash with those of others. Of course we can, to varying extents, transcend our partialities, and our faith calls us to do so, but it is rare to do so completely, and much more difficult for groups than individuals. Experience of life leads both persons and collectives to view situations differently. We are even divided within ourselves as workers and consumers. As workers, whether in manufacturing or in services, and at whatever level (including the professional), we are concerned with preserving jobs and improving pay and conditions, but as consumers in general we are sensitive to feather bedding which keeps up prices and charges. Economic factors are very strong in this ideological element in thought. The theories of Karl Marx were seriously flawed, but his insight here is permanently valid. How else do we account for the fact that at a general election, faced with the same party programmes and leaders from which to chose, we know that the electors of Barnsley will produce a large Labour majority and those of Bournemouth a large Tory one. The different economic and social positions of the electors leads them to see things differently.

Now it is entirely proper for people to argue in the public forum for their particular personal and group interests, and there is no reason why Christians should not join in. In doing so all will claim that they are also advocating what is in the wider public interests, thus paying tribute to the influence of the idea of the common good. It is a rare striker who says we are flexing our muscles and exercising our power to secure all we can get and hang the public interest. All must be challenged to take seriously the claim that even in conflicts there is a common good to seek. They must be prepared to admit that there is a good other than their good which must be allowed for, and that the public debate must be listened to in order to identify it, and that some tolerable adjustment must be made to allow for it. This would be a realization of the common good for the moment, provisional and always open to further adjustment.

4. The common good requires some public consensus on a reasonable doctrine of the good. It cannot be based solely on Christian doctrine. We are back here at a point previously made. Christians should believe that a broad basic moral consensus is realizable among humans, and that even adumbrations of the theological virtues of faith, hope and love can be discerned among them and should be looked for. That is why adherents of religious faith and secular philosophies need to be in contact to work at this. Hans Küng, who has been powerfully advocating this in recent books, is quite right. We cannot, of course, expect that there will be universal agreement; for one thing we have to allow for the fanatic, found among adherents of all faiths, but we need to work together to oppose them.

5. The common good can be regarded in one light as a Kantian regulative ideal, one to be purchased amid the power struggles of different interest groups in a civic culture whose decision procedures allow for it to take place at all levels (for all kinds of subsidiary voluntary organizations are training grounds). Such a culture will need a legal framework to prevent any person or group entrenching on the rights of others. But if the common good is to be sought it requires more than a legal level playing field. It requires a certain generosity of spirit which has to be fostered. It is hardly necessary to mention how important are the churches in this respect. They need to be less preoccupied with their own survival and more with a civic responsibility for human flourishing. This is as important as the evangelistic bark. Both need pursuing. (I don't see much of the former in the Decade of Evangelism, which seems to me to be a damp squib.) This picture of the common good is rather like Habermas' picture of

free and open enquiry without deception in an ideal speech situation with general communicative interaction. Presented like this it is a legacy of Marxist utopian thought in Habermas (for the Frankfurt School has shed most of Marx's implausible theories). But Habermas' picture could also be classed as a regulative ideal, as in Reinhold Niebuhr's paradoxical phrase, an 'implausible possibility'. It should always be striven for, and always be an inspiration. While we rejoice at its practical realization we cannot settle down in contentment with it. We are lured on. The common good in this respect is very congenial to the dynamics of the Christian faith.

Thus the very partiality of our achievements makes us exercise our hermeneutics of suspicion in relation to it. Community is a weasel word. Some communities are repressive, all have repressive dangers to guard against. Minorities can be sat upon. Liberty must never be forgotten. Village life is a good example. Many yearn amid the anonymity of much city life for the community of the village. How far the traditional village still exists is a question, but it must not be idealized, for it has its repressive side. So do some church groups. Again, some communities are basically nostalgic, fearful of the future and social dynamism. A classic example is the handloom weavers at the time of the Industrial Revolution. We deplore the way the *laissez-faire* philosophy treated them, but there could have been no future for them. Who are the handloom weavers of today? Are any church groups like them?

However, I do not want to end on a warning note. It is evident that I have something of a cross-bench position on the theme of the common good, in that I recognize that the criticisms advanced by Atherton and Dumas have some force. (The third criticism, that derived from post-modernism, I regard as dangerously mistaken.) But basically I am not cross-bench. I think the concept of the common good is fundamental to Christian social theology and that there should be no question of abandoning it. Especially it is a call to each Christian and to the churches to take civic responsibilities seriously. We cannot think that God is concerned only with the well-being of Christians. We are put into this world as human beings, made in his image, not as Christians. We are globally involved with those of other faiths and philosophies, cheek by jowl with them. We must assume God wants them all to flourish and not destroy themselves in conflicts. A common good must continually be sought. What contribution can Christians make today to that search?

19

The Moral Order of a Free Society

The question put to me is, 'How far does freedom rest on a moral tradition?', with two subsidiary themes; (1) 'How far does capitalism encourage selfishness?' (2) 'What is the place of Christianity in Western Civilization?' Underlying the discussion, which is deliberately set in the context of the Christian faith, is a theology of civil society. However, the first two questions require us to discuss within such a theology of civil society the relation of Christian moral affirmations to those of other faiths and philosophies. It is clear that making moral distinctions is a characteristic of human beings as such; and that in the plural societies of the 'West', with which we are concerned, freedom must rest on a moral basis which is not exclusively Christian. And I take it that the free societies of our theme are 'Western' types of political democracies which stand for two things, majority rule and respect for minorities. The second is important because political democracy will not work if the majority feels it can ride roughshod over minorities (a point which the Protestants in Northern Ireland need to take on board more fully). Political democracy of this kind does not necessarily accompany a market economy, which is also a background to this discussion. The recent examples of Chile under Pinochet and the partial switch to a market economy in China indicate this. But political democracy is congenial to a market economy.

It is not necessary to dwell upon the place of Christianity in Western civilization. With its heritage from Judaism and from the Greeks it has clearly been fundamental. Indeed of all the civilizations studied by Arnold Toynbee two generations ago, our Western one is the only one in which Christianity has powerfully woven itself into the social structures. That is why it has been meaningful to speak of Christendom in the past, and to refer to the present as a post-Christendom situation. For we have now been much affected by a secular humanist outlook, due to the vast technological and cultural changes since the Renaissance and the Enlightenment, together with a far more intimate contact with adherents of other traditional faiths. How does the Christian legacy relate to the political free, plural, market society of today? A brief historical survey is necessary to put this question in perspective.

Christianity, as its name implies, is centred in the ministry of Jesus Christ. In his teaching and actions the concept of the kingdom, or rule, of God is central. He lived what he taught; and his understanding of the nature of God's rule over his world was paradoxical in the extreme. God rules in righteousness not by punishing human wrong doing but by bearing the consequences of it himself. These consequences led Jesus to his death, seen by the earliest Christians not as a disaster but a triumph. The kingdom of God has far reaching ethical implications. Part of them are in line with the common moral insight of humankind, such as the Golden Rule, 'Always treat others as you would like them to treat you' (Matt.7.12). However, part go far beyond it, radicalizing love for one's neighbour, and requiring unlimited forgiveness of wrongdoers (Matt.18.22). Indeed the more one learns of love, as understood in the Christian faith, the more far-reaching and inexhaustible it becomes.

Civil society is not the focus of the kingdom of God, but it presupposes it. Caesar has his place and his claims (Mark 12.17). The kingdom remains a radical challenge, always searching for an expression in civil society, but never fulfilled in any particular expression, and always pointing forward. At first the expectation of the imminent return of Jesus (his *parousia*) obscured the problem of the relation of such a radical gospel to civil society, but as this expectation faded it soon became clear. Since then the problem for the church and for most Christians has been how to maintain this radical stance when there is no expectation of the imminent return of Jesus. It cannot be said that they have been very successful. The tendency has been to take a static view of established institutions and to sanctify them. This was more plausible when the speed of social change was slow. And that is why the advent of dynamic capitalist economies, with the rapid social changes that accompany them, was such a shock, a shock with which Christianity has been trying to come to terms ever since.

By the end of the first century of the Christian era the ethical teaching of the pseudo-Pauline Pastoral Epistles (I and II Tim. and Titus) had domesticated the radical kingdom teaching of the Gospels. Love has become one virtue among several, and the household codes are static and patriarchal. After the conversion of Constantine (whatever that was) the emphasis on the status quo became stronger. Radical ideas remained, but the tendency was to say that they belonged to the time before the fall, and that the established order, particularly the state, was the remedy for the sins which were the result of the fall. An hierarchical view of society, particularly stressing the duties of those low in the hierarchy to those above them, was characteristic. However this was at any rate a corporate view of society even though it was static. A market economy was to challenge both aspects. Positive social change, as we think of it, was not in mind. If anything the fear was of social decay, as evidenced by the rage and despair expressed by St Jerome at the news of the fall of Rome. Later, Luther was to think it far on in the history of the world, and that the best that could be hoped for was that God would enable rulers to fend off the forces of disorder and decay. The 1662 Book of Common Prayer of the Church of England prays for the punishment by the rulers of wickedness and vice and the maintenance of true religion and virtue. It thanks God for creation and preservation. There is no thought of social change, or the remedy of social evils; an understanding of social justice plays no part in public worship. How could such static and patriarchal social teaching cope with capitalism?

It had great difficulties. Traditional teaching on usury was the first challenge. The twists and turns of the discussion over three centuries are very illuminating. I have discussed them elsewhere and will not dwell on them now.[1] In the Roman Catholic Church traditional moral theology continued to be taught in seminaries and Catholic universities, but in practice it was losing influence until relaunched by Pope Leo XIII in his Encyclical *Rerum Novarum* in 1891. In Anglican and Puritan circles traditional social teaching, somewhat modified, continued for some time, but it collapsed at the end of the seventeenth-century.

One of the causes and results of the collapse was the breakaway of various sciences from the mediaeval framework within which they had operated, in which theology was the queen of the sciences. Of the social sciences economics, or political economy as it was called, was the first to develop independently. England and Scotland led the way because capitalism developed first in Britain. A number of clergy were pioneers in this. Before the advent of specialized professions a well-educated clergyman had the possibility of advancing the frontiers of knowledge in many areas. Lacking any sense of a tradition of Christian social ethics some of them argued on first principles against the prevailing mercantilist teaching in the eighteenth century. They said that God, as Christians understand him, could not have created a world in which one nation could only prosper at the expense of others. Mercantilism must be false. However, the next serious challenge came from a clergyman himself, Malthus. His theory of population was thought to be scientifically established, so that it could not be rejected on first principles. But it was so dismal that a theodicy had to be worked out to justify the ways of God to humans, if the inequalities and miseries of the social order which it analysed were indeed endemic. This task preoccupied several Christian thinkers in the first three decades of the nineteenth century.[2] The result was that a world of absolute scarcity, as Malthus led them to understand it, was to be administered according to the laws of competition in a free market. These laws were regarded as much a fixed element in the created world as were the laws of physics (as then understood). The social order which enshrined them was seen as divinely instituted for the moral discipline and training of sinful humanity. The very spontaneity of the laws of supply and demand warned against an attempt to modify them on behalf of, or by, the poor. It could not succeed. Since scientific evidence could develop outside the traditional theological framework, theology had to incorporate it into its account of God's rule of the world. It was a pioneering but flawed effort. The theology devised to deal with it was therefore flawed as well. Later the political economy in which it was expressed was to shed by the end of the century the part theological and part philosophical trappings which had accompanied it, and economics as we know it today emerged. It is concerned with the *relative* scarcity of resources compared with the possible alternative use of them; and with the market as an ideal means of maximizing the productivity of these relatively scarce resources, in so far as that is what humans want to do. In so far as humans put other values first, as to some extent they nearly always do, economics cannot prescribe their preferences; but it can tell them the probable economic cost of what they are doing.

To return to the situation around 1840. The theological post-Malthus justification of *laissez-faire* was dominant. At this point F. D. Maurice, one of the greatest nineteenth-century theologians, returned to first principles and said that to regard competition as a law of the universe and as the basis of human relations is a lie. This basic insight heralded the Christian socialist movement, which dates from 1848. Beyond that insight Maurice did not go. He himself had not only an organic but an hierarchical view of society. He was not a socialist in any standard use of the term. The immediate so-called Christian socialist experiments were short lived. But later in the century, and in this century, various Christian socialist movements have developed, almost all acknowledging a debt to F. D. Maurice. In 1960 they all came together, some long-standing groups, some relatively new, in one Christian Socialist Movement. It has produced several collections of papers and lectures, all but one of which I have appraised in review articles. The latest appeared in March 1993, *Reclaiming the Ground*, and it is on this that I now want to comment.[3]

However, at this point I need to insert a biographical paragraph. What happens in one's late adolescence is often very decisive for one's future attitudes. In my case, as an undergraduate at the London School of Economics, I was much influenced in three ways. The first was by classical economic theory. All my teachers in economics were in that tradition and most of them politically could be called Gladstonian liberals. Through them I came to understand the market as an ideal concept. Next, because I majored in modern economic history, I was much influenced, personally and intellectually, by R. H. Tawney, who was a Christian socialist. Indeed nearly all the teachers I came across in politics, history and sociology were on the left politically. Thirdly, I was one of the first in this country to read the acute social and political theology of Reinhold Niebuhr, often called Christian realism. Ever since then I have been trying to keep these three balls in the air, with varying emphasis between them, and doubtless with varying success. It has put me on the political Left, but I have never been theologically happy with the theology of the various Christian socialist groups or with many of their criticisms of capitalism. Dealing with their latest book will, among other things, raise the question of capitalism's alleged encouragement of selfishness. After that I shall come to the moral order underpinning a free society, and the relation of Christianity to it.

The aim of *Reclaiming the Ground* is to re-unite the ethic of Christianity to democratic socialism. This alerts us at once. We have seen already that the ethic of Christianity is directly related to the kingdom or rule of God as taught and lived by Jesus, and that it bears witness to a radicalism which cannot be exhausted by any one social and political order. Indeed, John Vincent, in the one sharp theological chapter in the book, points out that the kingdom of God bears witness to a radicalism beyond socialism, and at the same time points us towards the state of the poor as a prime concern.

We shall of course want to know what is meant by democratic

socialism. The structures of it are not clear in this book, but I think it rightly stresses equality as a socialist concern. I shall return to this shortly.

The symposium makes a powerful criticism of the working of our present market economy in three respects. (1) The state of the poor; the Easterhouse estate in Glasgow being taken as an example. (2) The existence of a semi-permanent underclass; whilst at the same time refuting the contention of the New Right that it is the welfare state which has produced it. (3) The fact that the pure theory of the market ignores the community structures which underlie it. Many people, not only on the Left, will agree. The next question is this. Since we have good reasons to suppose that no economic system will be without flaws, and since capitalism has undoubtedly brought many benefits, what is a better alternative? Here the book is very general. Bob Holman refers to 'an insufficiently controlled capitalism'; Tony Blair to the need to get beyond a stale debate on state intervention versus *laissez-faire*; and Paul Boateng on wealth creation does not get beyond a reference to the inadequacy of an 'unregulated free market'. There is a passing reference to 'co-operation not competition', but John Smith says that governments must appeal to self-interest. It is said that self-improvement must be combined with personal responsibility; and John Smith commends John Gray's conception of an 'enabling state' in a recent Institute of Economic Affairs pamphlet, *The Moral Foundation of Market Institutions* (1992).

None of this gets near policies and structures. Indeed two of the contributors, Holman with a stress on local communities, and Vincent writing on prophetic minorities with radical experiments, and on parabolic actions in alternative communities, seem to give up on questions of macro economic policies and structures. In terms of ideals Tony Blair, with references to Tawney, stresses equality as the main concern of democratic socialism, equality for the sake of proper relationships between human beings. He says this is central to Christianity. Beyond that he makes only the most general claims for Christianity, as far as social theology is concerned; that inherent in it are demands for personal and social change and hopes for a better world. Most Christians, apart from the most pietistic, would now agree with him as against the social pessimism so prevalent in Christendom in the past. It leads to a question not central to the present discussion but which is worth mentioning. In view of its radical origins in Jesus' life and teaching focussed on the kingdom of God, how is it that Christianity has been so socially conservative in practice, and how far should it be, if it be granted that Christians should not acquiesce in avoidable social evils? Presumably only if they can persuade themselves that any feasible alternative at a given time would be worse than the status quo. John Smith says that Christians need not be socialists, though he does not say why. Perhaps because some may well stress other values congenial to Christianity, such as freedom. He also points out that those of other faiths may, and will, also be socialists. Blair, however, gives a hostage to Christian critics by saying that democratic socialism is based on a fundamentally optimistic view of human nature and, referring to Tawney, on a sense of the human potentiality of every man and woman. It is true that Tawney did stress the fundamental soundness of the judgments of the ordinary citizen, Henry Dubb (as he called him) as against the alleged moral superiority of intellectual and wealthy élites, but he was not starry eyed about humans in general, even though he was not as subtle in analysing the interplay of human vices and virtues as was Reinhold Niebuhr. The latter was particularly effective in bringing out the insidious corruptions which prey on our virtues, much more serious than our obvious vices. Blair's blindness to this is characteristic of much Christian socialism. It enables those of the Right to score an unwarranted victory on those who understand the politics of imperfection, or Original Sin, to use a classic term. Indeed, as I have maintained elsewhere, arguments on the basis of human sin and irrationalism tell as much against the Right as the Left.[4]

This book is true to the main tradition of Christian socialism in that it shows no trace of being waylaid by the chimeras of Marxism, which betrayed many of the secular Left. Moreover it no longer makes much of the traditional Christian socialist criticisms of capitalism, chiefly three: (1) competition in itself is ethically dubious; (2) so is profit; production should not be for profit but for use; (3) the motive for economic activity should be service, not self. I will refer to these in a moment. Secularly, the traditional nationalization programme of the Labour Party has also disappeared from the book. Clause 4 of the Constitution might not exist. The strength of the book is in its stress on equality, and the need to criticize the ideology of individualism prevalent in capitalism. But is this a strength? Before assessing this I turn to those three traditional Christian socialist criticisms of capitalism, as a useful background to a consideration of equality.

1. Competition. I do not see any reason why Christians should be suspicious of competition as such. Both co-operation and competition

are part of one's natural and spiritual growth, and discovering one's capabilities. There must be a division of labour in society, and that will mean some grading according to standards such as cost, quality, natural talent and acquired skills. That will mean that there will be successes and failures in our human communities. We all have to learn how to cope with successes and with failures. Our civic structures as well as voluntary associations should guard against the relatively successful despising or marginalizing the relative failures.

2. Profit. There is no reason to reject profit as such, either as a motive for production or a directive as to what should be produced. Those who talked of production for use and not for profit did not understand the theory of the market, that it is the judgment of what goods and services consumers think to be useful that in principle secures that they will be provided, and profits made. No better way of deciding the allocation of relatively scarce resources in the present, and between present use and future consumption, is on offer. This, however, is subject to the social framework within which the market is scheduled to operate, of which more will be said later.

3. The stress on service not self. How far does capitalism encourage selfishness or, in the words of the ecumenical Oxford Conference of 1937, does it enhance acquisitiveness? It obviously tends to; but care is needed in thinking about this. First of all the self must be valued. Those who loathe or despise themselves are incapable of service to others. Concern for the self is not the same as selfishness. We must not ignore or underrate ourselves as unique persons. There is a proper place for egoism; we are to love our neighbours as ourselves. Indeed egoists can go a long way to what an altruist would approve, in seeing the wisdom of helping others to achieve their goals in order to achieve a tolerable level of social order and stability which is in their own best interests to achieving theirs. Even a distributive ethic on an egoist basis would be likely to stress need as a main criterion rather than desert, and for the same reason, though it would not be likely to be concerned with the disadvantaged beyond a fairly minimum level, unless they constituted a serious threat to the social order.[5] So I am well aware of the need to foster 'disinterested good will', and here the Christian churches have a major role to play. But society cannot be run on disinterested good will; it is too fitful.

A social order needs to achieve structures which foster the harmony of self interest with the common good. Or, as William Temple said, the art of government is to arrange affairs so that self interest prompts what justice demands.[6] Nevertheless, the structures of capitalism do very easily lead to greed and corruption. The pure theory of the market is an ideal construction. In reality there is much scope for twisting it whilst playing lip service to it, especially by the free rider who makes a buck by flouting what he hopes his rivals will stick to. Dealing with this is a matter of political economy and politics, not economics. And politics itself needs a built-in monitoring of structures against the abuses of combined political and economic power, and the corruptions of selfishness to which it can give rise. The monstrous abuses of the combination of political and economic power in the collapsed Soviet-style command economies are witness to this.

I come now to equality as the legitimate legacy of socialism, including Christian socialism. It is this which Tawney stressed, on behalf of an equality of respect, and for the sake of freedom and fellowship; not an equality of result, nor merely an equality of access, which by itself would lead to an unpleasant meritocracy. In my experience a stress on equality is often met with incredulity. It is asked whether one can be so naive as to stress equality in the face of the obvious human inequalities. But at a fundamental level Christians must affirm it. Both as created in the image of God, and re-created to new life in Christ, Christians see human beings as equally precious in the sight of God, whatever differences there are between them in sex, colour, talent or character. The question is, 'How far should this fundamental equality be expressed in social policy and structures?' Differences between Christians arise here. Some take an otherwordly line. It has been argued, for instance, that the text of the funeral service is the same for rich and poor alike, and that this expresses their equality before God in time and for eternity. This evasion is less heard now than a century ago. Others stress the value of liberty as fundamental to the Christian life. Men and women must make their own decisions before God; no one else can live someone else's life for them. Collective processes must not undermine personal choices. As for fraternity both radical and socialist may stress it; the former its voluntary nature, the latter the need for corporate structures to foster fraternity. And those traditional heirarchies which have a sense of *noblesse oblige* bear witness to it in their own way.

However it is not only Christian socialists who stress equality. A powerful statement, and one which has influenced me, came from the humanist Walter Lipmanns in 1927:

There you are, sir, and there is your neighbour. You are better born than he, you are richer, or you are stronger. You are handsomer, nay you are better, wiser, kindlier, more likeable. You have given more to your fellow men and taken less than he. By any and every test of intelligence, of virtue, of usefulness you are demonstrably a better man than he, and yet – absurd as it seems – these differences do not matter, for the best part of him is untouchable and incomparable and unique and universal. Either you feel this or you do not . . .

If the role of the Christian socialist is to stress equality, leaving to others to stress liberty, they can accept a central role for the free markets as the best device so far achieved by human beings to deal with basic economic problems which any society has to face. But they will be very conscious of its ideal character and the defects which in practice are inherent in it, and for which a political correction is needed. There are many collective needs it cannot meet, and disputes between right and left are likely to be about the extent of these. It also leads, particularly through inherited wealth, to great inequalities of purchasing power in the market. Resources are drawn to provide luxuries for some whilst the poor do not have the purchasing power to secure necessities. The assignment of productive resources seems more and more arbitrary. Therefore some redistribution of resources by state policy is required, the nature and extent of this being a standard content of political controversy. It is inequalities that need to be justified, particularly as to whether they do or do not work in favour of the disadvantaged, as Rawls argues in his *A Theology of Justice*.[7]

I come now explicitly to the moral order of a free society. I agree with Michael Novak that democratic capitalism needs a moral theory about itself, above morality on which most citizens can be counted to agree. Any society must have some presuppositions to hold it together. The market economy needs to examine its moral presuppositions, for if it ignores them or fails to promote them, it is in danger of undermining itself. This struck me forcefully in visits to Hong Kong, an astonishingly successful economy in which nearly everyone seems to be engaged in making money all day and every day. It seems to me it relied implicitly on the residual strength of the Confucian family ethic, which it did not attend to, and which if left to itself for many more decades it might undermine. Novak in all his social theology books writes eloquently of the positive moral features of a market economy, most recently in a booklet published by the Institute of Economic Affairs, *God in the Market Place* (1993). He makes little use of the negative arguments of the New Right, that capitalism is the economic order for dealing with sin.

In this booklet after some favourable comments on a recent book of mine he makes three criticisms of it;[8]

(1) That I ignore the democratic capitalist model of society as against the social market or democratic socialism models. But in fact the book criticizes recent New Right advocates of the market economy as ethically unsatisfactory because of the individualistic ideology which usually goes with it. (2) I assume non-capitalist economies create less inequalities than capitalist ones. I make no such assumption; indeed I do not consider them because they are irrelevant to our situation, where some form of market economy is the only option available. (3) I do not refer to the ambiguities of socialism. But the critique I gave of traditional socialism does this; indeed one of the aims of the book is to stress the ambiguities (or trade offs, to use a homely phrase), which any society encounters in balancing different values and policy considerations against one another. So I do not think, with respect to Novak, that these criticisms amount to much. My criticism of him is that he underplays the defects of the market and is not critical enough of the philosophy of individualism which has been associated with market economies.[9] Obviously to stress the importance of individual liberty and freedom of choice is to set a decisive value on each person. This can be on Christian grounds, as I have already mentioned, or on secular humanist grounds, such as that human beings are rational creatures, or that they are all of the same species, participating in one and the same reality. However, further reflection shows that the human beings who are to be seen as precious in themselves only truly became themselves in relation with others. They need freedom *from* unnecessary restrictions, but also freedom *for* creative relationships with others; a properly human community.

Community is somewhat of a weasel word. It can refer to a society which stresses order and security rather than freedom, which is conservative and hierarchical. Or, at the other extreme, a society of equalitarian solidarity. It is a word in common use, and has other words in our vocabulary related to it; common, commune, communion, communication, communism. So it resonates in human experience. Christianity has indeed its distinctive origins, but its theology has roots in the common experience of human living; it develops this and deepens it. So it is with community. In Pauline theology the term *koinonia*, which we translate as communion or fellowship, refers to the deep relation men and women have in and with God and one another in the church, neatly expressed in the Grace 'The Grace of our Lord Jesus Christ, and the love of God, and the communion of the Holy Spirit (II Cor.13.14).[10] So Christians have strong grounds for standing for freedom in the relationships between persons of equal ontological status as the foundation of social and civic life. And in a time when we are growingly conscious of moral and social diversity in a plural society, we need to seek some common ground for community in other faiths and philosophies, and promote it. I understand, for instance, that a Chinese character signifying person has also the thought of 'betweenness' associated with it. If so it is a heritage of a quarter of the world's population. It is also a sense of community which make family structures so important, where children can grow into responsible individuality in a community context. At the level of civil society a *koinonia* ethic should offer a basic security and significance to citizens, free from restrictions of colour or gender; it should encourage co-operative activities, and approach realistically institutional barriers in society, where a community ethic requires a better balance of power rooted in justice.

Some such understanding of persons as inter-dependent social beings can be spelled out in more detail, in ways in which Christian theology can co-operate with all men and women of good will (to quote a phrase occurring in recent papal social encyclicals). One such is by the Belgian theologian Louis Janssens. 'The human person is (1) a subject (2) an embodied subject (3) part of the material world (4) inter-relational with other-persons (5) an independent social being (6) historical (7) equal but unique (8) called to know and worship God.[11] All but the last could be agreed to by secular humanists. Kevin Kelly, who quotes this, adds, 'Whatever promotes or violates the good of the human person considered in this comprehensive way is respectively morally right or wrong. This is the basic criterion for a person-centred morality.' The recent European Values survey suggests that in a less coherent and systematic way it is akin to what the majority of those canvassed would affirm.[12] The last seven of the ten commandments are a desiccated version of it. Also, in another field, an effort is being made to articulate a cross-culture medical ethic, based on the four principles of respect for human autonomy, benevolence, non-maleficence, and justice as fairness.[13] There are good grounds for thinking that these are in fact implicit or explicit in the way the medical profession is trying to guide itself in face of the explosion of issues in medical ethics in the last twenty to thirty years.

It is all the more important to stress this because of some current attempts to allege the almost total absence of any common moral and ethical understanding in the post-modern world.[14]

I am not suggesting that all this is clear cut, but I am suggesting it needs to be thought through as the moral basis of a free society. It needs cultural institutions which foster human flourishing in these respects. Values will be held in tension. The freedom associated with democratic capitalism is too individualistic. The market left to itself without correctives also treats labour as a factor of production in the same impersonal way as it treats land and capital. We also need social structures which embody mutual giving and receiving between citizens, not leaving it to the arbitrariness of individual good will. This is what the welfare state is designed to achieve. In so far as it falls short it has lately been attacked for the wrong reasons. Freedom needs balancing by the stress on equality; but if this is taken too far it can become restrictive and inhibit the dynamism which has been the mark of capitalism. Adaptability, inventiveness, innovation, enterprise, curiosity are all much more stressed in modern dynamic societies than in the static societies of the past, including that of the New Testament. They have all bettered human life. And that betterment is needed by the two-thirds of the world it has so far largely passed by. But moral depth is needed, or the new powers at our disposal will lead to disasters. However, humans also need stability and social security. Most of us fear dynamism if our personal interests are threatened. We need social structures which help us to adjust. The hopelessness of the underclass created by our Western market economies is a scandal.

Disagreements about particular policies will always persist, partly depending on which value is thought to need stressing at a particular time. Dynamism and security both need stressing. Both need to be maintained simultaneously. The best policy may not be some intermediate half way between them; it may incline at any one time sharply towards one or the other. My judgment is that in view of the strong individualist theoretical and practical thrust in Britain in recent years it is time for a more corporate stress; and that we have something to learn from our West European and Scandinavian neighbours in this respect. Details of policy will always be problematic; but all parties relate their detailed proposals to some ideological framework, and it is this I have been discussing. It is the general direction not the details of policy with which I have been concerned. And I think it is the job of Christian theology to advance a critique of ideologies, whilst at the same time being self-critical about its own.[15]

20

Business Ethics and the Pastoral Task

Business has had a dubious ethical record recently. It has rivalled only miscarriages of justice in media attention. As a reminder of some of the British scandals I mention four. At the trial following the Guinness takeover of Distillers four of its directors were said in court to be 'carried away with greed and ambition'. There was the negligence involved in the English Channel ferry *Herald of Free Enterprise* disaster. There have been the details involved in the shut down of the Bank of Credit and Commerce International; and most recently the Maxwell Pension Fund fraud.

At the same time there has been a huge growth in the study and teaching of business ethics, particularly in the USA, from which most of the literature comes. It involves basic questions of morality in business and wealth creation, including the moral implications of a capitalist system which is now the triumphant survivor of the collapse of Soviet and command style economics. Business schools increase in number. The Harvard Business School, perhaps the leader, received in 1987 an endowment of twenty million dollars for the teaching of business ethics from a former chairperson of the Securities and Exchange Commission. *The Journal of Business Ethics*, a monthly from Amsterdam focussing mainly on the North American scene, has now a British counterpart, *Business Ethics: a European Review*, launched by Blackwells in January 1992 under the editorship of Professor Jack Mahoney, SJ, who holds the chair of Moral and Social Theology at King's College, London, and who has established there a Business Research Centre of which he is the Director.

In the USA by 1988, of the two thousand biggest corporations 92% had established ethical codes of practice. In the UK about 33% have. What kinds of ethical questions are being raised? They cover a disparate and wide range. I mention a few. One is the ethics of corporate finance. In modern capitalism the separation of ownership from management and control of a company is endemic. The private shareholders, who in the last resort are the owners, no longer take much, if any, serious entrepreneurial responsibility. They are more like punters betting on the success of a horse in a race. It is a type of private property unthought of when what became the traditional Christian defence of private property was advanced by St Thomas Aquinas.[1] The recent government privatizations have shown that the property-owning democracy which it is intended to create is not seriously expecting to take any risks, but to make an easy gain from a bargain sell-off. In the USA more efforts have been made by small shareholders' campaigns to influence the business policy of corporations than in this country, but the odds are heavily stacked against them, and the effort involved means that it can only be an occasional effort. The potentially effective shareholders are pension and life insurance funds, but they tend to take a distanced stance from the running of the enterprise. Should they become more involved and less like punters? Those who administer church funds, like the Church Commissioners of the Church of England, need to consider this. It is where the growing ethical investment movement can stimulate reflection and influence action.

As it is, management concerns in research and development which involve longer-term considerations are often frustrated by short-term market considerations. Moreover, if shares are held by a distanced and detached fund the only means of disciplining a management which has become ineffective is by a takeover, and that is a blunt instrument.[2] Continuous fine-tuning is preferable.

Many issues arise in connection with accountancy and auditing. Should there be a rotation of auditors? Should auditing be separated from consultancy? Vardy, writing as a Christian, gives many examples of the moral dilemmas which can arise in this area. In one example he says he once adjusted the business forecast figures of a firm to prevent a bank closing down; 33 jobs were saved.[3]

Two issues which are widely discussed need only to be mentioned in passing here. One is the enormous increases in salary which top executives have secured or been given in the recent past; the other is the terms and conditions of loans to Third World countries, and the problems of renegotiating repayment. But a third, which is coming to the fore, warrants a brief comment: 'whistleblowing'. This can be internal within a company or external in relation to the public. Loyalty to the company with respect to confidentiality can conflict with personal and professional integrity and civic responsibility. Since whistleblowers are always assumed to be guilty unless specifically exonerated, they are likely to be victimized.

Then there is sexual or racial discrimination in employment, especially at upper managerial levels. It may be formal, or, because of the cultural air we breathe, informal. White males are in a predominant position of power. It is difficult to correct, for explicit corrective preferences can bear harshly on those who have no responsibility for the injustice in question. But questions of distributive and compensatory justice are never easy.

In quoting a selection of issues one can easily move into areas of industrial ethics, like those arising over the status and power of trade unions, or in connection with industrial espionage. However, I am trying to keep some distinction between them. Problems of ethics in industry have had their own organs of discussion for some time whilst business ethics is a relatively new field. The examples given suggest that conflicts of interest and loyalties arise, as we would expect, in a business context as much as in others.

They can be dealt with on different levels. However, there is one level which must be set aside here. That is an ethical criticism of the fundamental basis of capitalism. Some traditional Christian socialist criticisms have been of this nature. Competition has been held to be unChristian. Profit has been thought of as a dubious criterion. Hence the market itself, in which both play a key role, is suspect. These criticisms have lost their force among many who held them, especially as it has become clear that the Marxist theories have no alternative effective way of running an economic system hidden beneath the distorted Communist power structures. Both economically and politically Marxism is discredited. Much has been written on this, and I have contributed to it; and I am not going to repeat it here.[4] Obviously if the basis of capitalism is unethical, unless business ethics admits this, it is tinkering with an inherently unsatisfactory structure. My own view is that there is a fundamental difficulty in the pure theory of the free market; it treats labour, which is a personal factor of production, in the same way as it treats land and capital which are impersonal factors of production.[5] Persons should not be treated as things. But this can be corrected by social policies in the political realm if we regard the market as a useful tool for some important human purposes. It is a neat device for settling a range of fundamental economic problems of production and distribution, but there are many areas with which it cannot deal; we must not give it a pseudo-divine status, nor bolster it by an ideology which turns market relationships into a complete philosophy of human relations in public life. This said, there is nothing basically unethical about profits and competition. We can return to the different levels at which business ethics can be discussed.

The first is that of good public relations. Business goes along with non-commercial concerns of its customers. Consumer pressure is not easy to build up, but it can build up and, if the cause is good, is worth the effort of building it up, if it is proportionate to the significance of the cause.[6] The Body Shop has done well out of its stance against animal experiments in the area in which it trades (though it is not alone in this and has suffered in the current recession). Growing consumer pressure is pushing for catalytic converters in car engines, and has induced the government to accelerate the use of lead-free petrol by a tax advantage. Carrying this kind of reasoning further, many companies realize that a good reputation is part of the value of their product. Perrier withdrew all its bottled water for a time after some of it had been contaminated with benzene. A further step is to realize that it pays to behave well to your employees, or suppliers, or to take an interest in the communities where your works or retail outlets are. Marks and Spencer have a good reputation for their treatment of their employees and for firm but fair dealing with their suppliers.

All of this 'honesty is the best policy' type of ethical reasoning is useful as far as it goes, but something deeper is needed. For one thing the market by no means always rewards virtue. And there is always the 'free rider', the firm which works at a minimal ethical level, and will cut corners on the assumption that its competitors, or most of them, will not. Most companies probably get along reasonably well by conforming to the letter of the law and not practising fraud or overcharging (even if they can get away with it), or paying below minimum wage rates. This raises the question of the role of codes of practice and of law in business ethics. But before discussing this we need to stress a commitment to certain basic moral convictions which need to underlie business ethics, and operate at a deeper level than those we have mentioned. This is the basis on which the new journal *Business Ethics* operates.

Philosophers are continually discussing whether indeed such a basic morality can be established and on what basis. It would take us too long to survey this now.[7] Most people assume, however, that there is one and that without it human society could hardly persist. We count on most people following it most of the time. Some, indeed, give the minimum adherence to it that they can get by with. Some give not even that (and many of them will find themselves in prison). Those who infringe it generally give lip service to it. Groucho Marx hits this off in his saying, 'The secret of life is honesty and fair dealing; if you can fake that you've got it made.' The free rider again! Behind any such ethical basis there is a view of the nature and significance of the human person which it presupposes. In other words there is a faith. Vardy says his is 'People matter'. What possible bases are there for such a faith?

A secular humanist faith will say that people matter because they are rational beings and this gives them a special place in the chain of being. (Their relation to 'nature' is a separate issue.) Or they will say that people matter because of a fellow feeling for those of the same species. Vardy himself brings in God only in the last chapter to make clear his basis. Christians hold that people matter because, in the well-known phrase, they are made in the image of God. They are also remade through the work of Christ. Humans are sinful, but they have not lost their dignity in the sight of God, nor their responsible freedom in moral matters.

Christians therefore have strong grounds for the conviction that people matter, but they do not have a blueprint for the social and political order, or for business ethics as part of it. They cannot bypass questions of justice as fairness by talk of love of neighbour. But their faith provides a strong challenge to improve the state of affairs they inherit in the light of the radical nature of God's way of ruling the world as disclosed in the life of Jesus. They need a firm theology of civil society. It will be built in Christian experience down the centuries, for the ones presupposed by the various New Testament writings are related to the context of the Christian church at that time and cannot simply be transposed into the twentieth century. In my view there is much cogency in the Lutheran 'two realms' theology, properly understood.[8] Like other theologies it is easily corrupted.

A main Christian task then, in business ethics as in civil society, is to fortify a common morality and to seek allies in promoting it. In a plural society it will mean seeking in what ways other religious faiths and philosophies support it, and working with adherents of them where they do. That is why those who stress *in this context* the distinctiveness of Christianity are not helpful. An example is Brian Griffiths, who was head of Mrs Thatcher's 'Think Tank' in Downing Street. He is well aware of the unsatisfactoriness of the possessive individualistic philosophy which has usually gone with capitalism (as distinct from its institutions), but thinks it is a satisfactory economic system if operated by Christians.[9] The unreality of this is evident.

Because of the powerful stimulus to greed and corruption to which market forces lead, some strong regulatory instruments are needed in addition to the force of basic moral commitment. A conference on the resurgence of capitalism at Lancaster University in 1991 had the appropriate sub-title 'Riding the Tiger'. What, then, of the role of codes of practice and of law?

Codes of practice need to be reasonably specific. It is not sufficient to issue orotund statements about observing the spirit and not just the letter of the law, or on aiming to contribute to the well-being of the community. These are merely a public relations puff. How are conflicts of interest to be handled? For instance that of the share-holders, the managers, the employees, the customers and the neigh-bourhood? What about the taking of bribes where, for instance, they are routine in business, as in Saudi Arabia? (In my experience this is the one issue that really worries Christians.) What about accepting gifts from a customer? What of the whistleblower at odds with his or her firm? In the USA some 10% of major corporations have set up an independent ethical ombudsman as a channel for whistleblow-ers. But I do not know how well they have worked. Some 20% have ethics committees at board level, and some have regular ethical audits on the conduct of the corporation. Such codes of practice can be a help to 'good' people in making good decisions; they may also restrain 'bad' people from assuming that everything is ethically permissible if the firm benefits financially, or that they are acceptable if other people do it. At least it may induce in them second thoughts.

Law is the most rigorous way of enforcing ethical standards. But by comparison it is inflexible and cumbersome. Nevertheless there is a necessary place for laws. Usually they are imposed after great scan-dal in which many people have suffered. They must be able to be enforced or law is brought into disrepute, and that means carrying general consent. What, for instance, should it do about the tobacco industry, which is compensating for a decline in business in economi-cally developed countries by pushing its products in developing ones? Prohibit it? Tax it heavily? What would be the likelihood of evasion, as in the case of prohibition in the USA? In general, law involves inspectors and court cases, often complex and legally expensive. The use of law involves a nice political judgment. It certainly cannot be ruled out, and there has in fact been a big increase in financial reg-ulating in the last decade, and there is more to come. Backing is needed in the use of law at every level from self-interest upwards. Chlorofluorocarbons are a case in point. The damage they cause to the ozone layer, once discovered, was quickly appreciated, and governments in the West began the process of limiting by regulation their production. A prominent ally in the USA has been the Du Pont corporation, the biggest producer of chlorofluorocarbons, because it thinks it is well ahead in the process of producing a cheap substitute.

In conclusion, how can the church exercise the pastoral care of those continuously involved in the difficult decisions with which business ethics deals? First by helping them to realize that ambiguities and trade-offs are inherent in ethical decision-making. It is true that clear-cut issues do crop up from time to time: the right decision is clear even if costly to implement. The choice is whether to take it or fail morally. Usually, however, it is a case of balancing factors and choosing what on the most plausible interpretation of the available evidence seems the best option. There can be no more certainty than the nature of the situation allows. Many Christians have a lurking suspicion that there is a clear 'Christian' answer if only the church would teach it, or if they themselves were sensitive enough to find it. So they suffer from a continuous spiritual debility. But not only are there the problems of getting at the empirical data of an ethical issue, and also of assessing the data, but also of assessing risks, evaluating their likelihood and the legitimacy of taking them. We are each likely to have worked out on the basis of our experience broad moral considerations to bear in mind (principles is probably too formal a term), but in particular cases these may conflict and point in different directions, so that we have to assess priorities in the case. All this involves an art of discernment. Christian teaching can help us by criticizing false or inadequate ideologies, and Christian worship and prayer can give us a deeper vision and confidence, but neither can usually give us a clear-cut answer to these detailed questions. Church guidance had best remain at a middle level between basic theological affirmations and detailed policies. If it can do so (and complexities may be such that it is not always possible) it can suggest the general direction in which to go whilst leaving each of us as a citizen in our job to work out the details.[10]

Here we would be much helped by reflection with other Christians, and others whose information and perspective can be drawn upon. There is nothing to equal corporate reflection in helping us to become more articulate and discerning in relating the insights of the gospel to the world of business, and to the wider context of social and political policy in a plural society. Such groups can be of many kinds. They can consist of Christians (and possibly others) in the same kind of jobs, or in different ones; from one church tradition or ecumenical; from one congregation or from several. Clergy would be one element but not dominant. Of course such groups involve time and effort. Many who spend their days in difficult decision-making want to leave it behind when they leave work and not be troubled further. They may appreciate what are sometimes called the consolations of faith but not its challenge. We need to be helped out of such an attitude.

The need is to avoid two dangers. One is a general moral gospel radicalism, cast in personal terms which people cannot relate to their collective responsibilities in their jobs, which leaves them with a perpetual uneasy conscience, and without the means of mitigating it. The other is a bland gulf between worship and work in which strength is drawn from worship but it does not illuminate work. This is a common difficulty which draws much criticism.

We need a robust faith to live amid the ambiguities of ethical decisions. There will be failures and disappointments and we must learn from them. There will be successes, which must not make us complacent. In this situation the church can give a strong back-up to the growing attention to business ethics, both by its own members and by the general public.

21

The Ethical Legacy of
John Maynard Keynes

At a recent colloquium in Canada I heard Keynes referred to as ethically 'an empty box'. Yet he himself took ethics seriously. It will be wise if this adverse verdict is in our minds as we consider his ethical legacy. There are three stages in our inquiry. First, what was his general ethical position? What was the intellectual and social context in which he acquired it and which made it so cogent to him? Did he modify it in later life? Then we must look at the way in which he applied his general moral philosophy to the economic order in the shape of *laissez-faire*, and his hopes and forecasts for its future. Third, we need to appraise his views on the relation of ethics to economics, and on the ethical problems of living with uncertainties in making economic decisions on which he laid so much stress.

Keynes' Basic Ethical Stance

There is no doubt where to begin. In September 1938, at his home in Sussex, Keynes read a paper on *My Early Beliefs* to a Memory Club, the members of which were friends of his. The paper was not published in his lifetime, but in his will he expressed the wish that of his unpublished writings, this alone should appear, together with a memoir on *Doctor Melchior: A Defeated Enemy*, who was a German Jew with whom he negotiated at the Peace Conference of 1919, and for whom he came to feel a distinct rapport. Both are very fine pieces of writing, showing both Keynes' sensitivity and his skill in the use of words to express it.[1]

Keynes arrived in Cambridge as a 'fresher' in 1902. Immediately he came under the influence of G. E. Moore, a moral philosopher, whose *Principia Ethica* was published in 1903. This book had an immense influence for decades among moral philosophers in the

Anglo-Saxon world, and it is still constantly referred to in any survey of twentieth-century moral philosophy. It was in a private club, the Apostles, which Keynes was soon invited to join, that he met Moore. In *My Early Beliefs* Keynes says:

> Now what we got from Moore was by no means entirely what he offered us. He had one foot on the threshold of a new heaven but the other foot in Sidgwick and the Benthamite calculus and the general rules of correct behaviour. There was one chapter in the *Principia* of which we took not the slightest notice. We accepted Moore's religion so to speak, and discarded his morals. Indeed in our opinion one of the greatest advantages of his religion was that it made morals unnecessary – meaning by 'religion' one's attitude towards oneself and the ultimate, and by 'morals' one's attitude to the outside world and the intermediate . . .
>
> Our religion closely followed the English Puritan tradition of being chiefly concerned with the salvation of our own souls . . . our religion was altogether unworldly – with wealth, power, popularity or success it had no concern whatever, they were thoroughly despised . . .
>
> I have called this faith a religion, and some sort of relation to neo-platonism it surely was. But we should have been very angry at the time with such a suggestion. We regarded all this as entirely rational and scientific in character. Like any other branch of science, it was nothing more than the application of logic and rational analysis to the material presented as sense data. Our appreciation of good was exactly the same as our appreciation of green, and we purported to handle it with the same logical and analytical technique which was appropriate to the latter . . . Russell's *Principles of Mathematics* came out in the same year as *Principia Ethica*; and the former in spirit furnished a method for handling the material provided by the latter.[2]

The aim was to make vague notions clear by using precise language and by asking exact questions. 'What *exactly* do you mean?' was a question often asked in the club. There can, of course, be no quarrel with this. Its error was the further assumption that if precise questions could be formulated, issues long in dispute in moral philosophy would be seen to have a clear answer; and a problem was the exclusion of the realm of mystery, ambiguity, and imagination from serious consideration in preoccupation with extreme literalness in the use of everyday words. Ambiguity appeared slipshod.

In his chapter 'The Ideal', Moore maintained

No one, probably, who has asked himself the question has ever doubted that personal affection and the appreciation of what is beautiful in personal affection and the appreciation of what is beautiful in Art or Nature, are good in themselves. This is the ultimate and fundamental truth of Moral Philosophy. It is only for the sake of these things ... in order that as much of them as possible may at some time exist ... that anyone can be justified in performing any public or private duty ... they are the *raison d'être* of virtue ... it is they ... that form the rational ultimate end of human action and the sole criterion of social progress ... These appear to be truths which have been generally overlooked.[3]

Moore thought of himself as a pioneer. It did not seem probable to him that they might be questioned.

Keynes says that this religion was 'a very good one to grow up under'.[4] However, he reflects that it is remarkable how oblivious Moore 'managed to be of the qualities of the life of action and also of the pattern of life as a whole. He was existing in a timeless ecstasy ... The New Testament is a handbook for politicians compared with the unwordliness of Moore's chapter on "The Ideal".[5] Keynes sees no reasons to shift from these fundamental intuitions, and indeed he did not, but he says they are 'much too few and too narrow to fit actual experience'.[6] Nevertheless, the life of passionate contemplation and communion enabled the Apostles to escape from the Benthamite tradition that is 'the worm which has been gnawing at the inside of modern civilization and is responsible for its present moral decay. We used to regard the Christians as the enemy, because they appeared as the representatives of tradition, convention and hocus-pocus. In truth it was the Benthamite calculus, based on an overvaluation of the economic criterion, which was destroying the quality of the "popular Ideal".[7]

Further, Keynes goes on to say that the Apostles also ignored Moore's discussion of the duty of the individual to obey general rules. They claimed the right to judge every individual case on its merits. 'We repudiated entirely customary morals, conventions and traditional wisdom. We were, that is to say, in the strict sense of the term immoralists.'[8] This he says has deeply coloured the course of their lives. As far as he is concerned it is too late to change. 'I remain, and always will remain, an immoralist.'[9] However, he goes on to say that this attitude was flimsily based and disastrously mistaken. In a powerful passage his diagnosis is as follows:

> We were among the last of the Utopians ... who believed in a continuing moral progress by virtue of which the human race already consists of reliable, rational and decent people, influenced by truth and objective standards, who can safely be released from outward constraints of convention and traditional standards and inflexible rules of conduct, and left, from now onwards, to their own sensible devices, pure motives and reliable intuitions of the good ... In short, we repudiated all versions of the doctrine of original sin ... We were not aware that civilization was a thin and precarious crust ... only maintained by rules and conventions skillfully put across and guilefully preserved. We had no respect for traditional wisdom or the restraints of custom. We lacked reverence ... for everything and everyone ... We completely misunderstood human nature, including our own. The rationality we attributed to it led to superficiality of judgment, but also of feeling.[10]

Finally, Keynes follows this disavowal of the overemphasis on the rational in life by denying the existence of any authority or standard to which he can appeal if what he thinks of as normal behaviour is under threat; and he ascribes a tendency of his still to do so as perhaps 'some hereditary vestige of a belief in the efficacy of prayer',[11] an example of his tendency to produce wild asides in conversation and in writing, which characterized his undergraduate days and which never quite left him.

So much for the substance of his account of his early beliefs. Why did it seem so convincing to him in the Cambridge of the early 1900s? As a boy he had had a conventional church upbringing. The family, who lived in Cambridge, had Nonconformist connections. His father, John Neville Keynes, was a distinguished university teacher and administrator. Only since the Universities Test Act of 1871 had most of the offices and administration of the university been open to non-Anglicans, and had fellows of colleges of the university been freed from the requirement of subscribing to the Thirty-Nine Articles of Religion of the Established Church of England. The family attended Emmanuel Congregational Church on Sunday mornings. Maynard, as an adolescent, went to Eton College, perhaps the most socially distinguished and one of the most intellectually distinguished of English public (that is to say, in American terms private) schools. Like most of the public schools, it had an Anglican foundation. Maynard attended chapel and was confirmed at the age of fifteen. Letters home express criticism of chapel preachers, but the criticisms are in general terms of schoolboy disparagement, with no precise intellectual or moral specificity. His brother Geoffrey says that, although intellectually interested in religion, Maynard 'at the age of seventeen or eighteen passed painlessly, as did my sister and I, into a natural state of agnosticism'.[12] The only clue as to the reason for this loss of faith is a remark by C. R. Fay, a college friend. Keynes was staying with him in Liverpool and explained to him as they were on the way to church on Sunday that T. H. Huxley had exploded Christianity.[13] Christian beliefs to him and the club were irrational; they occasioned raised eyebrows and were not to be taken seriously.

In this easy assumption that science had exploded Christianity, Keynes was in tune with a powerful *zeitgeist*. *The Origin of Species* had been published in 1859, and in Cambridge, as elsewhere, many intellectuals lost their Christian and religious beliefs.[14] The Victorian order rested for the most part on a combination of evangelical religion and social deference. What was to replace it? It was a serious question involving religion, in Keynes' sense, and ethics. Huxley had advocated the retention of the Christian ethic but the rejection of Christian theology. Another possibility was the erection of an all-embracing metaphysics that would comprehend the whole of the universe in a tightly-argued deductive system, which would include a social philosophy. This was more characteristic of Oxford than Cambridge.[15] G. E. Moore represented a reaction from this in favour of philosophy of 'common sense', more in line with the British empirical tradition from Locke onward. It was an attempt to prick what was thought to be philosophical bombast and rhetoric, and to substitute candour, clarity, and a cool frankness that exposed superstition and cant, and called in question existing institutions and conventions. Moore was obsessed with the need for clarity as he understood it. It seemed to be a new dawn. Those influenced by Moore thought of themselves as the first generation to ask with sufficient care what were the two precise questions that it was a task of ethics to answer.[16] What states of affairs or kinds of things are intrinsically good and ought to exist for their own sakes? And secondly, what kinds of action ought we to perform? We have already noted Moore's answer to the first. He held that these goods are simple and unanalysable, and that we just recognize them when we think about the good. His answer to the second was those actions that will cause more good to exist in the universe than any possible alternative.

What this assumed, as Keynes was later to see, was a society sufficiently stable in its social and financial arrangements, and the place of a social and intellectual elite within it suitably provided with domestic servants, to enable the practitioners of Moore's ethic to devote their time to the acquisition of desirable states of mind. It was also influenced by a mood of automatic progress that was common in the early 1900s. Leonard Woolf, for instance, returning from Ceylon in 1911 and a member of the Bloomsbury Group, thought that the world was on the brink of becoming civilized. And he was not typical among Keynes' associates.[17] D. H. Lawrence saw things differently, and it was reflection on his contemptuous dismissal of the Bloomsbury Group as 'done for' that prompted Keynes to write *My Early Beliefs*. Lawrence thought it corrupt. It was certainly parochial and class-bound.

It was at the Apostles Club where, as we have seen, Keynes chiefly absorbed Moore's philosophy, or that part of it that captivated him. It was a small, select, and secret society (of which details have only recently become widely known) whose formal title was 'The Society' or 'The Cambridge Conversation Society'. Founded in 1820, it had been shaped toward intellectual distinction in its earlier years by F. D. Maurice, perhaps the leading English theologian of the last century, but had become agnostic, and definitely anti-Christian. It met every Saturday evening in term for dinner, a paper, and discussion.[13] Moore, addressing the situation of a godless universe, set out to produce a moral philosophy that in fact supported conventional morality on a better basis than that of hedonistic utilitarianism. He thought of himself as pioneering a new path in moral philosophy by regarding the primary question not as 'What ought I to do?' but 'What is good?' Once that is established, the virtues then become a means to what is good, which must be pursued by proportionate reasoning. Keynes in *My Early Beliefs* does not bring out explicitly enough that there are three strands in Moore's thought that are intellectually separable. It is possible to hold any one or two of them without holding all three.

1. Good is a simple, undefinable concept. Decisions as to what is good depend on direct intuition in particular cases. This has continued to engage the interests of moral philosophers as a thesis in the logic of ethics. I doubt whether many now agree with it. It did not greatly interest Keynes and need not concern us.[19]

2. There is a plurality in ethics of what are valued as a good, not a concentration on one, such as pleasure with the classical utilitarians. By far the most valuable goods, as already mentioned, are 'the pleasures of human intercourse' and 'the life of passionate contemplation and communion'.[20]

3. Where ethics in relation to public conduct is concerned, Moore was an ideal utilitarian, maintaining that the rightness of an act derives from its consequences in producing the most good, as against the hedonistic utilitarianism of Jeremy Bentham, John Stuart Mill, and Henry Sidgwick. Moore rejected the hedonism but retained the consequentialism. In his view the best achievable states of affairs were bound to be complex wholes and in many cases would be the product of following conventional morality.

Keynes may have been partly teasing when in *My Early Beliefs* he says they were immoralists. True, at Cambridge they ignored the third element in Moore's teaching. Like many young (and not only young) intellectuals, they universalized their emotional needs in the guise of a rational philosophy. But subsequently many of them took up public causes in the spirit of classical consequentialist utilitarianism in which they had been reared. In practice, it often led them to support the cause of the underdog, even if in a paternalistic fashion.

Certainly this was the case with Keynes himself. He was no immoralist.[21] Indeed in *My Early Beliefs* he does in fact give illustrations of ethical issues discussed by the Apostles (even if of a somewhat bizarre kind), in which estimates of the relative value of the consequences of different answers were involved in resolving them. What he is particularly concerned with is the excessive weight given to economic criteria,[22] and, as we shall see, all his life he held that although considerable stress on these was a regrettable but necessary stage in economic development, it was one for which he expected the need to be outgrown in a century or a little more. Furthermore, the claim of the Apostles not to be bound by a general rule but to judge each case on its merits is one aspect of consequentialist ethics. There has recently been a vigorous discussion of this within Christian ethics in what is known as the situation ethics debate.[23] It has its difficulties – there is no general ethical position that does not have difficulties in that very awkward cases can be posited for it to resolve – but it is in no sense an immoralist position. Nor is it necessarily connected with an optimistic understanding of human goodness and rationality. Keynes' subsequent change to what is a more realistic (and a more

Christian) position did not involve any change in the consequentialist character of his method in making specific moral judgments.

An example of his later percipience is his analysis of the ineffectiveness of Woodrow Wilson at the Paris Peace Conference of 1919.[24] Keynes portrays him as too principled, too conscientious. His Presbyterian temperament became dangerous. Keynes says, with a touch of mischief, that his attitude to his famous 'Fourteen Peace Points' was akin to the verbal inspiration his forefather ascribed to the Pentateuch. In order to preserve them and his conscience intact the president deceived himself by agreeing to sophistries that kept the form of the points but undermined their reality. He had 'the theologian's capacity for self-deception'.[25] This revealing aside shows the prejudice Keynes harboured against the Christian faith, for the capacity of self-deception is notoriously not confined to theologians. Perhaps at the back of his mind lurked the thought that they ought to be most aware of it, when in fact they frequently held their position with a cocksureness that blinded them to it.

Keynes' basic perception of Wilson, however, shows a power of mordant analysis worthy of Reinhold Niebuhr. But like Niebuhr, he set it in the context of a larger hope. He wanted his book on the Paris Peace Conference, in which it occurs, to set in motion 'moral forces of instruction and imagination which change *opinion*. The assertion of truth, the unveiling of illusion, the dissipation of hate, the enlargement and instruction of men's hearts and minds must be the means.'[26] However, unlike Niebuhr, he did not see the necessity of harnessing power to interest in order to achieve a more just society, nationally and internationally, and to do this under the scrutiny of a transcendent source of judgment, such as the Christian understanding of the kingdom of God provides. This sets all interests within the larger perspective of the common good and puts a question mark against utopian hopes of completely fulfilling, in a future historical order, the vision that calls out our loyalty. Keynes was to some extent alert to this point. Burke's political philosophy influenced him to the extent of making him wary of deliberately creating evils in the present on account of the alleged future social benefits that would ensue, a cautionary attitude made necessary because our powers of prediction are so slight. In fact, he thought Burke went too far in defence of existing property arrangements, but he was never tempted by the Marxist willingness to intensify present ills as the means to a future utopia.[27]

Keynes was exceedingly able, self-confident to the point of arrogance, and often ruthless. He never lost his belief that stupidity and ignorance are the chief villains, that ultimately reason triumphs, and that social problems need to be solved by the application of intelligence.[28] He remained a rationalist, bristling with indignation at stupidity and prejudice, but still confident that an enlightened management of the economy by a popularly elected government would be possible, that an intellectual elite would be able to wear down prejudice and to persuade sufficient of the electorate by rational arguments, and that management would be in the hands of a similar elite of high civil servants such as he had met in the India office from 1906 to 1908.[29] This did not prevent him from expressing exasperation from time to time, as when he wrote to T. S. Eliot in 1945 concerning full employment that 'insufficiency of cleverness not of goodness is the main trouble'.[30] He never fully faced the corruptions to which the intelligent are liable, even if he did begin to appreciate the truth expressed in the term 'original sin' with respect to human beings in general.

Keynes' Ethic and *Laissez-faire*

Turning to specific examples of Keynes' ethical stances and their significance for us, I mentioned three that we should consider: (1) his view of *laissez-faire* and its place in his hopes for the economic future of humanity, (2) his view of the relation of economics to ethics, and (3) the attitude required of human beings who have to live with inherent problems of uncertainty about the future in making economic choices. But first of all, something about an issue of personal ethics needs to be said. It is clear that the use made by the Apostles of Moore's ethics was much conditioned by their cultural and social position as privileged intellectuals in a stable society and was not nearly so universal and culture-free as they imagined. In particular, it was affected by the predisposition of several of them to homosexuality. Keynes himself was bisexual. He had several homosexual relationships, some of them transient, the most prolonged with the painter Duncan Grant. Later he was happily married to Lydia Lopokova of the Diaghilev Ballet, whom he married in the St Pancras Registry Office in 1925, and who was to prove a tremendous strength to him, especially after his first heart attack in 1937.

It has been claimed that his homosexual expression of his bisexuality had much to do with his reformist and creative tendencies.[31] But this is doubtful. It was certainly a major element in the reaction of the Apostles to Victorian conventions, restraints and hypocrisy, particularly in the wake of the Oscar Wilde case. Indeed, it is only within the last three decades that homosexuality has become widely discussed and, within limits, accepted, and that we are aware both how much more we know about it and how much we do not yet know about it. Because it was underplayed in Harrod's life of Keynes, there is the temptation now that it has come into the open to assume it must have an overall significance that alters the perspective of everything in Keynes' life. This, I think, is a mistake. Just as it seems that homosexuality spans the whole range of human characters and has not any other traits that are particularly associated with it, so in the case of Keynes his homosexual expressions of his bisexuality do not seem to have any *special* place among the social and intellectual sources of his other ethical stances. Therefore I do not propose to say anything more on the matter.

I turn to his attitude to *laissez-faire*. Keynes' objection to *laissez-faire* was both practical and ethical. Practically, he claimed to show that it did not necessarily work. There has been an immense discussion of his analyses of it, particularly since the publication of *The General Theory of Employment, Interest and Money* in 1936. His desire to abolish mass unemployment and maintain a high level of income and employment led him radically to challenge accepted economic theory. He set out to demonstrate that the *laissez-faire* economy does not contain an automatic mechanism for the reconciling of conflicting interests. Instead a chronic lack of effective demand can lead to an equilibrium well below the level of full employment. The pursuit of private profit does not necessarily lead to public benefit, and in particular private virtue in the shape of saving (or thrift) can be a public vice (where there is insufficient investment and lack of demand). To correct this there can be no escape from political judgments, rather than the monetarist preference for a 'neutral' regulator of the economy. This evades, by reliance on an impersonal mechanism, the problem of political choices. Government action is needed to shift the economy out of its under-employment and keep it out.

I must leave it to professional economists to evaluate Keynes' technical and practical criticism of the *laissez-faire* economy, and whether it can solve the problem he pinpointed. My concern is with his ethical criticism that he has associated with it. Keynes made a sharp distinction between the immediate and the longer-term future. For the present he saw the need for a mixed economy, with some redistribution of wealth, as a condition of economic progress (or growth) and not an obstacle to it. Capitalism is a necessary evil for the moment. It delivers goods and services reasonably efficiently. It is capable of considerable reforms without affecting its basic performance. It channels potentially disruptive energies into relatively less harmful channels connected with moneymaking and money-loving. And it accumulates capital, without which it is impossible to 'solve' the economic problem.[32] In many ways it is extremely objectionable, but it is more efficient for advancing economic ends than any other system in sight.

So much for Keynes' short-term view. The longer-term one is very different. In his essay *The End of Laissez-Faire* he shows how the ethics and philosophy underlying its individualism draws upon diverse sources: the conservative individualism of Locke and Hume; the democratic egalitarianism of Rousseau and Bentham; a Darwinism that found competition in nature; and theories propounded by economists (who were helped by the incompetence and corruption of eighteenth-century governments and the undeniable material progress of the nineteenth century). Then he goes on to say 'It is *not* a correct deduction from the principles of economics that enlightened self-interest always operates in the public interest.'[33]

In the medium term Keynes says it is needful 'to move out of the nineteenth-century *laissez-faire* into an era of liberal socialism'.[34] In *The General Theory* he makes it clear that by this he does not mean a widespread state socialism, but controls to establish an aggregate volume of output to correspond as nearly as possible to full employment, involving a corporate decision as an organized community to achieve a common purpose. This will be the environment for the free play of economic forces to achieve the full potentialities of production, including the advantages of decentralization and of the play of self-interest. This individualism is the best guarantee of personal liberty and human variety.[35] In the class war he would be 'on the side of the educated *bourgeoisie*'.[36] At the same time his aim was the gradual euthanasia of the *rentier,* the functionless investor, as capital is deprived of its scarcity value within one or two generations.[37]

This thought leads to the remarkable optimism of the essay *Economic Possibilities for Our Grandchildren.*[38] Assuming that there are no important wars and no important increases in population (assumptions already falsified since 1931), the *economic* problem may be in sight of solution within a hundred years, and then humanity will be faced with its real and permanent problem, how to use its freedom from pressing economic cares to live wisely, agreeably, and well. There will be great changes in the code of morals:

We shall be able to rid ourselves of many of the pseudo-moral principles which have long hag-ridden us for two hundred years, by which we have exalted some of the most distasteful of human qualities (sc. the love of money as a possession) into the position of highest virtue ... I see us free, therefore, to return to some of the most sure and certain principles of religion and traditional virtue ... that avarice is a vice, that the exaction of usury is a misdemeanour, and the love of money is detestable, that those walk most truly in the paths of virtue and sane wisdom who take least thought for the morrow ... [Yet] for at least another hundred years we must pretend to ourselves that fair is foul and foul is fair: for foul is useful and fair is not. Avarice and usury and precaution must be our goal for a little longer. For only they can lead us out of the turmoil of economic necessity into daylight.[39]

This vision is astonishingly like Marx's picture of Communist society, except that Marx did not see that there would be any human problem in it because men and women would apparently live in a state of continuous harmony and goodwill. Keynes does think there will still be a problem of how to live wisely, agreeably, and well. But even leaving aside his already falsified assumptions, is there not an unreality in his vision? Since human wants are relative to possibilities, is it conceivable that in any future we can at present think of, let alone that of our grandchildren, we shall reach a state where there are no relatively scarce economic resources with alternative uses, the allocation of which is our basic economic problem? Further, is it not ethically naive to say that we must give minimum scope to ethical attitudes and motives that we think unsavoury until we have solved our basic economic problem, after which we will abandon them and take up virtue? It reminds me of a similar attitude taken by many in the last world war. We must abandon all moral scruples in order to defeat a monstrously evil enemy; there will be no holds barred, everything will be permitted. Then when victory is won, we will pick up again our traditional moral code (perhaps our Christian ethic) and build a new and morally better world order. Such an attitude forgets that the means used to achieve an end may so corrupt the process that it renders the end impossible of achievement. It was this attitude among the Allies in the war that led to their policy of unconditional surrender, and a peace settlement with unsatisfactory features from which Europe, and indeed the world, is still suffering.

Many of the attitudes to which Keynes refers are indeed distasteful, some radically so. Others are necessary aspects of the human situation, for example self and family love, that need harnessing by social institutions towards achieving a common good. We need social institutions that allow them scope while maximizing their potentiality for good and minimizing their potentiality for harm. This requires political wisdom. And it needs continual exercise, as institutions are shaped, refined, create new problems, and are further refined. Keynes is quite right that the theory of *laissez-faire* abandons the problem and naively leaves it to the spontaneous operation of the market. What he wanted for the immediate future, market forces operating in a more sophisticated social framework, is persuasive. However, he blackens economic morality too much. Maybe the unworldliness of Moore's ethic betrayed him. That, together with his elitist background, left him with an aesthetic distaste for the processes of economic life, even as he exploited them successfully himself. He made huge sums of money for his college at Cambridge, King's, and for himself; and he spent a lot on the arts and other good causes. To my mind his economic vision for us could better be expressed in a resolution to remove primary poverty from the Third World in one generation, which the rich Two-Thirds World could do if it would.

In another, *Essay in Persuasion*, Keynes says that the political problem is threefold: (1) to secure economic efficiency; this needs technical knowledge; (2) to achieve social justice; this needs an unselfish and enthusiastic spirit that loves the ordinary man; and (3) to respect individual liberty; this requires tolerance, an appreciation of the excellence of variety and independence, and a readiness to give an unhindered opportunity to the exceptional and aspiring.[40] This last remark gives too much scope for a meritocratic society, which would be an exceedingly unpleasant one. It is one thing to give scope to exceptional talent, but to say it must be unhindered obscures the common humanity of the gifted and the less gifted as the basis of citizenship. Apart from this, we can surely accept Keynes' fomulation of the political problem. How it is to be solved involves policies derived from a mixture of technical economic analysis, social and political diagnosis, and ethical evaluation. There is abundant scope for genuine differences of opinion here among those who are agreed with the general aims; and also with the need to deal with the challenge of a Hayek who calls the very conception of social justice a 'mirage'. But underlying the political problem is the likelihood that capitalism has been parasitic on a hangover of several precapitalist moral virtues that it has not itself fostered and, indeed, tends to undermine. That is why we need to embody fairness, altruism, and compassion in economic and social institutions that encourage citizens to behave *as if* they felt them, whether or not at any particular moment they do. Within this framework the market can be left to fulfil its function.[41]

Ethics, Economics, and Uncertainty

I turn now to the relation of ethics to economics in Keynes' thought. I doubt if Skidelsky is right when he says that, unlike Marshall, economics was not an activity through which his ethical beliefs found expression because he followed Moore who had cut the links between economics and ethics.[42] In a letter to Harrod in 1938 Keynes argues that economics is essentially a moral science and not a pseudo-natural science. It is a branch of logic, a way of thinking; and progress in it as a science of thinking is in terms of models, combined with an *art* of choosing models that are relevant to the contemporary world. Good economists are scarce because the gift of choosing good models is a very rare one. Economics employs introspection and judgments of value. On the other hand, it requires rigor to see that conclusions do properly follow from assumptions behind the model. On the other hand, motives, expectations, and psychological uncertainties are involved.[43] This double aspect of economics as a science and an art is not well teased out by Keynes, but it does in principle do justice to both modern economics and the older term 'political economy', out of which it grew and which is still in use in a few places. Economics has freed itself from the philosophical utilitarianism out of which it grew and has established theoretical models that can be handled mathematically and that are useful as heuristic devices *if* they are not mistaken for an adequate model of reality. By this means, the economist is apparently able to avoid value judgments and dwell in the value-free realm of mathematics. However, efficiency in the sense of maximizing resources is a value presupposed by the discipline; it also adopts a value that in fact does operate in mathematics, that of elegance in evaluating models. However, the economist cannot stop there when he is called upon to relate these models to the actual functioning of the various economies. More than logical deductions from the models is required and here we are in the realm of political economy. There seems to be a tendency for mathematical sophistication in economics to increase the more remote it becomes from actuality. Political economy, however, is full of empirical uncertainties (to which I shall shortly refer), which it can never fully resolve, and where the selection and weighting of significant facts is affected by value judgments. This is why there are continual policy disagreements among economists. But if the public is apt to get impatient with them, economists need to sell themselves better. Keynes had rightly a high view of their significance, as witness his famous toast at a dinner of the Council of the Royal Economic Society in 1945, to economists as 'trustees, not of civilization, but of the possibility of civilization'. Without their work the possibility of the various things that Moore had taught him to think of as self-evidently good, and which he himself cultivated all his life, would be hardly available – not even for the elite that he represented, still less for the wider community that he hoped within a century would share in them.

As we have seen, Keynes took an adverse view of the ethics of the free market, as something to be tolerated for a while longer until it has brought us to a level of productivity of goods and services when it will no longer be needed. In my view, this is too negative and too transitory a view. I think the free market is best viewed as a technical device to serve the human purpose of maximizing what can be produced by the allocation of relatively scarce resources with alternative uses, *in so far* as human beings want to pursue that aim compared with other social aims. It has potential moral dangers that require it to be put in a strong social and political institutional framework, which is a matter of political decision. At the same time, a greater realism is needed as to how far away in practice free market economies are from maximizing their productivity by bending to special interests through tariffs, quotas, monopolies, and other restrictions, and disguising the economic costs of doing so. Moreover, efforts to counter Keynes' ethical criticism of the free market by giving it a favourable moral status underplay the organic and interdependent nature of human society, and the damage to this that can be done by great social and economic inequalities. Society is prior to the individual person, who is moulded by it from infancy, and in so far as its institutions are inhumane and unjust is thwarted by it in growing to maturity. Yet that same person transcends society and, when adult, can challenge its institutional structures in the name of a greater justice and humanity. Paretian efficiency is consistent with gross inequalities. At the most, arguments deriving from it support *some* system of property rights rather than common ownership of everything – that is to say, a free market set within the framework of a redistributive system of income and wealth taxes. This is what Keynes came to advocate: in the long run, a better distribution of demand rather than an increased aggregate of demand.[44]

The other ethical issue that Keynes' thought raises in connection with economics is that of living with uncertainty, error, and ignorance. Models in classical economics presuppose, among other things, perfect foresight. Thus, rational expectation can be the basis of decision making. Rational expectation is the most important underlying difference between the conditions the theory assumes and those that exist in fact. For instance, the 'Quality Theory of Money' in its classic form was expressed in the formula $MV=PT$, where roughly M is the quantity of money, V its velocity of circulation, P is the price level, and T the volume of transactions. It assumes an identity in a fundamentally stable and decentralized economy, but in fact hides unproven assumptions about the significance and behaviour of each of the four components, and so is unusable for policy advice.[45] Keynes was primarily a mathematician by training who worked for years on probability theory in mathematical logic. As F. H. Knight pointed out in his classic work of 1921, risk is an actuarial matter, uncertainty is not. Probability statements involve judgments on the bearing of evidence on conclusions, not the forecasting of results.[46] In the *General Theory* Keynes stresses uncertain knowledge with regard to matters where decision and action are necessary, and yet on which there is no scientific basis on which to form any calculable probability. Uncertainty is particularly important in the case of investment, a central feature of his analysis. He says that an entrepreneur's decision to invest depends largely on his 'level of animal spirit'![47]

I take it that economics has to cope with uncertainty, error, and ignorance for three reasons: (1) It has no accepted laws as to how the economy actually works. It can establish trends, but it cannot be sure that they will hold in particular instances. For example, in the early 1970s, the rate of inflation in the United Kingdom was such that the real rate of interest on saving was negative. Contrary to expectation, the rate of saving showed a significant increase. (2) Even if models of how the economy actually works are identical between economists, different assumptions can be fed into forecasting, for example, the state of world trade, government policy, the rate of obsolescence of new inventions, or what will be the rate of interest a decade ahead. (3) Economists have to begin by some analysis of the immediate past, and it is a considerable time before they know whether they were right; complex empirical investigations never quite catch up.

For these reasons, decisions in the real world are made on the basis of guesswork, uncertainty, and conventional assumptions. The economist who has most stressed this is G. L. S. Shackle in his insistence that choice takes place in the face of vague, uncertain, and shifting expectations, hopes and fears. He refers to 'the irreducible uncertainty arising from the ultimate impossibility of (men) ever knowing whether or not, in any particular case, they have all the relevant information'.[48]

Living with uncertainty requires considerable moral and spiritual resources. At worst, it can be frenetic. The animal spirits to which Keynes refers can produce the atmosphere of a casino and expose what Edward Heath in a speech once called 'the unacceptable face of capitalism'. On the other hand, it can be paralyzing. Can it be creative and liberating? I think institutional controls are needed to keep these phenomena within bounds, but that is not my main concern. For living with uncertainty is an inescapable feature of human life. It is in how they set about this that human beings show their best qualities and their worst. Basically, we all need to draw upon resources that set us free to live creatively towards the uncertain future. The Pauline phrase is to walk by faith and not by sight. I quote this because I think the Judaeo-Christian tradition whose foundation Keynes assumed to be exploded has much to offer at this point. For it applies as much to ethical decision making as it does to basic doctrinal attitudes.

I understand why, in context, the young Keynes dismissed the Christian tradition so completely at the age of seventeen or eighteen. Much theology bumbled badly in coping with new intellectual outlooks of the nineteenth century. One can see how many young confident intellectuals became the 'cultured despizers of religion' to whom Schleiermacher had addressed himself at the turn of the century, as did Bishop Joseph Butler in the eighteenth century. The great eighteenth-century moral philosopher Joseph Butler, in his *Analogy of Religion*, wrote: 'It is come, I know not how, to be taken for granted by many persons, that Christianity is not so much as a subject of inquiry, but that it is, now at length, discovered to be fictitious. And accordingly they treat it, as if, in the present age, this were an agreed point among all people of discernment; and nothing remained but to set it up as a principal subject of mirth and ridicule, as it were by way of reprisals for its having so long interrupted the pleasures of the world.'[49] That comes pretty close to the attitude of the Apostles and Keynes. One would have hoped that someone as clever and with as wide sympathies as Keynes would have probed more deeply. Is there not a touch of intellectual and spiritual arrogance in those who refuse to do so? In my experience, social scientists, including economists, have been prone to this dismissive arrogance.

Everything works at bottom with a 'faith', in the sense of some fundamental presupposition about humans and their place in the universe on which they build, and behind which they cannot go. As we have seen, Keynes realized this.[50] Butler in his preface goes on to say with reference to the Christian faith 'that any reasonable man, who will thoroughly consider the matter, may be as much assured, as he is of his own being, that it is not, however, so clear a case, that there is nothing in it. There is, I think, strong evidence of its truth; but it is certain no one can, on principles of reason, be satisfied to the contrary.'[51] Because life's evidence is ambiguous, a choice of 'faith' has to be made, and in this sense agnosticism and atheism are also faiths. Keynes thought true belief to be important. He feared that our age has lost the possibility of believing in having true beliefs.[52] I am sorry Keynes did not give the Judaeo-Christian tradition more attention, because I think it makes more sense of more 'facts' than any other. It is hard to imagine Keynes outside it, for he had absorbed much from it. At its best, it is the best foundation for what he strove for all his life – concern for the good of human persons on the widest scale and for social and economic conditions that allow them to pursue the good as they perceive it. It might have sustained him, and he might have made a direct contribution to it, had he been explicitly inside it.[53]

Conclusion:

Ronald Preston and the Contemporary Ethical Scene

IAN S. MARKHAM

It is ironic. The Ronald Preston approach to ethics has become an industry, yet those specializing in Christian Ethics have rejected it. The Preston approach involves the following: we develop principles informed by our 'basic orientation'. We then engage with the specialists in the field – our secular experts – with the goal of arriving at certain policy recommendations. This basic method characterizes the growing arena of professional ethics in all its forms. Courses in business, accountancy, medical, veterinary ethics abound (just to name a few) and all use this same basic methodology. However, while the Preston approached succeeds in the secular world, it has been given short shrift in the theological and Christian worlds. The departure of Ronald Preston from Manchester was followed by Peter Baelz from Oxford and Gordon Dunstan from London. All three conceived the ethical task in similar ways. Although Anthony Dyson continued the Preston methodology, Baelz and Dunstan were replaced by Oliver O'Donovan and Michael Banner respectively. O'Donovan and Banner wanted *Christian* ethics to be recognizably and distinctively Christian. They joined forces with Stanley Hauerwas and Richard Hays to argue for a greater stress on the church as the location of Christian ethics and the Bible as the source of Christian ethics. The Preston approach hardly merited conversation: it was simply dismissed as unChristian and dated.

This short essay will defend the Preston approach. Although there are differences of detail between Preston and myself, these are insignificant compared to the gulf transfixed between us and O'Donovan and Banner.[1] I shall start by describing the main features of the Preston approach that I propose to defend. Then the main criticisms of this approach and the main alternatives will be described. I shall show that the main alternatives are very difficult for anyone wanting the church to engage the world to affirm. The Preston approach has triumphed in every other branch of ethics precisely because it is an approach that works.

Preston's methodology has a strong and proud ancestry. He stands in the classical tradition of seventeenth-century Anglican Moral theology, which has been rescued and renewed by Kenneth Kirk. In addition F. D. Maurice, William Temple, and perhaps supremely, Reinhold Niebuhr are important. The main complaint about Preston, which will be examined in detail later in the chapter, is that his 'Christian' ethics is nothing more than secular platitudes justified by using Christian language. Therefore it is necessary to make explicit the Niebuhrian theological framework that Preston uses.

As Durkin has shown, Niebuhr makes considerable use of certain theological myths around which his entire ethical system is built.[2] Although Lehmann is right to emphasize the position of christology, this is not central.[3] Although Minnema can point to Niebuhr's Gifford Lectures as clear evidence that the understanding of the human person is important, this is still not central.[4] Instead, as Tillich was the first to point out, Niebuhr's 'system' (in so far as the ever-changing Niebuhr had one) is built around the four primary myths of creation, fall, atonement, and parousia. This biblical religion, as Niebuhr calls it, or these primary myths, explain the deepest human needs and wants. They provide an analysis and solution to the situation of the human creature. So Niebuhr writes, 'Man does not know himself truly except as he knows himself confronted by God. Only in that confrontation does he become aware of his full stature and freedom and of the evil in him. It is for this reason that biblical faith is of such importance for the proper understanding of man, and why it is necessary to correct the interpretations of human nature which underestimate his stature, depreciate his physical existence and fail to deal realistically with the evil in human nature, in terms of biblical faith.'[5] Self-knowledge is made possible by an appropriate understanding of the significance of these myths. Put simply, the Niebuhrian method is that one should suggest policies compatible with the insights about humanity derived from biblical religion.

The ultimate ethical reference-point for Niebuhr is the law of love, supremely expressed in the cross of Christ. It is a standard which is both in and beyond history. This must be the ultimate point of reference against which all other historical systems should be judged. This is Niebuhr's first criticism of Natural Law. Niebuhr believed the law of love is reduced to a sort of addendum in Natural Law theories. His second criticism is that he believed Natural Law systems are intrinsically inflexible: 'But Catholic theory assumes that the requirements of natural law are absolute and inflexible, being contained in the reason which the creature shares with God.'[6] Not only is it historically impossible that any culture and age could provide the standard by which all human nature in every age should be judged, but this sort of claim undermines the law of love. Natural Law, for Niebuhr, is virtually synonymous with legalism. And Niebuhr believes that love can provide a standard against both legalism and relativism.

The actual policy recommendations Niebuhr proceeded to make show considerable sophistication. His sensitivity to the irrational potential for evil within humanity meant that he became a clear advocate of democracy.[7] His awareness of the social power structures made him an uncompromising critic of pacifism.[8] He is misunderstood as a prophet of sin and doom; in fact Niebuhr believed that once armed with the insights of biblical religion, one would avoid illusory utopian solutions, and start to construct genuinely hopeful and realistic options.

Preston's methodology is grounded in a Niebuhrian theology. This is clear from Preston's moving reflection on Reinhold Niebuhr in chapter 3. Preston talks of Niebuhr as a 'theological giant' and, along with William Temple, 'leading figures both in the church and state earlier this century'.[9] This grounding in Niebuhr means that theology and church are extremely important to Preston. When locating himself in terms of his vantage point, Preston starts with the acknowledgment that he is an Anglican priest working in Britain.[10] As such he affirms the existence of a God who is God of the whole world and a faith that has something to say to the whole world. This might seem banal, yet given the sectarianism of much contemporary 'Christian ethics' Preston is right to affirm these fundamentals. Then Preston explains in a direct echo of Niebuhr: 'The Bible gives us a general perspective on human life and destiny; a broad drama from creation, incarnation, redemption, and the church to the last things.'[11] Jesus remains supremely important for Preston. Jesus' teaching of the kingdom of God or 'the way God exercises his rule as King over the world'[12] is central to Preston. Unthreatened by the picture of Jesus emerging from biblical criticism, Preston is attracted to the radicalism of Jesus. Jesus, according to Preston, takes the common morality of his day (e.g. the Golden Rule) and then makes it more demanding. So forgiveness should be unlimited and enemies should be loved. And within these broad principles, Jesus then leaves us to work out the details sensitive to the ambiguities and complexities of this world. Contra to many of Preston's critics, there is a serious engagement with the Jesus traditions here. He does not want the radicalism evaded: Preston writes: 'The radical elements in Jesus' ethic are an authentic corollary of the radical stance of the Kingdom of God, calling us past the necessary struggles with justice to a fuller realization of love.'[13]

For Preston, the task of the theologian is to draw out the necessary principles from the Christian tradition. The *Imago Dei* is important because it affirms the intrinsic value of all people. The teaching of the kingdom sets an exacting standard for the treatment of the poor. The awareness of human sinfulness puts an appropriate break on all utopian hopes and expectations. Drawing on the tradition and scripture with imagination and clarity, Preston sets out the theological principles upon which he is going to build. Theology is important to Preston. This is the first component to the Preston approach: a drawing on the insights of the tradition to illuminate and clarify the difficult conceptual debates in society.

The second component in the Preston approach is to use middle axioms. W. A. Visser 't Hooft and J. H. Oldham formulated the concept of middle axioms. The purpose was to identify the factors that justified the move from theory to expression. J. Bennett took up the concept enthusiastically. Although 'middle axioms' have been extensively criticized,[14] for Preston the concept remains a valuable tool. The value is in the 'role' of the concept: it induces Christian humility. In much the same way that Duncan Forrester talks about 'theological fragments', which are insights sensitively applied to contemporary discussions, Preston uses middle axioms to ensure some sort of autonomy for the secular.[15] It ensures that Christian doctrine does not over-reach itself. Although the sovereignty of God touches every aspect of our lives, this does not mean that the church is the source of all expertise in every aspect of our lives. One does not turn to a catechism to decide how best the European Union is run. Middle axioms puts a clear distance between Christian doctrine and policy expression. Hence it is a device that insists on a little humility from the theologian.

This is linked to the third element of the Preston approach. Preston's initial training is in economics. He is acquainted from the inside with the assumptions made within that discipline. And he rejects entirely John Milbank's talk that the 'secular discipline of

economics' is parasitic on a set of assumptions fundamentally antag-
onistic to Christianity.[16] Indeed he cut his academic teeth on earlier
versions of such debates. Preston attacks the Malvern Conference of
1941 on similar grounds: it is simply wrong to believe that Christian
ethics can disregard the expertise of those in economics and sociology.
It is a conceit that is bound to marginalize our analysis and arguments.

There is so much good clear sense in the Preston approach that
one wonders why it has attracted so much hostility. The main reason
seems to be a preoccupation with 'distinctiveness'. Christian ethics,
so the argument runs, should not simply apply Christian language
to secular analysis but should be saying something 'different'. The
Christian voice in any group ought to stand out: one ought to be
able to see the difference.

The great inspiration to this distinctiveness campaign is Karl Barth.
Karl Barth, of course, was defined by his theological reaction to
nineteenth-century liberalism, which came partly as a result of a certain ethical insight. He believed that if his liberal theological teachers
were so wrong in supporting the obscenity of the First World War,
then it must be highly likely that they were wrong in theology. Nothing they said could be trusted. The themes of Barthian theology are
well known: God has acted in Christ; human attempts to discover
God are doomed to failure; Natural Theology and Natural Law are
wholly inappropriate. Instead, ethics is a branch of dogmatics. So
Barth writes: 'True man and his good action can be viewed only from
the standpoint of the true and active God and His goodness.'[17] Barth
formulates an ethic organized around Christ. Edward LeRoy Long
usefully summarizes: 'His own understanding of the Christian life
revolves about three points: (a) man himself cannot answer the ethical
question, (b) Christ does, and (c) when Christ does, the ethical dimensions of truly human existence are both authenticated and made possible without the distortions that are inevitable when the ethical
question is answered by man alone.'[18]

With this framework, the christocentric nature of Christian ethics
becomes paramount. The leading lights of this approach are Oliver
O'Donovan and Michael Banner. The framework for ethical reflection
is the church. The task is to link the theology of the church to the
problems facing God's world. The task is then heavy on Christian
doctrine but light on practical policies. A good example of this
is the rather tortuous St Andrews Day Statement devoted to the issue
of homosexuality. (Another issue on which Preston has led the way
by supporting the homosexual community.) Drafted by Oliver

O'Donovan and signed by Michael Banner, Markus Bockmuehl, Timothy Bradshaw, Ann Holt, William Person, and David Wright, it sets out a theological framework for discussion. Now to the credit of the group it is a wholly appropriate attempt to transcend the rather shrill, combative tone of the debate to date and find some way of moving the conversation forward. However, the problem is methodological. The Trinitarian affirmations will be shared by most Christians, yet most of us will not 'see' why the Group feel that the Trinity necessarily implies an inability to affirm homosexual relations.

The Group affirms the doctrine of the Trinity in three dramatic statements of principle; it then moves to application: 'There can be no description of human reality, in general or in particular, outside the reality in Christ.'[19] This means that our sexuality is not a defining characteristic of our humanity and therefore should not be given excessive significance. Then the fact that we are required to take up our cross means 'we are all summoned to various forms of self-denial'.[20]

This means that homosexuals should not complain if the cross they carry means no sexual activity. And finally it is the Bible (especially Romans 1.26–27) which must judge any secular or scientific description of homosexual behaviour. So they claim:

> Many competing interpretations of the phenomena can be found in contemporary discussion, none of them with an unchallengeable basis in scientific data. The Church has no need to espouse any one theory, but may learn from many. To every theory, however, it must put the question whether it is adequate to the understanding of human nature and its redemption that the Gospel proclaims.[21]

The St Andrews Day Statement exposes the inadequacy of this Barthian methodology. And this is for two reasons. First, it is possible to be Trinitarian and reach different conclusions. Rowan Williams offers 'unqualified agreement with the principles enunciated', yet is not persuaded by the group's application of those principles.[22] And Elizabeth Stuart states categorically: 'I have no argument at all with your three theological principles except that the full implications of these principles are not fully worked out.'[23] O'Donovan might retort it is good that the principles attract agreement given that it is a basis on which the conversation can proceed. But the problem with this is that it is difficult to see how the conversation is advanced if mutually incompatible conclusions can be deduced from the same doctrines.

The second difficulty is that the theology is being used for a political purpose. A crucial step in the group's argument is that homosexuality should be linked with 'race and class' and not with gender. At this point the group is vulnerable to a parallel argument that most contemporary Christians would reject, namely with slavery. Slavery after all was largely a class designation which was linked with race. If homosexuality does not define a person, then neither does the appellation of 'slave'. If homosexuality is a 'cross' that must be carried, then perhaps so are the duties of a slave. If the Bible is the determining context for interpretation of secular analysis, then perhaps the biblical analysis of slavery ought to be used to undermined those liberal calls for liberation. As a matter of historical fact a Trinitarian worldview has coexisted with a range of social expression: most people have not felt that the doctrine of the Trinity will advance ethical discussion very far.

If the Barthian enthusiasm for the Trinity is not going to get us very far, then perhaps the post-modern Radical Orthodox might have more success. John Milbank is the leading light of this group.[24]

John Milbank and his advocacy of 'radical orthodoxy' starts from the post-modern sensitivity that there is no traditionless basis for any position. So he deconstructs modernity by exposing its hidden assumptions. The Natural and Social sciences are exposed as manipulators of power. Natural science, explains Milbank, 'possesses no privileged access to truth and cannot, purely on its own account, build up a realist ontology. Its "truth" is merely that of instrumental control . . .'[25] The secular, on which the social sciences are parasitic, 'had to be invented as the space of "pure power"'.[26] Therefore disciplines such as 'sociology of religion' ought to disappear because 'secular reason claims that there is a "social" vantage point from which it can locate and survey various "religious" phenomena. But it has turned out that assumptions about the nature of religion themselves help to define the perspective of this social vantage.'[27]

Sociology has no privilege over theology: in so far as sociology can continue, writes Milbank, 'it would have to redefine itself as a "faith"'.[28]

Having deconstructed secularism, Milbank then constructs an account of Christianity as 'a true Christian metanarrative realism'.[29] This he believes is the only adequate response to Nietzschian nihilism. Christianity is located in a community – the church – and unlike the secular, which is built on an ontology of violence, the church is committed to an ontology of peace. He concludes the book: '[The] absolute Christian vision of ontological peace now provides the only alternative to a nihilistic outlook.'[30]

Preston is spot on in his criticisms of this approach reproduced in chapter 7. At this stage Milbank had not written his major work *Theology and Social Theory*. However, Preston both correctly anticipates the drift of Milbank's arguments and deals a devastating criticism of it. He writes:

> Milbank argues that the acceptance of Christian doctrine alters the entire intellectual picture so that there cannot be a single, non-controversial description of contemporary secular reality. Therefore there is no point in social theology engaging with so-called experts; instead it should be calling into question the terms on which secular analyses are made. There is some truth here. The assumptions of any discipline or any 'expert', explicit or implicit, need examining in terms of the understanding of the world, and human beings in the world, which they presuppose. But it does not follow that Christian theology requires such peculiar assumptions as to render other disciplines otiose, so that they have to be replaced by Christian ones, Muslim ones, agnostic ones, or whatever. If the entire intellectual picture is altered we should have to establish Christian mathematics and Christian engineering; or if the implications of this cause us to draw back, it would certainly involve Christian biology, psychology, sociology, and economics.[31]

Preston is correct. Challenging assumptions of any discipline is entirely proper. Talking of incompatible or incommensurable rationalities is just plain wrong. Granted different traditions 'weigh' factors in different ways. Granted also that the factors that count on any given topic vary from one tradition to another, but this does not make 'engagement' impossible. The fundamental laws of logic are shared. Translation and understanding of different traditions depends on this.[32] Engagement is not impossible nor is it undesirable.

Preston has a second criticism of Milbank in the same article. Christian ethics is in the business of offering some sort of policy recommendations to society. But complains Preston, 'When it comes to actual recommendations, Milbank bows out by talking of the "realism of the Cross", and of a creative disengagement from the so-called political realities. This prescinds from any of the choices offered us, and leaves us with all the problems of relating the cross to economic, social and political structures with which social theology has traditionally had to wrestle.'[33] For Preston, you judge the value of an approach to Christian ethics partly by its proposed policies. To offer none reflects on the poverty of the approach.

Preston is right. Christian ethics will not advance if it insulates itself from any secular criticisms by spurious philosophical considerations. Incommensurability means that other discourses have nothing to say to theologians and theologians have nothing to say to the world.

If one is in the business of defending an Anglican approach to ethics, then a version of Preston's approach is essential. An established church, coupled with a theology of the gatekeeper, willing and ready to engage with specialists outside the church, is the only way forward. Establishment cannot survive this sort of sectarian ethical methodology. (Although Preston would agree with this, he would actually go further and insist that there is no element of sectarianism in the Anglican theological tradition, not simply Established Anglicanism.) The theology of the gatekeeper places an appropriate obligation on the established church to represent all faith to Government. A pluralist culture will only allow Anglicans to be privileged by establishment provided it makes an overt attempt to open the gate to other faith traditions. And contemporary political discourse is not going to jettison the insights of economists and sociologists in favour of a 'radical orthodox' vision of a church built on an 'ontology of peace'. Anyway this latter proposal is tantamount to a plea for the conversion of society, not an engagement with it.

Ronald Preston's distinguished career remains a model for those who are in the same business. His theological method is sound; his major source, Reinhold Niebuhr, provided a robust theological resource. His theological humility is welcome. He would never have entertained suggestions that one can deduce solutions to contemporary problems from the doctrine of the Trinity. Although he agrees entirely that presuppositions made by other disciplines need to be carefully examined, he would never suggest that sociology is built on an 'ontology of violence'. He knows sufficient about sociology to know that this simply is not true. His acceptance of boundaries was never a denial of the distinctiveness of Christian ethics, but simply a recognition of the limits of Christian ethics.

The essays collected together in this book not only demonstrate the breath of Preston's work but also affirm the centrality of his method. They should be a model not only for students and clergy but plenty of professors as well.

After Word

RONALD H. PRESTON

My first after words must be ones of great gratitude to Canon Dr John Elford and Professor Ian Markham for their generosity in editing this book; generosity of time and generosity of spirit. I am also grateful to Archbishop Lord Habgood for his foreword, more especially because I am one of the very many who admire the wise and concise writings he has made over the years on a wide range of issues in church and state. For some time I had wondered whether to make a collection of some of my post-retirement essays, but the demands of new writing postponed any consideration of past writings. This undertaking entirely altered the situation, and it is on a larger scale than I had envisaged. It is also much better that others should decide which of my writings should be reprinted than that I should.

The selection has been made from essays originally appearing in journals, not books, these being less easily accessible. The two exceptions are the chapter on Christian ethics, which originally appeared in a large symposium covering all the main religious and philosophical ethical positions, and the one on J. M. Keynes which originally appeared in a book, *The Legacy of Keynes*, practically unknown in this country. The original publication in journals partly accounts for the fact (apart from the choice of the editors) that some areas of my writing do not appear here, e.g. the areas of criminal justice and medical and sexual ethics. The essays have not been revised; after some consideration it was thought better to let them remain as they were when originally published. I also refrain from commenting on them now – unlike St Augustine who, in his last years, surveyed all his previous writings in his *Retractationes*. At worst they are period pieces and at best they may still have something relevant to say. I thank the editors warmly for their own contributions.

One of their problems is that my basic theological stance has to be gathered from incidental passages and is nowhere systematically expounded. A word of explanation is perhaps needed. From 1949, when I began to teach Christian ethics part-time in Manchester university, my main effort was a course of about forty-six lectures each year on the foundations of Christian ethics, its history, its bearing on key areas of contemporary life and its relation to the ethics of other faiths and philosophies. I kept it up-to-date by revising it slightly each year. And that was all I had time for because of other responsibilities at St Anselm Hall and later at the cathedral. When I was appointed to the new Chair of Social and Pastoral Theology at the age of fifty-seven, I continued this course for several years until other commitments made it necessary to pass it on to others. At the same time I was teaching in new and more specialized courses, supervising research, external examining and carrying administrative duties in the faculty and university, so that there was little time for writing until I retired. Then I had to consider whether I should write a book based on these lectures, but decided that it would probably be better to concentrate on two areas where I had some special experience, issues in the areas of politics, economics and theology, and ecumenical and social ethics. Both are ever-changing and much time is needed to keep abreast. So the lectures have never been written up or updated since I ceased to give them.

The Middle Level

I now offer a brief comment on the chapters by the editors. First there is a vexed issue of middle axioms. John Elford has not understood my position on the role of experts. As he says, middle axioms is a wretched term, and very misleading. I now never use it. Its background in Dr J. H. Oldham's mind was a stress on the importance of the laity in their jobs in civil society together with suspicion of pronouncements on ethical issues by church synods and the like, on the grounds that they are likely to be ill-informed, and that they let those who pass them off too lightly, as if passing a resolution can achieve much unless it is clear what those who pass it are committed to by passing it. Nevertheless, churches might be expected to have some wisdom to pass on to their lay members in civil society, and in his view after proper investigation of the evidence in connection with an issue under discussion it is better for church bodies to speak at a middle level between generalities which are not specific enough to have precise content and detailed policies on which the evidence is likely to be uncertain. Christians who want to achieve the same direction of policy may disagree about the detailed policies to achieve it.

This middle level does not preclude groups within churches propagandizing for specific conclusions; it is official church guidance or instruction, issued with a certain authority, which is under discussion. Nor does it rule out specific proposals or criticism in clear cut cases (sometimes called boundary situations), but the vast majority of issues are not clear cut but of an ambiguous nature.

This is an attempt to move from Christian convictions based on the Bible and tradition to contemporary issues. In my experience both those who agree with it and those who do not are not very clear about it. My own systematic discussion is in an Appendix to the Scott Holland Lectures (*Church and Society in the Late Twentieth Century*, 1983) and is not referred to. In any case it needs clarification in some respects. I now attempt this.

Clearly some empirical judgment is involved in any comment on the contemporary scene. To urge the importance of full employment means an awareness that unemployment is a serious issue. The question concerns the level of empirical details involved. There are some statements that are so closely involved with Christian doctrine that the empirical element is minimal. F. D. Maurice, when faced with Christians who accepted the ideology of modern capitalism and said that to infringe the laws of competition in any respect was to go against a law of God as certain as a physical law, replied that the idea that competition is a total account of how human beings should relate to one another in society is a lie. In a Christian understanding of God it could not be true. Similarly broad presumptions (to use a term made popular by Wogaman) or principles have been drawn from Christian doctrine, such as that centres of power in society always need balancing because unchecked power is a prime source of injustice; or various slogans in the ecumenical movement such as the Just, Participatory and Sustainable Society. (The difficulty about the latest one which refers to the Integrity of Creation is whether the word 'Integrity' is the right one.) Examples such as these have often been referred to as middle axioms, but in my view this is a mistake.

Statements that fit the term are ones that include much more empirical detail. The more detailed they become, the less likely they are to be agreed, because of the difficulties of evaluating the evidence and forecasting the effects of specific detailed policies. The contention has been that if a fairly wide consensus on the evidence can be achieved it is useful for official church pronouncements to remain at a middle level between generality and detail, indicating the aim to be pursued, not one particular set of detailed policies by which to pursue it. This

should educate church opinion and put the onus on those who disagree to show why.

To take the theme of the church and the bomb, raised by Elford,
there is a strong case for saying on the basis of the Christian doctrine
of the Just War that certain types of nuclear weapons which the UK
possesses with its nuclear submarine, is so inherently indiscriminate
that there could be no moral (or rational) justification for using them.
To convince church and public opinion of this is important. The
question of how to get rid of them is one of detailed policy. Would,
for instance, unilateral renunciation be de-stabilizing? What other
options are there? The aim would be to work towards the international renunciation of them: there are alternative detailed policies
for achieving that. It is unlikely that official church bodies are in a
position to back one of them, though it is useful to have them distinguished and explored.

Working in this way depends on evaluation of evidence, some of
it expert and some personal experience. It is here that hazards of the
selection and evaluation of 'facts' arises and I have frequently called
attention to it. It is not a question of too much deference to experts,
as John Elford says, but of evaluating expertise because experts differ.
For example, in questions of medical ethics we cannot do without
the medical experts but we cannot leave them as sole arbiters in
ethical decisions. Is is the same in other areas.

We cannot be governed by experts. It is here that the public, and
the church public, needs guidance; giving it and monitoring it once
given is a hazard that has to be faced. It is, of course, a rough and
ready process, but there is no better one. As Aristotle pointed out,
we cannot expect more certainty in ethics than the nature of the
subject permits. Also ideological decisions within and between
Christians and between churches on ethical issues can be so great
that no middle level of agreement can be achieved. In that case it is
urgent to keep all sides in dialogue facing awkward questions that
others want to put to them, and always doing so as Christians.

Ecumenical Social Ethics

This leads to my root criticism of the study work of the World Council
of Churches since about 1981 in the areas with which I have been
mainly concerned. It is that instead of engaging in a sifting and enquiring debate between different stances on key ethical questions so that
they may face the awkward questions each wants to ask of the others,

it has in practice largely propagated one analysis and chosen advisors who themselves stood for it. Broadly it is a utopian ideology of the Left, which while properly criticizing the 'West' (which has most of the power and therefore the responsibility) lets the leaders of the Third World off the hook too easily. It has also taken from some sections of the 'West' some very dubious analyses. The result has been a dramatic fall in the quality of the study work coming from Geneva. An example of empirically weak study is given in the essay by Professor Charles Birch and myself in this book. On its theological method the WCC produced a study, *Ecclesiology and Ethics*, which is a tacit defence of it.

I produced a critique of this, which appeared in the *Epworth Review* in October 1998 with the title 'Faith and Order vs Life and Work: Ecclesiology and Ethics in the World Council of Churches'. It is not included in this book. My own position can be described as a 'realistic' approach to politics, both of the Left and the Right, as will be apparent from these essays. I remain an admirer of much of the work of the World Council of Churches, and am more of a committed ecumenist that I think is John Elford.

Other Religions and Natural Law

On Elford's backing of Cantwell Smith I would say that the issue is not what is common to the basic doctrines of all religions, but the values in civil society that they, at best, uphold, what, to use the traditional term, is the area of Natural Law. I think Küng focusses this well. And this links with my one comment on Markham's lively essay. The account he gives of Reinhold Niebuhr's attitude to Natural Law as inflexible and legalistic dates from pre-Vatican II days, when the old manuals of moral theology reigned. They have now been discarded. True there are differing attitudes within the Roman Catholic Church, and some of them, especially the more official utterances, are still inflexible and legalistic, particularly in sexual ethics, but there is much on different lines in the church, many moral theologians treating moral reasoning as 'natural' to human beings, and nature as dynamic, not fixed.

The Relevance of an Anglican Tradition

This is, I think, important. There is no suggestion that all Anglicans share it. It has been manifestly ignored by some and unknown to many, nor is it necessarily peculiarly Anglican, though it is congenial to the main stream of Anglican theology since Hooker. And behind him is Aquinas, and going further back the effort of the Early Church to use its Jewish religious and Greek ethical inheritance to achieve a civic theology which cannot be directly achieved by weaving New Testament texts together. After the Reformation the tradition of moral theology was continued both by Anglicans and Puritans of the Reformed tradition like Ames and Baxter. (It is Lutherans who have shied away from it, because in expounding their important doctrine of the Two Realms or Kingdoms they have made an extremely sharp separation between the two because they fear that explicit Christian reflection on the kingdoms of this world would lead to a religion of works.) Notable Anglican moralists in the seventeenth century were Sanderson and Taylor. Anglican moral theology differed from the current Roman Catholic variety in being at once more rigorist and more flexible. At the end of the century it faded out. Why? Tawney said bluntly that the church ceased to count because she ceased to think. Work needs to be done on how and why it faded.

One consequence was that when the new dynamic society produced by the agrarian and industrial revolutions got under way during the eighteenth century, producing many unpleasant side effects, Malthus and others, mistakenly thinking that the laws of competition were as fixed as physical laws, set out to produce a theodicy which justified their harsh effects on human beings by saying it was God's way of disciplining unruly humanity.

It was this contention that F. D. Maurice challenged. As I have mentioned, he said that on the Christian doctrine of God it could not be true. Towards the end of the nineteenth century there was a sustained attempt to renew Christian social theology as part of a renewed moral theology.

In the Roman Catholic Church, moral theology continued to be taught on the old basis, particularly in seminaries with the training of Confessors in mind, focussing on its precise differentiations of sins. In the early years of the twentieth century, Kenneth Kirk began to translate what was best in the manuals into an Anglican context in an effort to restore moral theology (or Christian ethics – the more 'Protestant' term) into the life of the church. Of his books, *Conscience and its Problems* (1927, reissued 1999) is the most accessible. In many ways he was a traditional figure; for instance he could write a chapter on marriage without mentioning (romantic) love. But although he was traditional in many of his views, his conclusions, for instance at the end of *Conscience and its Problems,* are very flexible and 'liberal'. I put that word in quotation marks because it is a weasel word. By it, I mean confidence in the ability of human beings to engage in practical moral reasoning with their fellows, together with a stress on their responsibility for doing so, and the need for structures in church and society alike which encourage it. That there has been a crass form of liberalism (culture bound), I acknowledge. I had to grow out of it myself, but that does not over-throw the traditional Christian doctrine of conscience as central to what we mean by a human being. I have lived through a period when theological attacks on liberalism have been made in the name of theological exclusivism by those who use the benefits of liberal insti-tutions to attack them. The latest arose from the deconstruction movement derived from French literary theory. Anyone who has wrestled with Marxism as I had to do as a young man, and has taken the sociology of knowledge seriously ever since, is not likely to underestimate the conditioning factors in human knowledge, including the importance of the communities in which we are formed. But to be conditioned is not to be determined; and I am no more impressed by current attacks on liberalism, in the sense of the ability of humans to communicate through the use of their reason, including their conscience, or reasoning on moral issues, than I have been with previous attacks on liberalism. I think theologians who build upon it make a great mistake; instead of bending to it they should criticize it.

Much of the incidental thought in Kirk's writing is naturally dated, but his basic exposition of the nature, authority and formation of conscience and its relation to church authority remains as the basis of the Anglican tradition of which I count myself an heir. It is also congenial to some tendencies in the Roman Catholic Church follow-ing the reform of moral theology after Vatican II.

Expansion in the Study of Christian Ethics

Serious study of moral theology or Christian ethics made slow progress in the UK. Scotland is a partial exception, where practical theology was taught in the divinity Schools, but for a long time it was mostly a 'hints and tips' type of Pastoralia. In the Church of England the acme of absurdity was reached in the middle 1950s when the bishops removed the paper on Christian ethics from the General Ordination Examination and substituted a third Old Testament paper in is place. This was probably due to the influence of the Biblical

Theology Movement which flourished roughly between 1935 and 1955.

Under this influence there was a tendency to assume that one could weave biblical text together on specific issues such as The (*sic*) Biblical Doctrine of Work or the State, and that was sufficient for the study of Christian ethics. Indeed, when I began teaching in Manchester university in 1949, its part-time lectureship in Christian ethics was the only academic job in the field in English and Welsh Universities, apart from the Chair in Moral and Pastoral Theology at Oxford (which Kirk had occupied). I felt intellectually isolated; the only scholars in the world I wanted to talk to were in the USA. Why was the UK situation like this? I can only hazard a guess. The UK has had a Protestant culture, stressing the Bible. When theology began to be studied in the universities, roughly from the beginning of the twentieth century, it tended to be introduced in the shape of biblical studies which could stand in their own right apart from confessional doctrinal differences. The Bible was also thought to embrace within itself its own bearing on the ethical issues of the modern world. Also it was thought that Christian ethics was generally accepted in the community. It was doctrines that were denominationally divisive. It was because in this sense Christian ethics was thought to be non-controversial that it was introduced into the Manchester BD from the beginning of the faculty in 1904. Since then it has become ever more clear that biblical studies cannot be separated from all other religious studies in this way, and now all branches of theology are included in Departments of Theology and Religious Studies. I have seen an enormous growth in teaching and writing in the field of Christian ethics since 1949. The Society for the Study in Christian Ethics is well established with its journal *Studies in Christian Ethics*. There is also the Association of Teachers of Moral Theology, primarily a Roman Catholic body, now thirty years old. At first it was essentially for those teaching in seminaries in this field, but as the number of those has diminished, so the number of Roman Catholics teaching in the field in universities has increased. From the start it had an ecumenical element and I have been a member almost from the beginning. I should like to pay tribute to the quality of the papers, the discussions and the openness and friendliness of the meetings and worship. Differences of opinion in the Roman Catholic Church as within other confessional traditions make it clear that, as the Lund Faith and Order Conference in 1952 said, churches should do together everything that conscience does not require them to do separately. They are far from doing it yet, but certainly in Christian ethics and moral theology there is everything to be said for doing so, and failure to do so will impoverish everybody.

Notes

Introduction: Ronald Preston's Theological Ethics

1. Preston's *Religion and the Persistence of Capitalism*, SCM Press 1991, is his contribution to the debate initiated by Tawney and continued by V. A. Demant. Chapter 3 of his *Religion and the Ambiguities of Capitalism*, SCM Press 1991, 'Understanding Economics and its Limits', is also important.
2. Particularly Reinhold Niebuhr's *Moral Man and Immoral Society*, Scribner 1932.
3. R. H. Preston (ed), *Theology and Change*, SCM Press 1979, p.150.
4. R. H. Preston, *Church and Society in the Late Twentieth Century*, SCM Press 1983, p.24.
5. Cf. R. H. Preston, *Religion and the Ambiguities of Capitalism*, SCM Press 1991, p.25.
6. See 'Facts and Fables in Ecology and the Integrity of Creation', chapter 12 of this volume.
7. See 'Convergence and Divergence in Social Theology', chapter 10 of this volume.
8. R. H. Preston, 'Reflections on Theologies of Social Change' in *Theology and Change* ed. Ronald H. Preston, SCM Press 1975, p.151.
9. R. H. Preston, *Explorations in Theology 9*, SCM Press 1981, p.3.
10. In Peter Singer (ed), *A Companion to Ethics*, Blackwell 1991, p.96.
11. Cf. J. D. Crossan, *The Historical Jesus. the Life of a Mediterranean Jewish Peasant*, HarperCollins 1991.
12. R.H. Preston, *Religion and the Ambiguities of Capitalism*, SCM Press 1991, p.131.
13. Cf. A. E. Bottoms and R. H. Preston, *The Coming Penal Crisis*, Scottish Academic Press 1980: R. H. Preston (ed), *Perspectives on Strikes*, SCM Press 1975.
14. R. H. Preston, *Confusions in Christian Social Ethics*, SCM Press 1994, pp.91–96.
15. Cf. R. H. Preston, *The Future of Christian Ethics*, SCM Press 1987, p.139.
16. See 'The Moral Order of a Free Society', chapter 19 of this volume.
17. Edwin Barker and Ronald Preston, *Christians in Society*, SCM Press 1939, p.147.
18. J. H. Oldham and W. Visser 't Hooft, *The Church and its Function in Society*, Allen and Unwin 1937, p.210.
19. R. H. Preston, *Explorations in Theology 9*, SCM Press 1981, pp.39–40.

20. 'Middle Axioms in Christian Social Ethics' in *Explorations in Theology 9*, pp.37–44.
21. *The Church and The Bomb*, Hodder/CIO Publishing 1982.
22. R. H. Preston, *Confusions in Christian Social Ethics*, SCM Press 1994, p.4.
23. Ibid., p.5.
24. Ibid., p.14.
25. Ibid., p.142.
26. Ibid., p.167.
27. Ibid., p.48ff.
28. Ibid., p.6.
29. Wilfred Cantwell Smith, *The Meaning and End of Religion*, SPCK 1978, p.194.

1. A Bishop Ahead of his Church

1. This chapter originally appeared in *Crucible*. Preston here explains why the official journal of The Board of Social Responsibility of the Church of England should publish this appraisal of Leslie Hunter, who was Bishop of Sheffield from 1939–62 (editorial note).
2. SCM Press 1933.
3. SPCK 1961.
4. L. S. Hunter (ed), *The English Church*, Penguin 1966.
5. John Habgood, *Church and Nation in a Secular Age*, Darton, Longman and Todd 1983.

2. The Collapse of the SCM: A Case Study

1. In *Religious Studies*, Vol. 20, No. 3, September 1984, pp.401ff. References to the SCM are on pp. 405, 408 and 411ff. In a book published in the same year, *Firm in the Faith*, Grove Publishing Co. 1984, Dr Bruce has a section on 'The Disintegration of the SCM' (pp. 75–77) in which he makes much the same general points, with illustrations derived from his PhD. in sociology from Stirling university in 1980: *The Student Christian Movement and the Inter-Varsity Fellowship: a Sociological Study of the two Student Movements* (available on microfilm). My references are mainly drawn from the thesis; this takes the analysis to about 1974, but hardly beyond that.
2. On p.2 of the article Bruce says that Liberal Protestantism was 'associated' with the ecumenical movement and that it was 'probably essential' to it.
3. The SCM archives are housed in a room to themselves in the Central Library of the Selly Oak Colleges, Birmingham, and are a very valuable source of material for the church historian of this century. As to persons, most of the second generation leaders are now dead; most of the third generation are alive, and the evidence of these, and of those involved in the traumatic 1970s, needs collating. McCaughey's book is *Christian Obedience in the University* (Studies in the Life of the Student Christian Movement of Great Britain and Ireland 1930 – 50), 1958.
4. The WSCF first experienced a marked change in the consciousness of Christian students at its Strasbourg Conference of 1960. The careful plans and

extremely competent speakers failed to connect with the outlook of the hearers who were less concerned with the life of the church and more with action in the world. The WSCF had a very stormy history in the period 1968–71. It was polarized between a more or less Marxist section, which had little use for the Bible or the church or worship, and an almost anarchist section which had staked everything on maximum spontaneity and the radical disruption of all existing structures in order that new forms of individual and corporate identity would emerge. The struggle between the two was carried out with great bitterness and factionalism and with practically no sense of overshadowing divine grace. It nearly killed the WSCF, which survived by regional decentralization. An account of this episode is given by Risto Lehtonen in an article 'The Story of a Storm' in *Study Encounter* (a quarterly publication of the World Council of Churches), November 1972. (Editors' note: This has now been expanded into a book of the same title, *Story of a Storm*, Eerdmans and the Finnish Society of Church History, Grand Rapids 1998. The work of the SCM University Commission is dealt with by Ronald Preston in the symposium edited by Marjorie Reeves, *Christian Thinking and the Social Order*, Cassell, London and NY 1999, pp. 141–55. See also R. H. Preston, 'A Theological Response to Sociology' in *Sociology, Theology and the Curriculum* ed L. J. Francis, Cassell 1999.) In the USA, the SCM equivalent dissolved itself. However, in South Africa it dissolved itself for a cogent reason; it was inter-racial, and government pressure made its work impossible.

5. The key book for the early period is *The Story of the Student Christian Movement* by Tissington Tatlow, SCM Press 1933, a large book of nearly one thousand pages, of which Bruce makes good use, together with his own researches. But although he mentions it he makes no significant use of the key book for the next stage by J. Davis McCaughey (see note 3 above). A brief book, J. Eric Fenn's *Learning Wisdom. Fifty Years of the Student Christian Movement*, SCM Press 1939, gives a theological interpretation of the period covered by Tatlow's narrative. An even briefer review covered the next decade, David L. Edwards' *Movement into Tomorrow. A Sketch of the British SCM*, SCM Press 1959. A presentation of the IVF postition is found in *Contending for the Faith. A History of the Evangelical Movement in the Universities and Colleges*, 1979, by Douglas Johnson, its General Secretary from 1924 to 1964.

6. Editor's note: Bruce's article was written in 1984, and Preston's in 1986. Since 1998, SCM Press, still one of the foremost theological publishers in the world, has been a division of SCM-Canterbury Press Ltd, itself a subsidiary of Hymns Ancient and Modern Ltd.

7. By contrast to Bruce, Martin Conway in *The Christian Enterprise in Higher Education,* Church of England Board of Education 1971, says of the SCM in the 1950s that it had the inner spiritual coherence of a relatively clear aim. What does Christ expect from his followers in this university, and what form does that mean that their fellowship in obedience should take?

8. See F. W. Dillstone, *Charles Raven : Naturalist, Historian, Theologian,* Hodder 1975, esp. p. 277 and p. 288. Opinions change quickly when one is an undergraduate. I was much influenced by Raven for almost a term after

hearing his Halley Stewart lectures 'Is War Obsolete?' before I concluded that his theology was not 'realistic' enough.

9. It is a pity that Bruce did not examine more closely the power structure in the IVF, not mentioned in its ecclesiology (any more than that of the Curia is in Roman Catholic ecclesiology). The SCM has always been troubled by the split with the IVF and has made periodical attempts to heal it locally and centrally. Local advances are always blocked by the IVF centrally. Its 1924 constitution precludes working with any who do not 'substantially' uphold its eight doctrinal affirmations, but 'substantially' can be interpreted strictly or less strictly. There is an impression that the influence of wealthy lay backers has been on the side of strictness, but the power structure within the IVF has never been investigated. In recent years there has been a much wider spectrum of views among evangelicals, and many are much more ecumenically minded, but this has been much less the case in the university world as far as the IVF is concerned.

10. A Christian concern for the university as an institution with a vital intellectual and social role developed in the SCM in the late 1930s, sparked off by the Oxford branch. It was vividly expressed in David Paton's *Blind Guides? A Student Looks at the University*, 1939. This is based on his experience as SCM Secretary in Birmingham University, 1936–39, and partly provoked by discussions in the National Union of Students at the time, whose ideological slant the SCM thought in need of theological criticism. The war halted the discussion from 1939, but in 1943 it was brought to the fore again by a book by Arnold S. Nash, *The University in the Modern World*, USA 1943; UK 1945. It caused the SCM to set up a commission which produced twelve University Pamphlets for discussion, edited by Ronald H. Preston (1946); and the WSCF to sponsor a book, by Sir Walter Moberly, *The Task of the Christian in the University*, 1949, and his *The Crisis in the University*, SCM Press 1949. Among those in the United Kingdom who took part in these discussions were Professors Donald Mackinnon, John Baillie, Dorothy Emmet, H.A. Hodges, and L.A. Reid, Michael Foster (Student of Christ Church, Oxford) and Sir Hector Hetherington (Principal of Glasgow University). A further book, Dermot Christopherson's *The University at Work*, 1973, shows a decline in perception. The whole theme is now due for a revival.

4. Christian Ethics

1. See Reinhold Niebuhr, *Christ and Culture*, Harper & Brothers, New York 1951.
2. Samuel Butler, *The Way of All Flesh* (1903); Penguin 1947.
3. Blaise Pascal, *Lettres Provinciales*, Paris 1956; Penguin 1967.
4. T. S. Eliot, *Murder in the Cathedral*, Faber 1935.
5. R. Robinson, *An Atheist's Values*, Clarendon Press 1964, p.149.
6. Aquinas, *Summa Theologiae*, 2a, 2ae, q40, articles 1–3.
7. A. Nygren, *Agape and Eros*, SPCK 1964.
8. J. Klausner, *Jesus of Nazareth*, Allen and Unwin 1925.
9. W. Manson, *Jesus the Messiah*, Hodder 1943.

6. *Not Out of the Wood Yet*

1. See R. Ambler and D. Haslam, *Agenda for Prophets,* Bowerdean Press 1981.
2. Alistair Kee (ed), *Seeds of Liberation. Spiritual Dimensions to Political Struggle,* SCM Press 1973.

7. *Christian Socialism Becalmed*

1. There is an account of the various Christian Socialist groups in the first chapter of my Scott Holland Lectures, *Church and Society in the Late Twentieth Century. The Economic and Political Task,* SCM Press 1983, 'The Legacy of the Christian Socialist Movement in England'.
2. I wrote an appraisal of this in an article in *Theology,* Vol.63, No.478, April 1960, pp.133–36, 'The Christian Left Still Lost'.
3. R. Ambler and D. Haslam (eds) *Agenda for Prophets ,* Bowerdean Press 1981. On this I wrote an appraisal in *Theology,* Vol.84, No.698, March 1981, pp.83–87, 'Not out of the Wood Yet: a Recent Christian Socialist Manifesto'.
4. *Facing the Future as Christians and Socialists,* co-ordinated by David Ormrod, Lecturer in Economic and Social History in the University of Kent.
5. Research needs to be done on several of these groups before it is too late. Already efforts to find the records of the Socialist Christian League (of which I was once a member) have failed, although it ceased to function only in 1958.
6. I have discussed this point in various places, e.g. *Religion and the Persistence of Capitalism,* SCM Press 1979, chs 1–4, and in the Scott Holland Lectures (see note 1 above).
7. The best study on this is *Competition: a Study in Human Motive* (1917) by William Temple and four other members of a small group, The Collegium, which he and a dozen or so kindred spirits ran from 1911. This study ends in a tentative advocacy of Guild Socialism as the next stage forward, a model widely discussed at the time. Beyond that it said a transformation of human nature is required.
8. *Facing the Future,* p.30.
9. Oscar Lange originally wrote in 1938 and Hayek's reply was in *The Road to Serfdom,* 1944; but Lange's work is better found in A. Nove and D.M. Nuli (eds), *The Economics of Socialism,* 1972.
10. Originally published in 1931 and reprinted several times since, with new material and new introductions.
11. E.g. Richard Layard, *How to Beat Unemployment,* 1986, which lies behind the Charter for Jobs campaign; and on income and taxation, cf. Tony Walter, *Fair Shares: an Ethical Guide to Tax and Social Security,* 1985.
12. E.g. the tone of recent articles in *The New Statesman* and *Marxism Today,* and the Fabian Society Pamphlet 516, Ian Forbes (ed), *Market Socialism: Whose Choice?,* 1986.
13. The best account of the Christendom Group is in John Oliver, *The Church and Social Order: Social Thought in the Church of England 1918–39,* 1968,

ch. 6. The Group went out of existence for a period, but the Christendom Trust has been reconstituted and sponsors research projects in line with its aims.

14. A particular example is illuminating. When he died Denys Munby was Reader in the Economics of Transport at Oxford university. His undergraduate course at Oxford was interrupted by the war. He was then reading Greats. He was attracted to the Christendom Group and accepted its economic arguments. We were friends and often argued. In the end I said I would not argue with him any more on economics unless he studied it; if he did and still accepted the Christendom argument, I would then take it seriously. When he returned to the university he did in fact change to reading modern Greats, abandoned the old arguments, and in the Appendix to his book *Christianity and* Economics, 1956, produced a detailed criticism of the economic assumptions and arguments in V.A. Demant's Scott Holland Lectures, *Religion and the Decline of Capitalism,* 1950.

15. 'The Body by Love Possessed: Christianity and Late Capitalism in Britain', *Modern Theology,* 3.1, October 1986.

16. Ibid., p.52.

17. Ibid., p.61.

18. Ernest Mandel, *Late Capitalism,* ET revd edn 1975; cf. also his *Long Waves of Capitalist Development,* 1980 and, more accessible, his chapter on economics in D. McClellan (ed), *Marx: the First Hundred Years,* 1983.

19. Mandel, *Late Capitalism,* pp.4, 11.

20. In a Jubilee Group pamphlet, *Nuclear Realism and Christian Realism: the Poverty of Niebuhrianism,* 1986.

21. 'The Body by Love Possessed', p.52.

8.   Fifty Years on from the Oxford Conference

1. 'The Evolution of Ecumenical Social Thought: Some Personal reflections' in *Faith and Faithfulness. Essays in Contemporary Ecumenical Themes: a Tribute to Philip Potter* ed Pauline Webb, World Council of Churches 1984, p.116. I myself found in the 1970s third year theological students becoming quite excited when required to read parts of the Oxford Conference volumes, as still much to the point.

2. The German title of the Oxford Conference was *Volk, Kirche und Staat.*

3. The proceedings of the conference, with an editorial reflection on it by J. H. Oldham, were published in the book, *The Churches Survey their Task,* Allen and Unwin 1937.

4. Tribute in this connection should be paid to Mark Gibbs, who died in 1986. In middle life he left schoolteaching to establish single-handed a movement to persuade churches to take the laity seriously. His library on the laity is being kept within the John Rylands University Library of Manchester.

5. I was Joint Secretary (together with Rose Terlin of New York) of a Youth Section of 100 members which had a parallel programme. The names of those involved include, among those from the UK, Professor Dorothy Emmet and Dr Nicholas Zernov.

6. Oldham's unique lay contribution to the British churches and the Ecumenical

Movement has yet to be publicly assessed; if he had been in holy orders it surely would have been.

7. All six, and the two books previously mentioned, were elegantly produced by Allen and Unwin and form a classic source of material. The six titles are (1) *The Christian Understanding of Man*, (2) *The Kingdom of God and History*, (3) *The Christian Faith and the Common Life*, (4) *Church and Community*, (5) *Church, Community and State in Relation to Education*, (6) *The Universal Church and the World of Nations*. In my judgment the second and third contain the biggest proportion of essays of long term importance.

8. The report of the Geneva Conference is entitled *Christians in the Technical and Social Revolutions of our Time*, World Council of Churches 1967. The four volumes of essays were published in the UK in 1966 by SCM Press. They are: John C. Bennett (ed), *Christian Social Ethics in a Changing World*, Z. K. Matthews (ed), *Responsible Government in a Revolutionary Age*, Denys Munby (ed), *Ecumenical Growth in World Perspective*, and E. de Vries (ed), *Man in Community* .

9. The MIT Conference Report was published by the WCC Geneva in 1978 in two volumes: Roger Shimm (ed), *Faith and Science in an Unjust World* and Paul Abrecht (ed), *Reports and Recommendations*.

10. I have elaborated these points with reference to the Geneva Conference in the first chapter of *Technology and Social Justice*, SCM Press 1970, a symposium I edited.

11. See *Octogesima Adveniens*, 1971, para. 4.

9. *Critics from Without and from Within*

1. *The Christian Understanding of Man*; *The Kingdom of God and History*; *The Christian Faith and the Common Life*; *Church and Community*; *Church, Community and State in Relation to Education*; *The Universal Church and the World of Nations*; all published with a general introduction by J.H. Oldham, Allen and Unwin 1938.

2. David Martin, *A General Theory of Secularisation*, Blackwell 1978, p.294.

3. E. R. Norman, *Church and Society 1770–1970*, OUP 1976.

4. Given in 1978 and published by OUP in 1979.

5. Ernest Lefever, *Amsterdam to Nairobi. The World Council of Churches and the Third World*, Ethics and Public Policy Centre, Washington DC 1979, p.60.

6. Universe Books, NY 1972

7. Paul Ramsey, *Who speaks for the Church?*, Abingdon Press, Nashville 1967.

8. Ibid., p.13.

9. R. H. Preston, *Church and Society in the Late Twentieth Century*, SCM Press 1983.

10. Ramsey, op. cit., p.146.

11. *Study Encounter*, No.2, 1968.

12. Ramsey, op. cit., p.32.

13. Editors' note: This theme is developed further in Preston's *Confusions in Christian Social Ethics. Problems for Geneva and Rome*, SCM Press 1994, as well as in 'Faith and Order *vs* Life and Work: Ecclesiology and Ethics in the WCC', *Epworth Review*, Vol.25, No.4, pp.69–75.

11. *Humanity, Nature and the Integrity of Creation*

1. This article also takes further chapter 5, 'The Integrity of Creation: Issues of Environmental Ethics' in my book *The Future of Christian Ethics*, SCM Press 1987. The chapter has an appendix, 'God in Creation: a Note on Moltmann's Gifford Lectures'.

2. There is a tendency in the WCC to leave studies unfinished or to neglect them, e.g. that of Faith and Order on 'God in Nature and History' (1987). Also it takes some five years for initiatives from Geneva to permeate a world constituency. In the case of the JPSS study it was just doing so when it was scrapped in favour of JPIC and when much still needed to be done on Participatory. Whatever the merits of the change there is very little information on how it came about. In the record of the Vancouver Assembly there is only one significant reference to it in David Gill (ed), *Gathered for Life*, World Council of Churches 1983, p.231.

3. There is also a tendency in the WCC to neglect previous studies in the same field, perhaps as new staff arrive with different approaches. For instance there was an important speech by Charles Birch on 'Nature, Humanity and God in Ecological Perspective' at the MIT conference on 'Faith, Science and the Future' (Vol. 1 of the record of the conference, pp. 67–73) which bridges the gap between Sustainability and what would later come to be called the Integrity of Creation, but it is neglected now. A few months earlier the occasional publication of Church and Society, Anticipation (No. 25, January 1979) published the report of a conference in Zurich in 1977 on 'Humanity, Nature and God' with contributions by John Austin Baker, Klaus Koch, Charles Birch, Charles Hartshorne and Paulos Gregorios which have not been drawn upon.

4. 'From Oxford to Nairobi: Lessons from Fifty Years of Ecumenical Work for Economic and Social Justice' in the *Ecumenical Review*, April 1988.

5. The concept of the Integrity of Creation is picked up by Pope John Paul II's latest social encyclical *Sollicitudo Rei Socialis*, 1987 para. 26, and the Vatican is involved in the preparatory work for the 1990 convocation though it will not co-sponsor it.

6. The WCC studies are considerably influenced by the ecology movement with its Green parties, Greenpeace, Friends of the Earth and other groups. Care is needed. The ecology movement is itself deeply split. 'Shallow' ecology has to be distinguished from 'Deep' ecology. As radical feminists turned in the 1980s to an emphasis on goddesses and a hatred of men, so Deep ecologists are spurning humanity and embracing a kind of animism. This is far beyond what the Norwegian philosopher Arne Naess, who invented the term in the 1970s, intended. From a position that all life has its own intrinsic value it moves to the position that Nature is more important than humankind, which is only one of its myriad species. Hence wilderness becomes primary if all species are to thrive. An example of this outlook in the WCC material (it is not typical) is the writer who says: 'Every time I walk on grass I feel sorry because I know the grass is screaming at me.'

7. The Book of Revelation is unusual in that it pictures a millennial provisional peace before the common apocalyptic expectation of a final cosmic battle and a new heaven and a new earth.

8. I quote part of some privately circulated verses by a friend of mine, additions to Mrs Alexander's hymn 'All things bright and beautiful':

The darkness-loving cockroach	The tsetse killing cattle
The rat that carries fleas	The vampire sucking blood
Mosquito, louse, bacillae	The Lord God both created
All bearers of disease.	And saw that they were good.
The hairy-legged spider	All things dark and dangerous
That eats alive her mate	All creatures great and small
The fly that tastes the dunghill	All things vile and murderous
Then vomits on your plate.	The Lord God made them all.

9. I am of course aware of the continuing debate in the Roman Catholic Church on this reconstruction not least because in some areas, notably that of sexual ethics, the Curia is unhappy with it.

10. This perception is important because the recrudescence in some Anglo-Saxon countries in the last decade of a nineteenth-century individualist philosophy (often called the New Right) goes a long way to undermine, if not to deny, it.

11. Cf. W. H. Thorpe, *Animal Nature and Human Nature*, Gifford Lectures, Jonathan Cape 1974.

12. This term was coined by Peter Singer, professor of philosophy in Monash University, Victoria, Australia. Cf. his *Animal Liberation*, Cape 1976.

13. Perhaps the best contribution so far on this point is the report of the core group on 'Towards a Theology of Nature and a Theocentric Ethic' at a meeting of the Church and Society Sub-unit at Glion, Switzerland, in 1987. However, the crucial section (III) does not meet the questions I have raised. On the Integrity of Creation it refers to the paper by D. J. Hall (see note 15 below).

14. In a paper on 'Salvation for Elephants' contributed to the Glion meeting (see note 13 above).

15. The most considerable attempt so far to give a theological underpinning to the concept the Integrity of Creation is an article by Douglas John Hall, professor of Christian theology at McGill University, Montreal: 'The Integrity of Creation: Biblical and Theological Background to the Term' in *Reintegrating God's Creation*, a paper for discussion, Church and Society Study Documents 1987. It should be read for a different view from mine.

16. Rosemary Radford Ruether, 'Ecology and Human Liberation, a Conflict between the Theology of History and the Theology of Nature?', *To Change the World: Christology and Cultural Criticism*, SCM Press and Crossroad Publishing 1981, pp. 53–70.

17. The Church and Society document (note 15 above) contains a select bibliography on 'The Wholeness of God's Creation' by Ans van der Bent. The radical diversity and uneven quality of the material are evident. If I had to single out one book as the most useful it would be Robin Attfield, *The Ethics of Environmental Concern*, Blackwell 1983.

12. *Facts and Fables in Ecology and the Integrity of Creation*

1. This article is unique amongst those in this collection in that it was written jointly with another author, Charles Birch, formerly Challis Professor of Biology in the University of Sydney.
2. D. Gill (ed), *Gathered for Life*, World Council of Churches 1983, p.231.
3. Donald Worster, 'Nature and the Disorder of History', *Reinventing Nature: responses to post-modern deconstruction* ed Michael A.E. Soule and Gary Lease, Island Press, Washington DC 1997, p.72.
4. L. C. Birch and P. R. Ehrlich, 'The "Balance of Nature" and "Population Control"', *American Naturalist*, 101, 1967, pp.73–98.
5. H. G. Andrewartha and L.C. Birch, *The Distribution and Abundance of Animals*, University of Chicago Press 1954; also H.G. Andrewartha and L.C. Birch, *The Ecological Web*, University of Chicago Press 1984.
6. Paul R. Ehrlich, *A World of Wounds: ecologists and the human dilemma*, Ecology Institute Press, Oldendorf/ Luhe 1997, p.6.
7. R. C. Lewontin, *Biology as Ideology: The doctrine of DNA*, Harper Perenial, NY 1993, p.118.
8. Ibid., p.119.
9. Michael E. Soule, 'The social seige of nature', *Reinventing Nature: responses to post-modern deconstruction* ed Michael E. Soule and Gary Lease, Island Press, Washington DC 1997, p.143.
10. H. G. Andrewartha and L. C. Birch, *The Ecological Web*, University of Chicago Press 1984, p.82.
11. S. T. A. Picket and P. S. White, *The Ecology of Natural Disturbance and Patch Dynamics*, Academic Press, Orlando 1985.
12. Paul R. Ehrlich, *A World Of Wounds: ecologists and the human dilemma*, Ecology Institute Press, Oldendorf/ Luhe 1997, p. 101.
13. Charles Darwin, *The Origin of Species by Means of Natural Selection*, Modern Library edn, NY 1859, p.52.
14. A.N. Whitehead, *Process and Reality* (1929), corrected edn ed David Ray Griffin and Donald W. Shelbourne, Free Press, NY 1978, p.105.
15. Michael E. Soulé, 'The social seige of nature' in Michael Soulé and Gary Lense, *Reinventing Nature*, Island Press, Washington DC 1985, p.143.
16. Richard Levins and Richard Lewontin, *The Dialectical Biologist*, Harvard University Press 1985, p.21.
17. Jarred Diamond, 'New Guineans and their natural world', *The Biophilia Hypothesis* ed Stephen Kellert and E.O. Wilson, Island Press, Washington DC 1993, p.268.
18. Gary P. Nabham, 'Cultural Parallels in viewing North American Habitats', *Reinventing Nature: responses to post-modern deconstruction* ed Michael Soule and Gary Leach, Island Press, Washington DC 1997, pp. 87–101.
19. Paul Ehrlich and Anne Ehrlich, *Extinction: the causes and consequences of disappearance of species*, Random House, NY 1981, pp.109–116.
20. Key documents on the Seoul conference are D. Preman Niles (ed), *Between the Rock and the Rainbow: Interpreting the process of mutual commitment (covenant) for Justice, Peace and the Integrity of Creation*, World Council of Churches and D. Preman Niles (ed), *Justice, Peace and the Integrity of*

Creation: Documents from an Ecumenical Process of Commitment, World Council of Churches. For a later Orthodox view see Gennadios Limouris, *Justice, Peace and the Integrity of Creation: insights from Orthodoxy*, World Council of Churches 1990.

21. Larry L. Rasmussen, *Earth Community, Earth Ethics*, World Council of Churches and Orbis Books, Maryknoll 1996.

13. *Laborem Exercens: Pope John Paul II on Work*

1. His poems *The Quarry* (1956) and *The Car Factory Worker* (1957) reflect his experience in industry.

2. The text refers to Jesus as a manual worker at a carpenter's bench for most of his life. This is, of course, widely assumed on the basis of the Greek word *tekton* applied to him. It seems rather to bear a general meaning, our word 'artisan' perhaps being the nearest translation.

3. The text glosses over the snobbish treatment of manual work in Ecclesiasticus 38.24ff.

4. I am not sure if this is strictly true, nor exactly what is to be drawn from it except the truism that every feature of distinctively human life derives from man. If capital is not taken seriously man will not get far; indeed his life will be nasty, poor, brutish and short for a different reason from that advanced by Hobbes.

5. This is not noteworthy in advanced industrial countries where a gulf between the more affluent workers and the rest, and between those employed and the unemployed, is growing. At the 1983 General Election one third of Trade Union members voted for Mrs Thatcher.

6. There is also not much evidence of this in advanced industrial countries.

7. Understandably Marxism is the intellectual foil to the Pope in this encyclical.

8. In an impromptu session at a steel works at Terni, north of Rome, in March 1981, John Paul said that workers are not instruments of production and should share in management; and that the church seeks social justice, and *all* those who do so walk in the way of the gospel. (Cf. Peter Hebblethwaite, *Introducing John Paul II*, who points out the similarity of this to Rahner's 'anonymous Christians' which John Paul had previously criticized.)

9. There are passages on agricultural, disabled and migrant workers.

10. In the chapter 'A Breakthrough in Ecumenical Social Ethics' in a symposium, *Technology and Social Justice*, SCM Press 1971, pp.15–40, which I edited.

11. The divorce of ownership and management has become increasingly the case for the last fifty years.

12. The symposium *Property: its Duties and Rights* ed Charles Gore, 1913, is still relevant.

13. This is in the passages inserted personally by Pius XI in the draft by Oswald von Nell-Breuning, SJ, who was the sole papal consultant, through the Jesuit Superior General.

14. The Mondragon co-operative in Spain is the most interesting example of what the Pope appears to be advocating. It now involves 18,000 workers. Producers' co-operatives have traditionally been weak in management, in access to finance, and in their constitutions. Mondragon has professional man-

agement, and its own bank. Its constitution provides that every worker must be involved in the ultimate control, but distinguishes ownership from day-to-day management; and requires every worker to build up a capital stake in the enterprise. Otherwise Yugoslavia seems to have been trying to develop industrial management structures along lines the Pope might approve.

15. No such change has taken place in the utterances of the *magisterium* on sex questions.

16. Let J. H. Oldham's *Work in Modern Society*, 1950, be one example.

15. *Centesimus Annus: An Appraisal*

1. I use the following abbreviations: RN for *Rerum Novarum;* QA for *Quadragesimo Anno* (1931); MM for *Mater et Magistra* (1961); OA for *Octogesima Adveniens* (1971); LE for *Laborem Exercens* (1981); CA for *Centesimus Annus;* PT for *Pacem in Terris* (1963); PP for *Populorum Progressio* (1967) and SRS for *Sollicitudo Rei Socialis* (1988).

2. John T. Pawlikowski, 'Modern Catholic Teaching on the Economy: an Analysis and Evaluation' in Bruce Gruelle and David A. Krueger (eds), *Christianity and Capitalism. Perspectives on Religion, Liberation and the Economy,* Centre for the Society for the Scientific Study of Religion, Chicago 1986; also 'Capitalism and Catholic Social Teaching', a paper written for the international conference on 'Religion and the Resurgence of Capitalism', Lancaster University 1991.

3. Cf. A. M. C. Waterman, 'The Intellectual Context of *Rerum Novarum*' in *Review of Social Economy,* November 1991.

4. Cf. RN para. 9f.; LE para. 14; CA para. 6.

5. Three useful books are: E. E. Y. Hales, *The Catholic Church in the Modern World: a Survey from the French Revolution to the Present,* 1958; R. L. Camp, *The Papal Ideology of Social Reform: a Study in Historical Development 1870–1967,* Leiden 1969; Donald Dorr, *Option for the Poor: a Hundred Years of Vatican Social Teaching,* Maryknoll 1986.

6. Behind the various statements on private property lies the teaching of St Thomas Aquinas on it, which it is thought necessary to affirm, although property was much more simple and personal then than today.

7. *Christianity and Social Order* (1942); 1976 edn, p. 65.

8. Cf. *Not Just for the Poor: Christian Perspectives on the Welfare State,* a Report of the Social Policy Committee of the Board for Social Responsibility of the Church of England, Church House Publishing 1986.

9. I have given an appraisal of Pope John Paul II's two previous social encyclicals in *Theology*: LE in vol. LXXXVI, no. 709, 1983, pp. 19–24; and SRS in vol. CXII, no. 750, 1989, pp. 519–25.

16. *Veritatis Splendor: A Comment*

1. One source for this and other texts is Peter Morgan et al., *On Human Life,* Burns and Oates 1968.

17. *Theology and the Economy: The Roman Catholic Bishops in the USA*

1. Canadian Conference of Catholic Bishops, *Ethical Reflections on the Economic Crisis*, prepared by eight of them in 1982.

2. *The Challenge of Peace: God's Promise and Our Response*, The Catholic Truth Society and SPCK 1983.

3. After a wide discussion a second draft appeared in October 1985, and a third in June 1986. The final text was passed by 225 votes to 9 in November 1986. It is preceded by a short Pastoral Message which stresses the main points, and says that the whole area should be taken seriously by Christians because for most the road to holiness is through their secular vocation. The text was published in *Origins*, NC Documentary Series vol. 16, no. 24, 27 November 1986. There is not a great deal of difference between the drafts, most between the first and second. The final one is a little less blunt than the first, but not much: and as a result of a meeting between the drafters and some Latin American Bishops and economists it contains a strong statement on the World Bank, the International Monetary Fund, and GATT (the General Agreement on Tariffs and Trade).

4. There is a rumour that the Vatican is not too happy with a national conference of bishops issuing teaching in this elaborate and thorough way, and that the American bishops have to some extent safeguarded themselves by copious references to Vatican documents and stresses on the consistency of its teaching.

5. In an article in *America*, 21 September 1985.

6. 1971, para. 4. The whole paragraph goes on to say that this should be done 'in dialogue with other Christian brethren and all men of good will'.

7. Weakland acknowledges (see note 5 above) that the relation between scripture and moral discourse has not yet been thought through by moral theologians, and that there are hiatuses in this respect in the document.

8. Cf. *Gaudium et Spes*, 1965, para. 36.

9. Cf. *Quadragesimo Anno*, 1931, para. 79.

10. See note 5 above.

11. Cf. William K. Tabb (ed), *Churches in Struggle: Liberation Theologies and Change in North America*, Monthly Review Press, NY 1986, chapter by W.K. Tabb, 'The Shoulds and the Excluded Whys: The US Catholic Bishops Look at the Economy'.

12. They are not readily available in the UK. The ones I have drawn on are: 'The US Catholic Bishops and the Pursuit of Justice'. Paul Heyne in *Policy Analysis 50*, Cato Institute, Washington DC 1985; Walter Block, *The US Bishops and Their Critics: An Economic and Ethical Perspective*, Fraser Institute, Vancouver 1986; *Economics, Theology and Social Order*, a Symposium, Center for Research in Government Policy and Business of the Graduate School of Management, University of Rochester, NY 1986 (Center Symposium Series CS18).

13. Cf. Ronald H. Preston, *Church and Society in the Late Twentieth Century*, SCM Press 1983, ch. 2, 'Christianity and Economic Man' and ch. 3, 'The New Radical Right'; and *The Future of Christian Ethics*, SCM Press 1987,

ch. 8, 'The New Right: A Theological Critique' and ch. 12, 'The Politics of Imperfection and the Politics of Hope'.

14. Cf. part of the argument in *Not Just for the Poor: a Christian Perspective on the Welfare State.* A report of the Social Policy Committee of the Board for Social Responsibility of the Church of England, 1986

15. Cf. *Church and Society in the Late Twentieth Century*, Appendix Two, 'Middle Axioms in Christian Social Ethics'.

16. See above, note 5.

18. The Common Good

1. There is some discussion whether the legacy of the Confucian ethic in South East Asia, with its stress on the community, including the family against the individual, lies behind the phenomenal economic success of Singapore, Hong Kong, Taiwan, South Korea and Japan. Max Weber thought Confucian traditionalism was a hindrance. It may be that traditionalism is breaking down but leaving a legacy of society still seen as a moral order, and morality as essentially concerned with communal relationships. I don't know. The nature of Confucianism and the secret of the economic success of South East Asia are both obscure.

2. It has been done in several ways. One is by frequently making small, and a small series of, almost imperceptible cuts; unemployment benefit was cut 17 times between 1979 and 1988. Another is by making a one-off change whose effect is negligible at first but becomes ever greater as times goes by; in 1980 state pensions ceased to be related to average earnings but instead to the rate of inflation. A third way is to make large cuts in public programmes: housing has taken a fearful battering since 1979, thus off-loading a major problem on to the future.

19. The Moral Order of a Free Society

1. On usury see Appendix 1, 'Usury and a Christian Ethic of Finance' in my *Religion and the Ambiguities of Capitalism*, SCM Press 1991 and Pilgrim Press, Cleveland, Ohio 1993.

2. On mercantilism and on Malthus see note 6, p.161 in my *Religion and the Ambiguities of Capitalism*.

3. The Christian Socialist manifestos have been:
Papers from the Lamb, The Malvern Press, 1959 appraised by me in 'The Christian Left Still Lost', *Theology*, Vol. 67, 1960.
Rex Ambler and David Haslam (eds), *Agenda for Prophets*, Bowerdean Press 1980 appraised by me in 'Not out of the Wood Yet', *Theology*, Vol. 84, 1981.
David Ormrod (ed), *Facing the Future as Christians and Socialists*, Christian Socialist Movement 1988, appraised by me in 'Christian Socialism Becalmed', *Theology*, Vol. 91, 1988.
David Ormrod (ed), *Fellowship, Freedom and Equality. Ten Tawney Commemorative Lectures*, Christian Socialist Movement 1990
Christopher Byrant (ed), *Reclaiming the Ground*, Hodder 1993. Four out of the six chapters are Tawney lectures.

On Christian Socialism see also:

'The Legacy of the Christian Socialist Movement', ch. 1 in my *Church and Society in the Late Twentieth Century: the Economic and Political Task*, SCM Press 1982, and 'The Christian Socialist Critique of Capitalism' in ch. 3, of *Religion and the Ambiguities of Capitalism*.

4. See 'The New Right: a Christian Critique' and 'The Politics of Imperfection and the Politics of Hope', chs 4 and 8 of my *The Future of Christian Ethics*, SCM Press 1987.

5. See Gerald J. Hughes 'Christianity and Self Interest', ch. 4 in *Christians and the Future of Social Democracy* ed Michael H. Taylor, G.W. & A. Hesketh, California 1981.

6. *Christianity and Social Order*, Penguin 1942; reissued by Shepheard-Walwyn and SPCK 1976, with an introduction by me, p.65.

7. John Rawls, *A Theory of Justice*, OUP 1972.

8. *Religion and the Ambiguities of Capitalism*.

9. The latter criticism has to take account of a book, *The Hemisphere of Liberty*, published in the USA in 1992 by the American Enterprise Institute, Washington DC, in which Novak writes about community with some eloquence, but still in my judgment overplaying the market as an instrument of community by giving more space to the individual. He distinguishes himself from the New Right by identifying himself as a New Conservative, and describes himself as an adherent of the Catholic Whig Tradition, involving ordered liberty, person, community and enterprise. It is a novel reading of Tradition, but its merits for today will doubtless continue to be discussed.

10. See *Changing Britain: Social Diversity and Moral Unity*, a Study for the Board for Social Responsibility of the Church of England, Church House Publishing 1987.

11. See Kevin T. Kelly, *New Directions in Modern Theology: the Challenge of Being Human*, Geoffrey Chapman 1992, p.30. Janssens' articles appeared in *Louvain Studies*, 1980.

12. For comments on the European Values Study see *Changing Britain*.

13. See the Symposium *Principles of Health Care Ethics* ed Raanan Gillon, John Wiley 1993.

14. See A. C. MacIntyre, *After Virtue*, Duckworth 1981 (and the lively discussion it has provoked).

15. This chapter originated as a dialogue between Ronald Preston and Michael Novak, Professor of Religion and Public Policy at the American Institute in Washington DC, arranged by the Institute of Economic Affairs in London and subsequently published by it under the title 'Christian Capitalism and Christian Socialism'.

20. *Business Ethics and the Pastoral Task*

1. Aquinas, *Summa Theologiae* 11, 11, question 66.

2. Cf. James I. Connor (ed), *Ethical Considerations in Corporate Takeovers*, Georgetown University Press, Washington DC 1990.

3. *Business Morality*, pp. 92ff.

4. Cf. *Religion and the Persistence of Capitalism*, SCM Press 1979; *Religion and the Ambiguities of Capitalism*, SCM Press 1991.

5. John Paul II stresses this in his encyclical *Laborem Exercens* (1981) but it is not so clear in his two later social encyclicals *Sollicitudo Rei Socialis* (1988) and *Centesimus Annus* (1991).

6. Cf. *Morality and the Market*, 1981: *Consumer Pressure for Corporate Accountability*, Routledge 1990.

7. Such a discussion has been particularly stimulated in the 1980s by Alasdair MacIntyre in *After Virtue*, Duckworth 1981 and two subsequent books; see the response of Jeffrey Stout in *Ethics after Babel* Beacon Press, Boston 1988.

8. Cf. K. H. Hertz (ed), *Two Kingdoms and One World*, Minneapolis 1974.

9. Cf. *Morality in the Market Place*, Hodder 1981 and *The Creation of Wealth*, Hodder 1984.

10. Cf. Appendix 2, 'Middle Axioms in Christian and Social Ethics' in Ronald H. Preston, *Church and Society in the Late Twentieth Century*, SCM Press 1983. The letter of Pope Paul VI, *Octogesima Adveniens* (1971, in the series from *Rerum novarum* of 1891), suggests something like this, following some passages in *Gaudium et Spes*, the Pastoral Consititution of Vatican II, 1965.

21.   *The Ethical Legacy of John Maynard Keynes*

1. John Maynard Keynes, *Two Memoirs*, Rupert Hart-Davies 1949.

2. Ibid., pp.82, 84, 86.

3. G. E. Moore, *Principia Ethica*, CUP 1903, pp.188–89.

4. Keynes, *Two Memoirs*, p.92.

5. Ibid., p.94

6. Ibid.

7. Ibid., p.96

8. Ibid., p.98. Later he and many of his friends were members of what came to be known by others as the Bloomsbury Group, a cultural coterie that flourished from about 1907 to the early 1920s, and where fine intellects were assimilated to the salon. It had a big influence on English attitudes in reacting against typical Victorian and Edwardian values.

9. Ibid.

10. Ibid., pp.98–99.

11. Ibid., p.100.

12. Geoffrey Keynes, *The Gates of Memory*, OUP 1981, p.20. His parents later ceased to attend church. The standard source of biographical details is R. F. Harrod's *The Life of John Maynard Keynes*, Macmillan 1951, which is now supplemented by Robert Skidelsky's *John Maynard Keynes*, 2 vols, Macmillan 1983. Quotations are from Volume 1, *Hopes Betrayed*; cf. also Charles H. Hession, *John Maynard Keynes: A Personal Biography of the Man Who Revolutionized Capitalism and the Way We Live*, Macmillan, NY 1984.

13. C. R. Fay, 'The Undergraduate' in Milo Keynes (ed), *Essays on John Maynard Keynes*, Clarendon Press 1975, p.37. T. H. Huxley was the distinguished scientist and Darwinist with whom Bishop Samuel Wilberforce of Oxford had a disastrous confrontation at the annual meeting of the British Association for the Advancement of Science, held in Oxford in 1860.

14. Owen Chadwick, *The Secularization of European Mind in the Nineteenth Century*, CUP 1975.
15. Examples of the Oxford Idealist philosophers are T. H. Green, B. Bosanquet and F. H. Bradley; and in Cambridge, J. M. E. McTaggart.
16. In a letter to Lytton Strachey in 1906 Keynes wrote, 'It is impossible to exaggerate the wonder and originality of Moore . . . How amazing to think that we and only we know the rudiments of a true theory of ethic: for nothing can be more certain than that the broad outline is true.' Harrod, *Life*, p.114.
17. Skidelsky, *John Maynard Keynes* (see n.12 above), p.251.
18. Cf. Paul Levy, *Moore: G. E. Moore and the Cambridge Apostles*, OUP 1979. Public knowledge has occurred in the wake of Sir Anthony Blunt and a famous spy case.
19. A stringent critique of Moore's position was given by C. D. Broad in a paper to the Aristotelian Society in 1934, 'Is "Goodness" a Name of a Simple non-Natural Quality?', *Proceedings of the Aristotelian Society* New Series XXXIV, 1933–34, Harrison & Sons. Two recent verdicts on it are that it is 'plainly false' and 'extraordinarily wrong headed'. Arguments in moral philosophy have actively continued since Moore between, for example, intuitionists on the one hand and emotivists and prescriptivists on the other, in which great attention has been paid to the precise analysis of language. This has been one main legacy of Moore. The fact that such disputes as that between deontologists and consequentialists do not get finally resolved does not mean that they are not worthwhile. Great clarity is certainly achieved.
20. Moore, *Principia Ethica*, chapter 'The Ideal', *passim*.
21. Cf. R. B. Braithwaite, 'Keynes as a Philosopher' in G. Keynes (ed), *Essays*. A better statement of ideal utilitarianism was to be given in 1907 by Hastings Rashdall, Dean of Carlisle, in *The Theory of Good and Evil*, 2 vols, Clarendon Press 1907.
22. Keynes, *CW*, Vol.8, p.329: Vol.10, p.455.
23. Cf. Joseph Fletcher, *Situation Ethics*, Westminster Press and SCM Press 1966; Paul Ramsey, *Deeds and Rules in Christian Ethics*, Charles Scribner's Sons 1967; Gene Outka and Paul Ramsey, *Norm and Context in Christian Ethics*, Charles Scribner's Sons and SCM Press 1968.
24. John Maynard Keynes, *The Economic Consequences of the Peace*, in *CW*, Vol.2.
25. Keynes, *CW*, Vol.2, p.52.
26. Ibid., p.188.
27. Skidelsky, *John Maynard Keynes*, p.155.
28. Cf. Elizabeth S. and Harry G. Johnson, *The Shadow of Keynes: Understanding Keynes, Cambridge and Keynesian Economics*, Blackwell 1978.
29. Cf. T. W. Hutchison, *The Politics and Philosophy of Economics: Marxians, Keynesians and Austrians*, Blackwell 1981.
30. D. E. Moggridge (ed), *Keynes: Aspects of the Man and His Work*, Macmillan 1976.
31. This is stressed in Hession's biography (n.12 above) in various places, e.g. p.203.
32. Keynes, *CW*, Vol.7, p.375, Vol.9, pp.294, 329. Cf. also A. P. Thirlwall (ed), *Keynes and Laissez-Faire*, Macmillan 1980.

33. John Maynard Keynes, *Essays in Persuasion*, CW, Vol.9, pp.287–88.

34. Keynes, *CW*, Vol.7, p.379.

35. Ibid., p.378.

36. Ibids. Vol.9, p.297.

37. John Maynard Keynes, *The General Theory of Employment, Interest and Money*, CW, Vol.8, p.376.

38. In Keynes, *Essays in Persuasion*, CW Vol.9.

39. Keynes, *CW* Vol.9, pp.32–31.

40. 'Liberalism and Labor', ibid., p.311.

41. Cf. F. A. von Hayek, *The Mirages of Social Justice*, Routledge 1976 (the second of his three-volume trilogy *Law, Legislation and Liberty*); Fred Hirsch, *Social Limits to Growth*, Routledge 1977; Ronald H. Preston, *Religion and the Persistence of Capitalism*, SCM Press 1979.

42. Skidelsky, *John Maynard Keynes*, p.209.

43. Keynes, *CW*, Vol.14, pp.209–10.

44. Cf. Amartya Sen, 'The Moral Standing of the Market' and Allan Gibbard, 'What's Morally Special About the Free Market?' in E. E. Paul, F. D Miller, Jr and J. Paul (eds), *Economics and Ethics*, Blackwell 1987.

45. Cf. J. C. Gilbert, *Keynes's Impact on Monetary Theory*, Butterworth 1982.

46. F. H. Knight, *Risk, Uncertainty and Profit*, Boston 1921, reissued by the London School of Economics 1960.

47. Keynes, *CW*, Vol.7, p.161.

48. G. L. S. Shackle, *Uncertainty in Economics*, CUP 1955, p.255.

49. Joseph Butler, *Analogy of Religion* (first published in 1736 and constantly reprinted) from the Preface.

50. Cf. n.2.

51. Butler, *Analogy*, Preface.

52. If Europe suffers from a decline, it will be due to spiritual causes, according to Keynes in a general introduction to a series of supplements on 'Reconstruction in Europe' commissioned by the *Manchester Guardian* in 1921. He goes on to say: 'We today are the most creedless of men. Every one of our religious and political constructions is moth eaten. Our official religions have about as much practical influence on us as the monarchy or the lord mayor's coach. But we no longer substitute for them the militant scepticism of Bentham and Comte and Mill, or the far-fetched abstractions of Hegel' (quoted in Hession, *John Maynard Keynes*, p.192). This theme is very similar to that of T. S. Eliot's 1922 poem *The Waste Land*.

53. This chapter was a contribution to an International Nobel Conference XXII on the legacy of Keynes, held in the USA in 1986.

Conclusion: Ronald Preston and the Contemporary Political Scene

1. For a brief discussion of some of the problems of emphasis in Preston's work see my revised edition of *Plurality and Christian Ethics*, SevenBridgesPress, NY 1999, pp.12–13, 43–46, 164–65.

2. See K. Durkin, *Reinhold Niebuhr*, Geoffery Chapman 1989. I am much indebted to this perceptive discussion of Niebuhr's work.

3. For Lehmann see C. Kegley and R. Bretall (eds), *Reinhold Niebuhr: His*

Religious, Social and Political Thought, Macmillan, NY 1961, pp.251f.

4. See T.Minnema, *The Social Ethics of Reinhold Niebuhr*, Kampen 1958.

5. R. Niebuhr, *The Nature and Destiny of Man*, Vol. 1, Nisbet 1941, pp.140ff.

6. R. Niebuhr, *Faith and History*, Nisbet 1949, p.211.

7. See R. Niebuhr, *The Children of Light and Darkness*, Nisbet 1945.

8. See R. Niebuhr, *Moral Man and Immoral Society*, SCM Press 1963. For an interesting discussion see R. Harries in R. Harries (ed), *Reinhold Niebuhr and the Issues of our Time*, Mowbray 1986, p.105.

9. See chapter 3 above, p.46.

10. See chapter 5 above, p.70.

11. See chapter 5 above, p.75.

12. See chapter 4 above, p.50.

13. See chapter 4 above, p.63.

14. Even the editors of this volume have been critical of 'middle axioms'. John Elford in the introduction suggests that it is problematic because it assumes a regard for expertise which is now redundant in our information-rich age. My criticism is that it does not pay sufficient regard to the 'cultural' dimension of Christian ethics. See my *Plurality and Christian Ethics*, SevenBridgesPress, NY 1999, pp.164–65.

15. For Duncan Forrester see his excellent study *Christian Justice and Public Policy*, CUP 1997. In my judgment, in the methodological debate in Christian ethics today, Forrester keeps Preston and myself company.

16. See Ronald Preston's review of John Milbank's *Theology and Social Theory* in *Theology*, September 1991.

17. Karl Barth, *Church Dogmatics*,111/4, T & T Clark 1961, p.3.

18. Edward LeRoy Long, *A Survey of Christian Ethics*, OUP, NY 1967, pp.150f.

19. 'St. Andrew's Day Statement' in Timothy Bradshaw (ed), *The Way Forward? Homosexuality and the* Church, Hodder 1997, p.7.

20. Ibid., p.7.

21. Ibid., p.8.

22. Ibid., p.13.

23. Ibid., p.71.

24. I examine John Milbank's impact on contemporary Christian theology in Britain in a forthcoming article for the *Expository Times*. The summary provided here is taken from that article.

25. John Milbank, *Theology and Social Theory*, Blackwell 1990, p.259.

26. Ibid., p.12.

27. Ibid., p.139.

28. Ibid., p.139.

29. Ibid., p.389.

30. Ibid., p.434.

31. See chapter 7 above, p.97. As already noted, Ronald Preston did review Milbank's volume in *Theology*, September 1991

32. This argument is made at length in my *Truth and the Reality of God*, T & T Clark 1998.

33. See chapter 7 above, p.98.

Writings 1994–1999

Most of Ronald Preston's books have included a list of his published writings, other than book reviews and short articles, since 1935. The following covers those since *Confusions in Christian Social Ethics* was published in mid–1994 and concludes the list.

1994
Confusions in Christian Social Ethics: Problems for Geneva and Rome, SCM Press 1994.
'*Veritas Splendor*: A Comment', *Studies in Christian Ethics*, Vol.7, No.2. See ch.16.

1995
'Living with the Ambiguities of Wealth and Poverty', *Christian Action Journal*, autumn.
'Orbanverplanzung', *Theologische Realenzyklopadie*, Walter de Gruyter, Berlin.

1997
'The Common Good', *Epworth Review*, January. See. ch.18.
'On to Harare: Social Theology and Ethics in the World Council of Churches', *Crucible*, January–March.
'William Temple Remembered', *Report Back* (journal of the WEA), spring.

1998
'Faith and Order vs Life and Work: Ecclesiology and Ethics in the World Council of Churches, *Epworth Review*, Vol.25, No.4, October.
'Facts and Fables in Ecology and the Integrity of Creation' (with Charles Birch), Liverpool Hope Press. See ch.12.

1999
'Looking Back on the Twentieth Century: Christian Ethics', *Expository Times*, Vol.III. No.1, October. See ch.5.
'A Theological Response to Sociology' in *Sociology, Theology and the Curriculum* ed Leslie J. Francis, Cassell.
'The Student Christian Movement and the Critique of Universites' in *Christian Thinking and Social Order: Conviction Politics from the 1930s to the Present Day* ed Marjories Reeves, Cassell.

Subject Index

Index of Names